Joycean Possibilities: A Margot Norris Legacy

Edited by Joseph Valente, Vicki Mahaffey, and Kezia Whiting

ANTHEM PRESS

Anthem Press
An imprint of Wimbledon Publishing Company
www.anthempress.com

This edition first published in UK and USA 2026
by ANTHEM PRESS
75–76 Blackfriars Road, London SE1 8HA, UK
or PO Box 9779, London SW19 7ZG, UK
and
244 Madison Ave #116, New York, NY 10016, USA

First published in the UK and USA by Anthem Press in 2023

British Library Cataloguing-in-Publication Data
A catalogue record for this book is available from the British Library.

Library of Congress Control Number: 2026941629

ISBN-13: 978-1-80136-052-4 (Pbk)
ISBN-10: 1-80136-052-9 (Pbk)

Cover Credit: Peter M. Zogby.

This title is also available as an eBook.

CONTENTS

Preface v

Part I Introduction: Margot Norris and the Ideal of Interpretive Possibility 1

1. Defining a Generation in Joyce 3
Joseph Valente, Kezia Whiting, and Vicki Mahaffey

Part II Personal Testimonies 13

2. California Joyce 15
Karen R. Lawrence

Part III Suspicious Readings 25

3. Wondering Where on Earth All the Children Came From? 27
Joseph Valente

4. Free Indirect Palaver 41
Kezia Whiting

5. "But Who Was Gerty?": "Nausicaa," *The Lamplighter* and the Styles of Modernism 57
Anne Fogarty

Part IV Joyce's Webs 73

6. *Ulysses*: Thoughts in Isolation 75
Michael Groden

7. Inorganic Form from James Joyce to Eleanor Catton 87
Derek Attridge

8. Joyce's "The Dead" and Shakespeare's *Romeo and Juliet*: A Reading of Memory, Adaptation, and Afterlife 105
Beryl Schlossman

9. Ephemeral Spectacles: Art, Political Theater, *Ulysses* 123
Ellen Carol Jones

Part V The Value of James Joyce: Ethico-Political Readings 141

10. "Foreign Words are the Jews of Language": Joyce's Philological Anatomy of Anti-Semitism and the Diaspora of Joyceans 143
Valérie Bénéjam

11. Always a Good Turn: Veterans of the Jewish Subject in Joyce 159
Marilyn Reizbaum

12. James Joyce's Humane Comedy 175
Michael Patrick Gillespie

13. Changing Perspective: Why Style and Structure Matter in *Ulysses* 189
Vicki Mahaffey

Part VI Possible Worlds 205

14. Hobgoblins in Dublin: Joyce's "Circe" and the World of the Work 207
Gregory Castle

15. *Finnegans Wake* as Fictional World Refusal 223
Paul Saint-Amour

Part VII Epilogue 239

16. The Reel Margot 241
Moshe Gold

Index 251

PREFACE

This dedicated volume proposes to honor the rich, varied, trenchant, and tremendously influential scholarship of Professor Margot Norris in a series of essays amplifying her illumination of Joyce's literary oeuvre along with several prominent lines she introduced and investigated. Our title is intended to mark the common denominator running, like Ariadne's thread, throughout Professor Norris' many-sided explorations of Joyce's labyrinth. For Professor Norris, the quiddity of Joyce's work, its elusive whatness, resides in its unfolding of multiple what elses, its opening up of alternative ways of regarding the novels themselves, the narrative or generic forms they destabilize, the world to which they refer, the heritages they tap, and above all the readers they address. These five categories, in fact—textual plurivalence, formal innovations, possible worlds, emergent histories, and variegated readerships—serve as anchoring points of the collection, each corresponding with one of the significant projects delineating Professor Norris' esteemed career. Prominent Joycean, Modernist, and Irish studies scholars of different nations and generations supply the essays under each heading.

Part I

Introduction: Margot Norris and The Ideal of Interpretive Possibility

Chapter 1

DEFINING A GENERATION IN JOYCE

Joseph Valente, Kezia Whiting, and Vicki Mahaffey

Margot Norris has defined a generation in Joyce studies in at least two senses of the term. She has been, for upward of four decades, an exemplary voice on Joyce's oeuvre, the ideal reader of our title. Invited to keynote more Joyce conferences than anyone in the history of the field, and by a wide margin, Margot Norris has combined preeminence as a theoretician, an exegete, and a historical critic of all things Joyce. She has anchored what has come to be known as the "Joyce industry" like no other figure since the heyday of Hugh Kenner. But she has also defined a generation of Joyce studies in the sense of delineating the outline or form of our collective project, of simultaneously marking and pushing the boundaries of the field in all directions. No approach to Joyce's work has been foreign to Norris' imagination or intractable to her powerfully prehensile intellect. To trace her career, accordingly, from the mid-1970s to recent times, is to follow the march of our investment in and engagement with Joyce's literary creation and its critical heritage—not that she has followed the prevailing footsteps, but that she has led the parade.

Appearing two years before Colin McCabe's *James Joyce and the Revolution of the Word*, widely credited with initiating the post-structuralist turn in Joyce studies, Margot Norris' *The Decentered Universe of Finnegans Wake* had already executed that paradigm shift with respect to Joyce's most challenging, experimental opus, a foray beyond not only the avant-garde bourne of modernism, but beyond the pale of a postmodernism yet to be born. In her own words, Joyce's last work assaulted "not only the conventional literary modes but also many of the epistemological presuppositions of our culture." Its means for accomplishing this radical demarché, on Norris' account, is to enact a narrative anatomy of the infrastructure of language as such, in which our "empirical belief in the separation of inner and outer, subjective and objective, mental and physical—completely disintegrates." By casting this Wakean "colliderscape," an environment where human characters are periodically "melting into their landscape to become river and land, tree and stone," Norris not only captures Joyce's disruption of the logic of identity at its most cosmic, but anticipates today's ecocritical indictment of the Enlightenment construction of the Anthropocene.

The 1980s brought the most far-reaching paradigm shift yet in the century-long history of Joyce studies, the long overdue introduction of a sustained political assessment of Joyce's writing, beginning with feminist debates over his representation of gender relations in turn-of-the-century Dublin. Here again, in landmark essays like "Narration under a Blindfold" and "Stifled Back Answers," Margot Norris occupied and even directed the vanguard. Each of these essays unfolds the text of a *Dubliners* tale, "Clay" and "The Dead," respectively, to reveal half-occulted narrative prompts to readerly skepticism of its own seductive surface. In either case, that resistance, actualized in Norris' analysis, brings to light what generations of Joyce critics had never before espied: Joyce's critique of the patriarchal assumptions leading to a seemingly foreordained justification of a woman's socially determined subordination (Julia Morkan, Maria, Greta Conroy), and a man's (Gabriel Conroy) defensive posture of socially mandated stewardship. At this point in her career, Norris led the effort to bend the arc of literary history toward justice, ushering in a phase of what we might call advocacy criticism to Joyce studies.

Her endeavors in this regard have at times admittedly overshot the mark or overstated the case for ethico-political judgment. For example, she accuses Gabriel Conroy on no clear evidence, and much contextual counter-indication, of making sexual advances to Lily, the caretaker's daughter, and she buttresses her argument with reference to Lily's "prettiness," which is nowhere remarked or even suggested in the text. From this insinuation, she infers, logically but hyperbolically, an analogy between the sexual politics of Gabriel Conroy and those of the murderer-rapist Lord Gregory of "The Lass of Aughrim," not to mention the murdering narrator of Robert Browning's "My Last Duchess." But more generally, the luminous fruit of her aggressive approach cannot be discounted nor denied. It was Margot Norris who alerted us to the paternal bias of the stories' narrative voice even at its most detached from the force field of Gabriel's consciousness. It was Margot Norris too who detected outright contradictions of fact in "The Dead"—regarding, for example, Julia Morkan's current position in her church choir—and showed how they formed part of a uniquely Joycean innovation, the self-critical, self-subverting narrative voice.

From this insight, Norris proceeded to develop a hugely influential method of "suspicious reading," answerable to the provocations of Joyce's double-edged style. By this device, a feminist approach to and even a feminist critique *of* Joyce's text melded ingeniously with the discovery of a latent feminism *in* Joyce's text. In "The Dead," for example, Norris finds the subtextual layers and intertextual frames sabotage the patriarchal modernism on display in the collusion between the passages of feigned narrative omniscience and the stylistic dominant of free indirect discourse. Her bravura reading of "Clay" takes this feminist strategy a step further, altering, fundamentally and permanently, our experience of the story and of ourselves experiencing the story. Norris was the first to identify the narrative voice in "Clay" as neither free indirect discourse aligned immediately with Maria's consciousness nor neutral third-person reportage, but narrative advocacy on behalf of Maria, a telling of her story as she would, unconsciously, have it told. Every subsequent reading of "Clay" has begun, perforce, with this premise in mind. Ironically, however, the tone of this narrative patronage is so euphemistic and so defensive as to highlight Maria's social abjection—as an unattached, credulous, quasi-institutionalized spinster—in the very attempt to eulogize her. Insofar as this strategy of denial attaches to Maria herself, it subjects her to a shade of mockery, for being a socially disqualified subject insensible of her own disqualification. Yet precisely in this self-torpedoed effort to salvage some measure of dignity for Maria, Norris has isolated one more ironic twist, a third dimension to the game of representational chess that Joyce is playing. The subtle blend of strained compliment and inadequately averted insult lends Maria an intensely poignant aura that enlists her readers' sympathy and, in so doing, arraigns them for the condescension that the text itself, on another level, has solicited. By this means, Joyce not only exposes the invidious gender basis, or bias, on which Dublin society of the time would discount a figure like Maria, but also the hold such gender bias might have on his readers. In alerting us to Joyce's constructive entrapment of his audience, Norris effected a decisive shift in the critical framing of Joyce's sexual politics: from a focus on the narrative content of Joyce's fiction, famously and reductively misunderstood by Gilbert and Gubar, to a focus on Joyce's stylistic performance, whose feminist impetus conforms more closely with Joyce's express admiration for his first and most durable model, Henrik Ibsen.

> The purpose of *A Doll's House*, for instance, was the emancipation of women, which caused the greatest revolution in our time in the most important relationship there is—that between men and women [...]

Although fashioned in the service of a determinedly feminist intervention, Norris' sophisticated anatomy of the incriminatory, self-ironizing turn in Joycean narration has the great advantage of being fully portable to other modes of critical advocacy. Take for example, her essay "The Work

Song of the Washerwomen," introduced in her book, *Joyce's Web.* She directs her attention to how the "double and devious" representational method that Joyce had honed in writing *Dubliners, A Portrait of the Artist* and *Ulysses* is brought to bear on a shrewd critique of colonial and class antagonism in *Finnegans Wake*—a remarking of complex social hierarchies as the residue of bourgeois efforts, likewise inscribed in the text, to "repress and occlude" them. In "The Politics of Childhood in the Mime of Mick, Nick, and the Maggies," Norris finds the modernist ideology of exceptionalist bildung, which still lingers in *A Portrait of the Artist,* to come under the illuminating pressure of Joyce's still more decisively double-edged writing of the Wakean palimpsest. Undercover of a lighthearted children's pantomime lurks the fractured signifiers of the deeply adverse "social and material condition that the entertainment, aptly enough, labors to mute." In the portmanteau, Joyce discovered the concentrated vehicle for the "internal subversion" to which, on Norris' seminal reading, his prose stylings had always been committed. Obversely, the "imperialistic imprint" on the children's game—that acculturative surface of metropolitan names and games, legendary and historical figures, rituals and mores—camouflages but cannot fully contain a fiercely "oppositional" energy that the children's game directs at "the big world they inhabit." Norris elaborates how the play of the children renders "adult power more brutally transparent" through an inventive form of "paedocentric bricolage," of which the portmanteau itself is a cellular condition of possibility.

In the 1990s, Margot Norris expanded her analysis of the productively rifted texture of Joyce's text to address its newly legible queer nuances. Her essay in the collection *Quare Joyce*, "A Walk on the Wild(e) Side," aptly subtitled "A Double Reading of 'An Encounter'," explores a textual play of disclosure and concealment, expression, and repression that speaks directly to the bivalent social disposition toward male, same-sex relations. Her signature technique of excavating the "self-commentary" embedded in Joyce's signifying practice reveals the simultaneous con/disjunction of homosocial attachment and homosexual implication in the story. The affective corollary for both the child-protagonist and his narrating adult self-comprises a sense of fellowship permeated with feelings of emulousness and disdain that effectively secrete (in both senses of the term) a nascent homophobic recoil. A sexual nervousness hangs over the representation of events and is communicated to the reader as an exegetical-cum-ethical nervousness, in doubts as to whether and how far their very attempt to categorize the tale's sexual undercurrents might manifest denial, displacement, or projection on their part, might bespeak biases or a socially conditioned insecurity. Joyce has, to Norris' mind, placed the story of the boys' encounter at once "in and out of the closet" and has thereby positioned his readers' encounter with the story provocatively and unsettlingly on the threshold.

Throughout her career in Joyce studies, whether working in the fields of post-structural semiology, narratology, or stylistics, whether adopting a feminist, Marxist, postcolonial, or queer theory approach, Margot Norris has consistently taken considerable care to parse the effect of any given Joyce text upon his readers, to consider the sort of literary episteme that his innovative formal and stylistic technique engenders. Seamlessly, ineluctably, her descriptive analysis of Joyce's textual performance bleeds into a prescriptive guide to the readers' interpretive performance—what narrative gambits should they take special notice of, what modes of ideological critique should be discerned and deliberated, what feints suspected, what lures resisted, and what incitements addressed in all of their complexities. Yet each of these instances of readerly response is less important in itself than for its reflexive and introspective meaning. Norris' distinctive concern for how Joyce's text might be read is alternatively about how Joyce's text encourages and enables us to read ourselves. The passage that Norris conducts from textual to readerly practice is a passage from an epistemology to an ethics of reading, and the immediacy of that passage attests to her sense, elaborated in all of her criticism, that the latter is always already at work in the former, whether we recognize it or not. All of this is to say that Norris has not only modeled the ideal reader of our title, she has sought to foster a particularly committed, engagé type of ideal reader in all of us.

Her scholarship in the twenty-first century has continued that quest by purveying a theoretical toolbox for navigating the "chaosmos" of Joyce's later fiction, *Ulysses* and *Finnegans Wake*, in a manner that at once respects and strives to organize its lexical, stylistic, and narrative heterogeneity. In her recent books, *Virgin and Veteran Readings of Ulysses* and *The Value of James Joyce*, Norris sets forth a hermeneutics explicitly centered on the reading experience, or rather on the disparate reading experiences that variously positioned subjects might undergo. Each such experience in turn is striated across several dimensions or frames of reference that Norris specifies, delineates, and taxonomizes by drawing upon a cutting edge branch of narratology known as possible worlds theory. In Norris's hands, possible worlds theory gives a certain ontological weight to Joyce's double writing—the central object and key discoveries of her scholarly endeavors—by converting the question of literary polyphony into one of literary heterocosm. But more importantly, the task of traversing these fully imagined possible worlds, of negotiating among their sundry and sometimes conflicting assumptions, values and priorities, trains and tests Joyce's readers, virgin and veteran, in the ethical responsiveness that is ever Norris's paramount concern. For throughout her long and illustrious career, Norris has always wanted to know, and sought to show, how becoming better readers—more sensitive, more reflective, more self-conscious, more self-critical—can contribute to our becoming better persons. This project forms the explicit focus of her most recent book-length essay, *The Value of James Joyce.*

This volume brings together leading and rising scholars of Joyce's fiction to appreciate, discuss, and extend the work of Margot Norris in each of its clearly defined directions. We begin with the personal testimony of Karen Lawrence, Norris's longtime colleague and friend.

The first critical section, the textual dimension, will engage with Professor Norris' exemplary vindication of the hermeneutics of suspicion in her monograph, *Suspicious Readings of Joyce's Dubliners.* Joseph Valente, Anne Fogarty and Kezia Whiting engage with Norris' exemplary vindication of the hermeneutics of suspicion in her monograph, *Suspicious Readings of Joyce's Dubliners.*

Valente's "Wondering Where on Earth All the Children Came From?" weighs the suspicious and skeptical exegetical strategy of Norris in *Suspicious Readings of Joyce's Dubliners* against the contemporaneous "surface reading" paradigm initiated by Eve Sedgwick. For Valente, skepticism alone respects and reckons with the various interpretive lures and ruses whereby narratives like those in *Dubliners* enact their own ideological intervention. Applying Norris's hermeneutics of suspicion, this essay investigates Joyce's short story "Eveline" for the purpose of determining why, to what aesthetic and sociopolitical effect, there appear toward the end of the story unnamed children whose very existence seems to have been ruled out from the very beginning. In the aporetic presence of these children, Valente discerns an augur of unstated, unacknowledged, inadmissible sexual violence, a traumatic obstacle to any futurity Eveline herself can imagine.

Like Valente, Whiting explores "The Dead" guided by Norris's suspicious approach to the story. She argues that the verbal repetitions that flicker through Joyce's free indirect style in *Dubliners* arouse the interpretive unease that Norris describes as an effect of Joyce's style, and point to the intersubjective and ideological makeup of the narration. Taking up Norris's description of the narration of "The Dead" as being "in league" with Gabriel, Whiting finds this collusion to be a marker of the textual enmeshment of character and narration.

Anne Fogarty casts a suspicious eye on the common reading of "Nausicaa" as a satirical denunciation of the trivializing romance fiction marketed to and consumed by women. She proposes instead that the subversive energies of "Nausicaa" are fueled not simply by a high-handed rejection of romance fiction, but by a complex interplay with the plots of women's fiction and the varying moral and political perspectives that they inculcate. Joyce incorporates and redisposes the motifs and plots of American and Irish nineteenth-century women's novels in order to confer Gerty with the moral authority not only to accuse Bloom but to call out the pretensions and elitism of modernist style with regard to those women's genres. Fogarty thus builds on Norris's explication of Joyce's own suspicions concerning modernism's elitism and cruelty.

The second section, the readerly dimension, will take up Norris' perspective in Joyce's Web, wherein she elaborates how Joyce's iridescent style, to paraphrase Hugh Kenner, spins out a far-reaching and densely reticulated intertextual net of signification, while simultaneously, paradoxically, reinforcing the sui generis tenor of his own representational practice. Derek Attridge, Michael Groden, Ellen Carol Jones, and Beryl Schlossman each contribute an essay on this topic.

In a poignant essay that recounts his own initially "isolated" reading of *Ulysses*, Michael Groden reflects on the passage of time and the concepts of return and belonging in his own encounters with *Ulysses* and its critical community as well as within the characters' experiences in the novel.

Taking off from Norris's acute attention to the reader's experience of the text, Derek Attridge considers the contribution of form separate from meaning to the experience of reading *Ulysses*. In "Inorganic Form from James Joyce to Eleanor Catton," Attridge challenges the critical understanding of form and meaning as inseparable, looking at the way Joyce's formal innovations loosen the connection between form and content. In discussing "inorganic form," Attridge demonstrates that formal devices can operate free of representational work, instead contributing to the reader's pleasure, potentially altering our apprehension of our own world. Attridge suggests that Catton, using astrological mapping to structure her narrative in *The Luminaries*, follows Joyce's new path by creating works in which content is determined, to some degree at least, by form.

For Schlossman, Norris's intertextual reading of "The Dead" finds an anti-Romeo and Juliet trope that presents "stifled back answers" to the festivity and hospitality of the Morkans' party. In further elaborating on Joyce's references to *Romeo and Juliet*, Schlossman investigates Shakespeare's adaptation of earlier literature, and Joyce's further uses and betrayals of these texts. The adultery, commodification, and romantic love from *Romeo and Juliet* reverberate through Joyce's modernity.

In "Ephemeral Spectacles: Art, Political Theater, *Ulysses*," Ellen Carol Jones shows how Joyce's intertextual web extends beyond the written word to social events and cultural rituals. She specifically demonstrates that the "Messianic scene" of "Circe" both critiques and parodies religious and political spectacles in Ireland deriving from the urban festivals and processions that flourished throughout monarchical and imperial Europe. Focusing in particular on royal processions, Jones examines their power to colonize public space and memory. She further builds on Norris's critique of modernist elitism, arguing that in "Circe" Joyce critiques the subversive, even revolutionary, function of an avant-garde or modernist experimental art in a colonial state.

The third section, the ethico-political dimension, grows out of Norris' attention to Joyce's use of experimental narrative and symbolic structures, to address social issues in distinctively literary ways. One particularly rich vein in Margot Norris's criticism, tapped into by Marilyn Reizbaum, Valérie Bénéjam, Michael Gillespie, and Vicki Mahaffey in this section, is her recognition and valorization of the democratic tendency of Joyce's work, his "remarkable generosity in his embrace of all that is human" (2). Through their discussions of Joyce's narrative idiosyncrasies and experimentation, Bénéjam, Reizbaum, Gillespie, and Mahaffey each point to the radical equality posed by Joyce's writing.

Valérie Bénéjam yokes Norris's narratological study of anti-Semitism with her preoccupation with the circulation of gossip to examine in dissemination of anti-Semitic stereotypes in *Ulysses.* In studying Joyce's linguistic anatomy of anti-Semitism, Bénéjam claims that Joyce exposes anti-Semitism as a contagious physiological and linguistic disease that produces mechanical, thoughtless speech. Bénéjam ends by turning to the diasporic linguistic program within *Finnegans Wake* as a reminder to Joyce critics of their responsibility to be faithful to Joyce's program of defamiliarization and demystification, of resistance against sedimented clichés and any form of uncritical usage of language.

Marilyn Reizbaum, like Bénéjam, extrapolates on Norris's discussions of Jewishness in *Ulysses.* Reizbaum describes Norris's confrontation of multiple interpretations as both generous and intolerably ambiguous, in order to consider what she calls the "gorgeous didacticism" of Norris's discussion of Jewishness and anti-Semitism in Joyce's work. Reizbaum, in examining the "slow reveal" of Bloom's Jewishness and the Ballad of Harry Hughes in "Ithaca," parallels Norris's discussion of "The Dead" and the inextricability of politics and art in his staging of sexist attitudes and behavior to his staging of anti-Semitic scenes.

In "Joyce's Humane Comedy," Michael Gillespie points to the influence of Balzac's *La Comédie humaine* on Joyce through each writer's fascination with the mundane details of everyday life in combination with a humane vision informing their depiction of central characters. Gillespie demonstrates Joyce's complex characterization and character development of Stephen in particular, arguing that the range of situations and attitudes informing Stephen are portrayed with sympathy and understanding.

Vicki Mahaffey's essay, too, addresses Joyce's complex portrayal of the human. Joyce allows us to see the characters in *Ulyssses* (as well as ourselves, and its author) not as heroes or villains, but works in progress. Mahaffey demonstrates *Ulysses*'s insistence on the reader's flexibility. For Mahaffey, Joyce's narrative techniques prod the reader to change perspectives, and unsettle our habitual and even mechanical way of understanding a text. These narrative techniques counter attempts to oversimplify or categorize people, instead representing the multiplicity of the individual. Mahaffey focuses in particular on the Homeric parallels of *Ulysses*, which, she argues, enable the reader to see and understand beyond the characters' perspective while still sympathizing with them.

The fourth and final section, on alternative realities, enters forthrightly into dialogue with Norris' recent essays that usher the postmodern "possible worlds theory" into the orbit of Joyce studies. Gregory Castle and Paul Saint-Amour extend the application of this paradigm to *Ulysses* and *Finnegans Wake*, respectively.

While Margot Norris, in her possible worlds reading of *Finnegans Wake*, describes the book as "an entirely virtual construction that makes no attempt to present itself as actual but rather flaunts its virtuality," Paul Saint-Amour instead argues that while Joyce's book is a work of fiction, it is not, in fact, a fictional world. Saint-Amour's argument rests on the role of coincidence in creating fictional worlds, and, for him, a novel such as *Finnegans Wake*, in which diegetic coincidences cannot happen, is not a fictional world in the possible-worlds sense. Instead, the *Wake* lets our actual world be *its* actual world. Saint-Amour ends by engaging with Norris's combination of possible worlds theory and environmentalism in her reading of the "Anna Livia Plurabelle" chapter, focusing on the "weak environmentalism" of its call on specific readers through potential recognition triggers that bind particular readers to particular waters.

Gregory Castle's reading of "Circe" rests on the question of the reader's responsibility to the fictional world and characters that possible worlds theory opens. He argues that while possible worlds theory, and Margot Norris's use of it in her reading of Joyce, suggests that the reader's responsibility to characters and fictional worlds has its roots in the "actual world," in "Circe," these relations, and the obligation and wish worlds they sustain, are confounded in a process of permutation that has neither duration nor extension so that responsibility becomes, for both reader and characters, a purely textual matter.

Hopefully, this roster denotes how the concept of possibility will give the collection, as it has Margot Norris' research, and as it did Joyce's literary monuments, a kind of floating foundation (what seismic architects call base isolation), that ensures consistency in and through flexibility. The essays, to shift metaphorical register, speak to one another but in different idioms, each of which Margot Norris herself has helped to make legible and compelling in the several fields where the work of James Joyce has such salience.

Part II

Personal Testimonies

Chapter 2

CALIFORNIA JOYCE

Karen R. Lawrence

In a residential neighborhood of Irvine, California, two streets intersect: California and Joyce. That Joyce's name appears on a street sign in the University Hills faculty housing area of UC Irvine is only partly an accident, as many streets refer to famous writers and intellectuals. "California Joyce" is a fitting, even "overdetermined" title for my essay in a volume celebrating the influence Margot Norris has had in shaping the direction of Joyce Studies. Most importantly, she and I were faculty colleagues at UC Irvine, where she spent the bulk of her academic career. By the time I was recruited to UC Irvine as Dean of Humanities in 1998, Margot was already a friend from Joyce symposia, where she had delivered stunning plenary talks and was always a star at symposium *Finnegans Wake* charades. In fact, it was through my attendance at the 1993 Joyce conference "California Joyce," hosted by Margot along with Vincent Cheng and Kimberly Devlin, that the seeds of my interest in moving to UC Irvine and California were sown. The conference held at UC Irvine introduced Joyceans from all over to the powerful crop of academics who taught Joyce at neighboring southern California universities. The focus of the conference was Joyce and film—very California—and it was that taste of southern California Joyce and Joyceans, as well as a coffee shared with other conference-goers on the sunny campus patio, that beckoned five years later when I was offered the position of dean at Irvine. I have written elsewhere of the difficulty of that decision to uproot our family, during which I identified with Eveline in *Dubliners*, as she decided whether to leave her home to go with a sailor named Frank, and it was Margot whom I called to discuss the wisdom of the move.[1] She herself had moved from Michigan to Irvine years before, recruited in a similarly strategic way, in her case, during the winter months in a cold climate (I was moving from Salt Lake City). In our discussion, though, we focused on the intellectual climate at Irvine, including the robust Joycean community, and she enthusiastically encouraged me to come. My family and I moved to Irvine and remained there for nine years, at which point I left

Figure 2.1 Intersection of California and Joyce streets in Irvine, California.

to become president of Sarah Lawrence College. After a decade at Sarah Lawrence, I returned to Southern California, where I now serve as president of The Huntington Library, Art Museum, and Botanical Gardens. I am delighted that The Huntington Library houses, among other items, several first editions of *Ulysses*, a typescript of "Penelope" with Joyce's handwritten edits, and postcards from Joyce regarding Samuel Roth's piracy of *Ulysses*. In my Huntington office a display case contains some of my proudest Joyce possessions, including a few special Joyce editions. Occupying pride of place is my photograph of the street signs at the California/Joyce corner at UC Irvine, which for me marked the happy crossing of geography and academic field. Margot was the titular genius of that Joycean space.

But if the lure of California is forever associated in my mind with both Margot and "sunny Jim," Margot's presence is indelibly woven as well in the European landscape of Joyce symposia, the memory lanes of those of us who have spent a lifetime traveling in Joyce's wake. In this essay, I want to highlight influential Margot Norris sightings throughout that landscape, both on stage and on the page. They are what I would call "Margot moments," vivid memories that capture Margot's representations in writing as well as her in-person performances. I am confident that I can speak for others when

I say that over her illustrious career, Margot Norris has been a major part of the Joycean experience, indelibly imprinting her own interpretative powers on the consciousness of James Joyce and James Joyceans.

I read Margot Norris several years before I met her. I was in graduate school, working on my dissertation on Joyce (which, with revision, became *The Odyssey of Style in* Ulysses[2]). And I was beginning to read political, psychoanalytic, and poststructuralist theory, adding to my study of narrative and reader response criticism. Along came a book called *The Decentered Universe of* Finnegans Wake*: A Structuralist Analysis.*[3] "(Stoop) if you are abcedminded,"[4] Margot quoted, and proceeded to show the *Wake* dramatizing its own need for a tour guide—mind the gap between manifest and latent content, stop, get down, and pay attention to the language, if you want to make it through this exhibit, exhibition, exhibitionism of language curated by James Joyce. I knew a good guide when I saw one, and Margot led me through a book I had feared during my intensive immersion in studying and writing about Joyce's work. Many years later when I came back to Margot's work to review her short book, *The Value of James Joyce* (2016) for the *JJQ*, I admired all over again the exegetical powers in her earliest book. "It is in her exegesis of the *Wake* that this unparalleled interpreter demonstrates that the complexity and intelligibility of the language is inextricable from the comedy of the common man and woman. It is here that she sees linguistic play as a renewable source of a multiplicity of viewpoints rather than a detraction from the main show."[5] I still deeply admire the fact that Margot launched her career in Joyce criticism with a brilliant book on the *Wake*, as she took on what Andrew Malraux once called "the steep face" of Joyce's genius. Her career has been an ongoing critical project of reading Joyce's works, backwards and forwards, starting where Joyce ended, with his "book of the dark." Identifying in the *Wake*'s language a kind of "literary free association" borrowed from Freud's analysis of dreams, Margot unearthed in this language "the unconscious of the earlier books," which are Joyce's "daybooks."

Beginning with the "steep face" of *The Wake*, Margot has spent much of her extraordinary career identifying conscious and unconscious counterparts in Joyce's oeuvre. No one moves more fluidly back and forth over this terrain than she, the consummate guide through the echo chambers of Joyce's fiction. Margot's expert maneuvers rely partly on her stunning recall of most of the sentences in Joyce's oeuvre. That might seem like an exaggerated statement, but I do not believe it's far off. Margot has read and reread Joyce's novels more carefully than almost any other Joycean I know, giving her the ability to trace their adumbrations and echoes, re-imaginings and recycling, and above all, their incessant disguises. Margot's readings produce uncanny results, with familiar things turning up in all sorts of unfamiliar and unexpected places.

My first vivid recollection of Margot performing her interpretive magic tricks occurred at the 1986 Copenhagen Joyce Symposium, in her plenary address, "Joyce's Heliotrope," (subsequently published in the volume *Coping with Joyce*.)[6] In a purple dress, which mimed the color of the heliotrope, the flowering plant that provided the main trope of her talk, Margot offered "a valentine" to the audience. She invited us to join her in pursuing the figure of the heliotrope throughout Joyce's works, beginning with its appearance in "The Mime of Mick, Nick, and the Maggies," the child's guessing game in *Finnegans Wake*. Coaxing the audience to cultivate what she called "erotic hermeneutics" (*CJ* 8), she followed the journey of the heliotrope, the flower that bends toward the sun in "a desirous motion," enacting "a romantic ballet or a seductive dance." Reading backwards from "The Mime of Mick, Nick, and the Maggies" she led us through a "journey into the old love stories of Joycean figures," tracing the protean manifestations of the heliotrope back to its avatars, models, and prototypes in "Nausicaa," *A Portrait* and "The Dead." Displaying her command of the Joycean archive, Margot wowed the audience with this game of hide and seek conducted through the textual corridors of Joyce's earlier fiction. Spellbound, we followed her, as familiar scenes in the early fiction yielded extraordinary new meanings; conversely, the three girls performing for Bloom in "Nausicaa uncannily materialized in "The Mime of Mick, Nick, and the Maggies" (*CJ* 10). In "Joyce's Heliotrope," Margot excavated the "occluded perspectives from the earlier works," retrieving the "infantile experience and feeling" in *Ulysses*, *A Portrait*, and "The Dead." Her performance transformed critical excavation into a demonstration of the pleasure of the text.

Margot's focus on the child's guessing game in *Finnegans Wake*, leads to a related "Margot Moment" at the 1990 Joyce Symposium in Monaco, where a large group of Joyceans played a favorite adult guessing game, *Finnegans Wake* charades, a fixture at Joyce symposia. At these ritual events Margot's presence on your team was a pretty sure bet to get you to the finish line. The particular moment that I remember most, however, is more personal, and DOES involve a child guessing, in this case, my own child, Jeffrey Lawrence, who attended the 1990 Symposium with our other family members when he was 7 years old. The only child I remember being present, Jeff was mesmerized by the adults' raucous nonverbal performances. Although I can't recall who was performing, I remember that our team had guessed some parts of the Wakean clues performed. For that brief moment, the Wakean charades again became a child's guessing game when Jeff piped up with the final word that led one of our team members to identify the entire Wakean phrase. At the risk of overinterpreting this moment ("I have often thought since on looking back over that strange time that it was that small act, trivial in itself … that determined the whole aftercourse of both our lives," 7.763–65), it has become part of our family lore, *associated with,* if not really *causing* Jeff to become a successful English professor, now tenured (though I hasten to add, not a Joycean).

In 1993, my family accompanied me to enjoy California and the beach while I attended the California Joyce conference at UC Irvine hosted by Margot Norris and other California Joyceans. This time, they joined me only for some of the virtuoso performances of Joyce in film and on stage. With a nod to the explicit theme of "Joyce, Modernism, and the Social Function of Art," Margot and her co-hosts welcomed non-academics and non-scholars to the conference, culminating in the enthusiastic and large audience that attended Fionnula Flanagan's on-stage performance of Molly's soliloquy.

Apropos of Flanagan's climactic soliloquy, the conference poster—blue, pink, and palm-treed, like California, was inscribed with a section of "Penelope," yoking the two landscapes of California and Gibraltar (see Figure 2.2). In the passage, Molly remembers Gibraltar, with its "sea crimson sometimes like fire and the glorious sunsets and pink and blue and yellow houses and

Figure 2.2 Official poster of California Joyce conference in 1993.

the rosegardens [...] where I was a flower of the mountain yes." Joseph Strick, whose 1967 film of *Ulysses* was screened at the conference, was both a presence and a topic of discussion. Both the filmic and political challenges presented by Joyce's texts were a major focus. The "libidinal aspect [...] of intellectual activities" that Margot invoked in her heliotropic performance in Copenhagen (*CJ* 3) were in full flower with Flanagan's performance as well as in Strick's film. The social function of art figured prominently, with Terry Eagleton as a plenary speaker. The pronounced turn toward social critique evident in the conference program was reflected as well in Margot's own turn toward a more historical, cultural reading of Joyce in the book she had published a year earlier, *Joyce's Web: The Social Unraveling of Modernism.*[7]

With *Joyce's Web*, Margot began a sustained *rereading* of her own work as she continued to reread Joyce. As she continued to pursue the deliberate omissions in Joyce's fiction, she began to acknowledge what she identified as her *own* earlier methodological occlusions, faulting, in particular, her "ahistori[cal] approach to *Finnegans Wake*" in *The Decentered Universe.* In *Joyce's Web,* she adopted instead a more feminist, materialist approach to Joyce, excavating the social and historical contexts of Joyce's works omitted from her previous analysis. In doing so, she sought to bring to light what she calls a "bourgeois" disavowal of history that is camouflaged within modernism's doctrine of the autonomy of art. In *Joyce's Web,* she posited a new figure for the Joycean author: the crafty, stay-at-home Penelope rather than either the proud artificer Daedalus (in *A Portrait*) or the polytropos Odysseus (in *Ulysses*). In contrast to the aloof modernist artist "paring his fingernails," this avatar weaves and unweaves the narrative as it is told. According to Margot, the discourse of the narrative simultaneously embeds its own unravelling, in a "dispersed field of silent counterdiscourses" (JW 7) which contain their own "ideological self-corrections." She argued that Joyce embeds in the narrative texture a "system-imminent critique" (*JW* 4) of modernism's myths and occlusions. As the writer becomes his own Penelope, the image of the reader is transformed as well, now a textual sleuth on the trail of material history. In a series of ground-breaking chapters on *Ulysses, Finnegans Wake,* and *Dubliners,* Margot counseled the reader to mind the gap of historical context.

In Margot's next book, *Suspicious Readings of Joyce's* Dubliners (2003), the textual sleuth in *Joyce's Web* gave way to the "suspicious" reader.[8] Activating Paul Ricoeur's "hermeneutics of suspicion," itself based on Nietzsche and Freud, Margot identified the suspicious reader of *Dubliners,* who takes on the gaps and miscues of the gnomic and gnomonic short stories of *Dubliners.* The "payoff" for this reader is neither libidinal content nor occluded history, for this suspicious reader cannot get to the bottom of things even in the "counterdiscourses" in the text. Instead, according to Margot, the short stories of *Dubliners* become a model for the way fiction presents "conflicting ethical readings" (*SR* 13). The duplicitous narratives of the stories refuse to yield any secure position, and the suspicious reader runs an "ethical risk" no matter how she "adjudicate[s] the moral conundrum posed by each story" (*SR* 13). Suspicious reading means maintaining uncertainty of judgment and interpretation even after the sleuthing of silences is done. The signature operation performed in each story is the creation of a kind of double consciousness in the reader, as the suspicious reader experiences a "moral and psychological splintering of knowledge" (*SR* 20) between a hypothetically "innocent" reading on the "surface" and a more "transgressive" one (*SR* 23). In this model, neither innocence nor experience wins out. Instead, the reader holds two implied subject positions, at once "virgin" and "veteran," each persona equipped with a different level of knowledge and skepticism. In the end, the reader must beware of both of these implied reader positions, since the moral of Margot's reading in this analysis of *Dubliners* is an anti-moral: readers cannot exist in a confident morally superior position to the characters but, instead, are implicated in the "undecidabilities" (*SR* 26) of the text.

This notion of virgin and veteran readers reemerged powerfully in a series of books Margot subsequently published, including the titular *Virgin and Veteran Readings of* Ulysses.[9] In this group of essays exploring *Ulysses* in terms of narratology's "possible worlds theory," Margot continued to cast her reader in the roles of innocence and experience. Extending the view of the double consciousness of the veteran Joyce reader that she identified in *Suspicious Readings*, in this study, she was less concerned with moral hazards. Instead, she focused more on the "ontologies" of the fictional world constructed narratively, positing a first-time "virgin reader" who can't "know" what is coming next, and a "veteran reader," who has the "knowledge of the whole work, including the ending," and thus can more "fully" understand *Ulysses.* Still absorbed by the problems of gaps, miscues, and incompleteness, Margot took on each chapter balancing the first-time reading of the "virgin" with the wiser, more experienced rereading of the "veteran." Again, a double consciousness was at play, a dual casting of the implied reader, but now with ontological questions of fact and fiction at the fore.

Virgin and Veteran Readings of Ulysses was an outgrowth of a new California Joyce conference called "Joyce Redux" hosted at UC Irvine. By this point, I was in New York working at Sarah Lawrence, and administrative duties precluded my attendance at a west coast Joyce gathering, though I continued to follow both Joyce's and Margot Norris's work. When I read the book, I noticed that her note to the reader suggested a kind of valedictory—she wrote, "my complicated journey [...] ends here." By that time, she had retired from UC Irvine. But luckily for all readers of Joyce, Margot has kept on considering what first-time and more experienced readers of Joyce "know" and how and when they know it. The terms "virgin" and "veteran" are resilient and have again come into play in a series of short books by Margot for general audience, presented in the context of her own career as superb master teacher and prolific scholar. For example, in *The Value of James Joyce,* Margot continues to explore the important operations of reading between the lines and minding the gaps.[10] In this book, with students and other first-time (and intimidated) readers of Joyce specifically in mind, Margot becomes a kinder, gentler version of tour guide. Here, the career-long teacher of Joyce focuses on the first-time "virgin" reader who might be too afraid of Joyce to read him. Margot plays tour guide and coach with encouragement and assurance, not by counseling suspicion or a warning to the reader to "stoop, if you are abcedeminded." In *The Value of James Joyce,* Margot makes a case for the pleasures of the text for a nonspecialist. She argues that despite Joyce's notoriously difficult language, his work is about and for the ordinary person.

And so, my last "Margot moment" brings us to 2016, when I had the pleasure of reviewing *The Value of James Joyce* for the *JJQ*.[11] The review afforded an opportunity, as does this essay, to look back at the continuities of her work and on her rereadings, refinements, and retakes in her long, hugely successful career as both scholar and teacher. In the review, I wrote, "Norris has insistently asked what it feels like for the Joycean reader not to know, probing the anxieties and ethical dilemmas that arise when we are in the dark." In this short book, she leads the general reader to discover Joyce's "democratic impulses," and to Joyce's "remarkable generosity in [Joyce's] embrace of all that is human" (*VJJ* 2).

Margot's bravery as a critic and her own remarkable generosity as a human being have been evident in every appearance on stage and page during her long career. As a faculty member at UC Irvine, she was remarkably generous, humane, and fiercely intelligent. As Dean of Humanities, I had the responsibility of "reviewing" her work in a different capacity, every year between 1998 and 2007, as part of the evaluation process at The University of California. These "reviews," too, were pleasures, one of the perks—scholarly and personal—amidst the competing claims of playing such an administrative role. One of the best "perks" was the opportunity to support Margot's well-deserved nomination to become Chancellor's Professor of the Humanities at UC Irvine, a capstone to her extraordinary career. Then, as now, with this volume of essays, it is fitting for us to celebrate Margot's personal qualities and scholarly accomplishments.

Notes

1 See Karen R. Lawrence, "Living with Joyce: Grand Passion and Small Pleasures," in *Who's Afraid of James Joyce?* (Gainesville: University Press of Florida), 1–12.
2 Karen Lawrence, *The Odyssey of Style in* Ulysses (Princeton: Princeton University Press, 1981).
3 Margot Norris, *The Decentered Universe of* Finnegans Wake (Baltimore: The Johns Hopkins University Press).
4 James Joyce, *Finnegans Wake* (New York: The Viking Press, 1939), 18.
5 *JJQ*, 53, no. 3–4 (Spring–Summer 2016), p. 348.
6 *In Coping with Joyce: Essays from the Copenhagen Symposium*, ed. Morris Beja and Shari Benstock (Columbus: Ohio University Press, 1989), pp. 3–24. Hereafter cited parenthetically in the text as *CJ*.
7 Austin: University of Texas Press, 1992. Hereafter cited parenthetically in the text as *JW*.
8 Philadelphia: University of Pennsylvania Press, 2003. Hereafter cited parenthetically in the text as *SR*.
9 *Virgin and Veteran Readings of* Ulysses (Palgrave Macmillan, 2011).
10 Cambridge: Cambridge University Press, 2016. Hereafter cited parenthetically in the text as *VJJ*.
11 Karen R. Lawrence, Review, *The Value of James Joyce* by Margot Norris (*JJQ*, 53, no. 3–4 Spring–Summer, 2016).

Part III

Suspicious Readings

Chapter 3

WONDERING WHERE ON EARTH ALL THE CHILDREN CAME FROM?

Joseph Valente

In 2003, Eve Sedgwick published an influential critique of the hermeneutics of suspicion, which in her view had grown all but synonymous with academic literary analysis itself, to its great detriment.[1] The key to her argument, and its fatal flaw, is a conflation of the various types of skeptical interpretive attitudes and approaches—suspicion, demystification, *anagnorisis*, unveiling, questioning generally—with a paranoid mode of reading, clinically understood: hence the title "You're so Paranoid, You Probably Think this Essay Is about You." For Sedgwick, the "strong" theories underwriting the dominant methods of contemporary literary scholarship and interrogation—Marxist, feminist, psychoanalytic, deconstructive and queer—cherish and militate for a rigorous *idée fixe*, which blinds their practitioners to the manifold semiotic and affective contingencies at play in their object texts. Averse to surprise, obsessed with "exposure," devoted to forestalling "negative affect," the hermeneutics of suspicion rewrites the documents studied in terms of its own defensive master code instead of taking them on their own terms.[2] To this paranoiac end, it treats any given text as symptomatic of whatever motives or pathologies its own grounding theory is primed to diagnose. In this searching for the hidden, yet presupposed cause of which the text is but a mediated reflex, the hermeneutics of suspicion, on Sedgwick's quite suspicious appraisal, is itself symptomatic of a reductively tendentious disposition.

To the often "ugly prescriptions" of the dominant paranoid approach, Sedgwick counterposes what she calls "reparative reading": one that attunes oneself to the contingencies of the text in question, allows oneself to experience the "joy-inducing" surprises they might offer, and (re)assembles the text on that basis.[3] Perhaps because Sedgwick herself has long displayed a thoroughgoing mastery of the suspicious interpretive mode that she latterly decries, her birthing of the reparative alternative remains notably underdeveloped. It did, however, prove suggestive enough to spawn an entire post-critical movement of exegesis known as "surface reading."

As articulated by its leading proponents, Stephen Best and Sharon Marcus, this (anti-) interpretive strategy contests not just the hermeneutics of suspicion and its associated methods (historicism, deconstruction, etc.), but also the "hermeneutics of depth," the search for any truth not "evident, perceptible, apprehensible in texts."[4] As its name implies, surface reading eschews the subtextual contradiction, disavowal, concealment, even latency, all the possible evidence of unconscious significance, ideological mesconnaisance or even textual reticence, in favor of salvaging or consolidating the apparent *vouloir dire* of the text, what it ostensibly wishes to say. "A surface," they hold, "is what insists on being looked at rather than what we must train ourselves to look through."[5] As a matter of practical engagement with literature, this injunction to an aggrandized superficiality translates as a determination to exclude from inquiry the textual "absences, gaps, ellipses" that have magnetized our scholarship, in preference for the manifest properties of the text.[6]

In the same year, 2003, Margot Norris introduced a dazzling body of work, under the title *Suspicious Readings of Joyce's Dubliners*, which reads as a concurrent refutation of Sedgwick's argument and a proleptic discrediting of the surface or "just" reading paradigm that followed.[7] Her volume is dedicated to the proposition that when it comes to literary modernism, and in particular to the arch-modernist fiction of James Joyce, the most authentically reparative approach is precisely a hermeneutics of the utmost suspicion. Skepticism alone respects and reckons with the various interpretive lures and ruses whereby narratives like those in *Dubliners* enact their own ideological intervention. Implicitly controverting Sedgwick's ham-handed identification of suspicion with paranoia, Norris amply demonstrates that a certain wariness in response to Joyce's richly equivocal narrative prompts forms a portal of discovery for all of the contingencies/possibilities that his text might harbor, rather than a strategy for filtering them out in the service of a preconceived master code or theoretical remit. Far from averting surprises, the hermeneutics of suspicion prove, for Norris, the most expansive and efficient means of *staging* them; far from devaluing "mere aesthetic pleasure," as Sedgwick complains, mistrustful reading, the counterpart of Joyce's own ideal of creative incertitude, joins the *plaisir du texte* with a *joie d'explication*, issuing in what Lacan calls *surplus jouissance*.[8]

Norris' critique of surface reading, though still implicit, is even sharper and more direct. She elucidates how Joyce's fluctuating, inferential narrative perspective and prismatic free indirect style encode absences and evoke silences with such immediacy as to indicate that the "gaps, fissures and ellipses" produced thereby do not lurk beneath or beyond the text, but linger on its surface, in the play of its signifiers and nowhere else. Indeed, for Norris, the narrative and the "silent discourses" that "supplement, interrogate and frequently dispute" the narrative are stitched inextricably in the fabric of each *Dubliners* story.[9] They are the warp and the woof of Joyce's text and, as such, are equally manifest on its pages. As Norris puts it, "My own sense of the 'text' constructs it as the narration supplemented by the questions and disputes produced by its elisions, gaps, and silences [...] what is not spoken or said nonetheless 'speaks' in the story."[10] The pressure of the unsaid, of the absented, is no less a presence than the impress of the words triggering that pressure. If as Best and Marcus contend, we should "see ghosts as presences, not absences, and let ghosts be ghosts, instead of saying what they are ghosts of,"[11] Norris' reading of Joyce's *Dubliners* counters with the insight that in the symbolic dimension, exemplified by Joyce's notoriously haunted cityscape, ghosts are presences indivisible from what they are ghosts of, the absences they comprise.

On Norris' astute reading, moreover, the "famous elisions" in Joyce's text, its "gaps, fissures, silences and lacunae," are not merely inscribed on its surface, they are "marked" there, "reported" in the narrative, their significance underscored no less forcibly than any turn of phrase.[12] In this respect, they serve as outward signs of an immanent counter-discourse lining the articulate narrative: not deep or repressed truths, but dissociated alternatives and contestations of the official line. They exist, in other words, precisely to provoke suspicion, and to provoke a specifically reparative manner of suspicion, nudging the reader to hold together the rifted tissue of the text, the manifest content and its manifestly implied but vacated supplement.

At the outset of *Dubliners*, Joyce introduces what is both a signal and an emblem of this interpretive dynamic, the structural key word gnomon, which names a complete geometric figure with a homologous section missing or, rather, excised. Taken on its own, the bracketed portion is an obvious correlative to the gaps and lacunae in Joyce's text, as Norris elaborates. If we think of the bracketed portion in its participation in the geometric figure as a whole, however, as a facet that belongs without being fully integrated, that is connected in the mode of detachment, the gnomonic piece might also be seen as an iconic trope for another still more strikingly superficial occlusion in Joyce's stories, *the loose end*. Now in a sense the loose end, rather than the omission, represents Joyce's primary means for inciting readerly interrogation. His first sustained attempt at narrative fiction, the epiphanies, can be seen as a series of loose ends, deliberately fashioned. By the time of *Dubliners*, he brought the loose end and the lacuna into close relation. The loose end serves as a key device for marking and remarking the fissures, evasions and elisions on the surface of the text. The loose end gives a certain positivity to textual vacuoles. It points to an immanence in the text while remaining fully present on its surface. The loose end is thus the plenary complement to the textual hiatus.

On the theory that extension is the sincerest form of scholarly flattery, my essay looks to augment Margot Norris' suspicious readings of Joyce's "famous elisions" with a focus on the loose ends that thread their way through the short story "Eveline," loose ends that no one to my knowledge, including Norris herself, has picked clean. Taking the imperative to suspicion to what I hope is an audacious yet constructive extreme, I will be looking to determine why, to what aesthetic and sociopolitical effect,

a) there appears in the middle of the story unnamed children whose very existence seems to have been ruled out from its beginning;
b) similarly, unnamed sisters appear at the beginning of the story only to disappear completely thereafter.

What decisive if understated role must we divine for these children to justify their previously excluded being-in-the-world? What corresponding role might be ascribed to the sisters and their unexplained vanishing from narrative consideration?

"Eveline" has long been a happy hunting ground for skeptical readers, beginning with Hugh Kenner's landmark article, "Molly's Master Stroke," which throws shade upon the motive and veracity—the frankness in short—of the sailor boy Frank, who promises a naïve, hapless Eveline a home, marriage, and a new improved life in Buenos Ayres.[13] Katherine Mullin counterbalances Kenner's derogation of Frank as "a bounder with a glib line" with a demystification of the anti-emigration propaganda and, specifically, the anti-emigration tale for which the *Irish Homestead*'s "Our Weekly Story" feature, where "Eveline" first appeared, was a prominent forum.[14] Mullin takes Frank himself to be both an agent of Argentinian recruitment and a parody of the predatory seducer and sex trafficker dear to the Irish anti-emigration campaign, and a similarly hapless Eveline to be pinioned, voiceless, between these clashing propaganda offensives. Norris breaks with this slighting, somewhat infantilizing attitude toward Eveline by, ironically, casting doubts upon her own motives and her candor if not her truthfulness. Norris disputes the impression that Eveline is besotted by Frank's charms or by the romantic fantasies of the fairy tale or penny romance to which his stereotypically handsome visage seems to allude ("his hair tumbled forward over a face of bronze" *D* 31). She is rather a person of "thoughtful calculation and consideration," who weighs the risks that Frank poses to her well-being ("He would drown her" *D* 34) against the benefits he might provide, not as a lover so much as a lever, a vehicle for extracting her from a tedious, laborious and injurious home life ("He would save her" *D* 33).[15] Exploring the "fissures in the ideological ideals of the *Irish Homestead* and the cooperative movement," Anne Fogarty turns a skeptical eye on the *Homestead*'s subtextual construction of "home," specifically the way that newspaper's inculcation of duty to a sanitized, sentimentalized version of the domestic status quo violated its own ambitious ethos of self-help and self-improvement. In the name of an ersatz nationalist solidarity, the cooperative movement's chief organ would deliver Eveline from "the sexual entrapment that Frank represents" back to "the violent predation of her father's house."[16]

The loose ends that I am isolating lead back still further into the recesses of the home life of the Hill family. They exist in the original version of the story published in the September 10, 1904 edition of the *Irish Homestead*, and they continued unchanged into the *Dubliners* volume, despite some modest but significant revision of the tale—including the addition of the line alluded to in my title, "Wondering where on earth all the dust came from" and the famous promises to Mother Mary Alacoque (D 29–30).[17] These loose ends would not, then, seem to be inadvertent, and so must be taken as purposeful.

Loose End I: The Children

The reader learns that among the quotidian hardships Eveline endures is the responsibility for seeing "that the two young children who had been left to her charge went to school regularly and got their meals regularly" (*D* 31). The reader is left to wonder, as Eveline does of the dust, "where on earth all the children came from?" Derek Attridge accounts for "the somewhat mysterious fact that she is caring for two small children" by suggesting that Eveline has become a "surrogate" for her deceased mother, whose dying request was for her "sole daughter," as he mistakenly says, to keep the home together. But this assumption cannot be correct.[18] If the two small children belong to Mrs. (and presumably Mr.) Hill, they would be Eveline's siblings, whom we are informed at the outset "were all grown up" and gone away (D 29). The fact remains mysterious. Margot Norris likewise deems Eveline a "surrogate mother" conscripted to raise her "deprecating father's" (and presumably her deceased mother's) children, a reading which comes a cropper on the same introductory passages of the story.[19]

If the children are to be ruled out as siblings, on Eveline's indirect testimony, perhaps they have come into the Hill household, and Eveline's care, by way of the time-honored Irish custom of fosterage. While this possibility is never overtly gainsaid, certain elements of Eveline's situation, her recruitment, and her ultimate response, militate against it. First of all, Eveline is an unlikely candidate for such an office, being only nineteen and unmarried. Secondly, she does not factor the children into her calculation about emigrating, which she would have probably felt the need to do had she taken them on a fosterage agreement. Third, at this time, for this class stratum, Irish fosterage would have typically involved close family or friends, for which Eveline would surely have given a thought before abandoning their offspring. She does, for instance, envision the reaction of the people at Clery's, her place of employment, to her departure, and yet she makes no mental reference to anyone to whom she might bear some responsibility as a foster parent. On the one hand, she calls to mind no current friends whatever. On the other, her brothers Ernest and Harry occupy her thoughts so insistently and prominently, it is hard to imagine that if either had "left to her charge" his children, she would have entirely omitted or barred that fact, that bond, from contemplation. So where *do* all the children come from and to whom do they belong? Why are they such a marginal item in Eveline's reported musings and thus in the story? Why are they forgotten as soon as brought to mind? All in all, the children seem to figure as loose ends in the life of Eveline no less than in the story "Eveline." Is the unaccounted for presence of these children evidence of something illicit, something to be kept out of view and even out of mind? That brings us to …

Loose Ends II: The Sisters

If I were to pose the question, how many siblings has Eveline, I suspect many of my readers, most perhaps, would say two, the deceased brother Ernest and the peripatetic brother Harry. But the correct answer, the *only* correct answer is that, like so much else in this story, we do not know. Remembering nostalgically her childhood play, Eveline refers to her presumably older brothers and sisters now grown up. Since unlike the brothers, the sisters are never mentioned again, and since unlike Harry, they are apparently to receive no farewell missive from Eveline, we tend to overlook them. Readerly amnesia follows the protagonist's amnesia. And since unlike the brothers, the sisters do not seem to count in Eveline's calculations, they are never counted. How many sisters? We do not know. What became of them? Why are they never mentioned again? Why are they, like the children, forgotten or blocked out as soon as recalled? Or, perhaps it is time to turn things around and ask a still more pertinent question about the children and the siblings both: *Why if they are to have such a fugitive, peripheral, unexplained place in the story did Joyce persist in keeping them around through the serious revision process between the impromptu newspaper entry and the long-delayed book?* Since the children and the sisters both lurk on the surface of the text without being fully incorporated into the narrative itinerary, their shared liminal status begs the question, is there a connection to be inferred between these two dissociated items, a common denominator that is not so much subtextual as paratextual: that is, a part of the text that is not just missing but present *as* missing, like the cut-out section of the gnomon, what Norris deems the reader's interpretive portion?[20] Can these two loose ends be tied together and woven seamlessly into the text? To start, we might consider the following question. Is it not plausible that the children "belong" in some way to one or more of these older sisters? And if so, why have they come home to roost, as it were, in the Hill's residence? And why then does the absentee mother go unremarked in Eveline's self-communion? How, finally, have the reasons for these children's presence slipped her consciousness altogether? The notion that something unacknowledged or inadmissible haunts this domestic space cannot but occur to suspicious minds. To solve this compound riddle, we now turn to another mother and …

Loose End III: "Derevaun Seraun!"

The description of Mrs. Hill's fatal decline is at once striking, even graphic, yet for all that cryptic, shrouded in mystery. Eveline's summary of her case, "that life of commonplace sacrifices closing in final craziness" (*D* 33), actually does nothing to diagnose or explain the craziness at issue. The mother's obsessive mantra, "Derevaun Seraun! Derevaun Seraun!" (33) is less telling for the constructions that can be placed upon it than for its intractable, mad illegibility. For it is precisely as word salad that her speech encapsulates the distressed opacity of her condition. To be sure, her gathering insanity can be understood as a simple effect of cognitive deterioration incident to her terminal illness, as in the case of Mrs. Dedalus in her last days (on the report of Buck Mulligan in *Ulysses*).[21] But there is also countervailing evidence to suggest a separate psychosocial cause that may have been exacerbated by the helplessness attending her physical ailment. Her dying wish to Eveline is not, it should be noted, to look after her father, or the family for that matter, but "to keep the home together" (*D* 33), a formulation that leaves open the nature of the company assembled there, especially since "Eveline," as the first story of adolescence, bears a marked structural relation to "A Boarding House," the initial story of adulthood. The call to keep the home together, while undoubtedly signaling the indispensable domestic role women were consigned to fulfill in Edwardian Ireland, also hints at some disruptive force that threatened to pull the "home" apart. Given the contingencies at play surrounding the children and the older sisters, it does not seem unwarranted to surmise some type of sexual intrigue, outrage, or scandal, which a customary social practice like fosterage would serve to conceal. With this in mind, and in the absence of any definitive grounds for Mrs. Hill's final "craziness," one might well speculate that she was driven to distraction by guilt, shame, or sorrow at her association with, awareness of, or connivance at the sexual violation—be it errancy or violence—that brought these children into her house and sent her own daughters away. A breakdown under the burden of such regret or self-reproach would, one might object, carry a melodramatic impact of the sort Joyce ordinarily eschewed, but then he does so here as well, leaving the matter in the conditional mode.

This scenario does, however, find reinforcement in, of all places, the conduct of Eveline herself at the close of the story. She and Mrs. Hill, mothers, surrogate and biological, are subjects of a psychic "crypt" not entirely unrelated to the material one the latter comes to occupy. As famously theorized by Nicolas Abraham and Maria Torok, a psychic crypt is a bulwark of repression, denial and forgetting that is transpersonal by definition, exceeding the bounds of the individual unconscious.[22] It is a defensive fortification organizing and binding an intimate group, like a family unit, around an unbearable, unaddressed enormity (taboo adherences or practices, guilty desires and their enactment, traumatic inflictions, sexual violence, etc.) to which the members are variously party, whether as perpetrators, victims, witnesses or accomplices. As the amphibolous name implies, a crypt both contains and encodes a corpus, which is to say it buries a corpus only to translate it into another form, one that can be read strictly from the perspective of group interaction. In this instance, Mrs. Hill's cataleptic symptomatology, the "foolish insistence" of her repeated nonsense phrase (*D* 33), is replicated in a (literally) muted but more extreme key in Eveline's last stand on the pier, where she is unable to make sense, to give a legible "sign." The parallel afflictions become more meaningful in consideration of the effect that Eveline's earlier "vision of her mother's life" has upon her. The specific language used—"laid its spell on the very quick of her being" (33)—points to something deeper than an identification with the "commonplace sacrifices" her mother had made or even alarm at the spectacle of her deepening mental debility. The word "spell," with its overtones of stupefaction and bewilderment, combines with the almost redundantly emphatic phrase "the very quick of her being" to suggest a shared source of existential distress so intimate and harrowing as to become dissociated from the conscious thought and conduct it nonetheless shapes. In this light, I would submit, Eveline's cataleptic disposition on the dock signifies more than terminal indecisiveness, inescapable constraint or even that well-worn Joycean trope of paralysis. Her body registers a full-on traumatic seizure, the embodied encrypting (in every sense) of a memory or affect lost to conscious processing, lost like her mother's "mind" somewhere on the trail of those loose ends. As the loose ends themselves, the inexplicably present children and the inexplicably absent sisters, betoken a scandalous sexual impropriety, the devastating if unconscious damage evidently visited upon Eveline and her mother indicates that the offense in question hits very close to home, involving them both personally if not directly.

In their essay, "Eveline at Home," Derek Attridge and Anne Fogarty observe that the story "nightmarishly reverses the fairy tale plot" (featured in Charles Dickens' "Donkeyskins") where the girl evades her "incestuous father."[23] Nevertheless, they confine their brief against Mr. Hill to what is recorded overtly in the text: the past commission and present threat of physical, as opposed to sexual, violence. But what if Joyce's inversion of the classic fairy tale narrative is more precise; what if Mr. Hill represents a renewed version of the "incestuous father," and those "mysterious" children are the fruit of his depravity, hidden in the plain sight of fosterage, their mother(s) having been ushered off to conceal the crime? What if the historical pattern of this family puts Eveline in the crosshairs for an assault more grievous, a violation more abominable, than a battering—though she cannot bring herself to recognize as much? Consider that when Eveline broods upon the likelihood of domestic abuse at the hands of her father, her mind goes to an idiomatic phrase, "gone for her," that carries an undercurrent of sexual pursuit. Her bodily response to paternal menace likewise carries unconscious erotic connotations; indeed, her phrase "given her the palpitations" might well have been taken from the same penny romance as Frank's "face of bronze" (30, 31). And although she claims her father had never "gone for her" previously (unlike Harry and Ernest) "because she was a girl" (*D* 30), she registers no such explicit gender exemption for her sisters. Her failure to mention them *at all* in this context might be an indication of their irrelevance, but it is more likely a signifier of her repression. She goes on to regret the loss of protection that her departed brothers might have offered her, without any suggestion that her sisters received the desired fraternal guardianship. Such evidence of the defensive cast of Eveline's mental formulation of past familial dysfunction supports a reading of her brothers' gender-specific abuse as screen memory: a painful remembered truth masking a positively intolerable, likewise gender-specific truth.

But if sexual abuse is centrally at issue in "Eveline," why does Joyce take pains to camouflage it, secreting it within the surface of his story? Correlatively, why do I, following the lead of Margot Norris, hold my reading to be not only suspicious but also reparative, or reparative in its very suspiciousness? Sexual abuse, and especially domestic or incestuous sexual abuse, is not coterminous with the assault itself, but comprehends the atmosphere of silence and concealment in which it both occurs and continues to infuse the life experience of its victims, witnesses and associated parties. The trauma of domestic or incestuous sexual abuse, for everyone involved, persists in its unconscious ramifications precisely to the extent that it overwhelms and impairs conscious apprehension. Joyce does not, then, shroud the story's deep truth, sexual abuse, in a web of disavowal and misrecognition; he does not occult the reality of sexual abuse as a determining factor of the Hill family fortune. Rather, he represents sexual abuse in full, as a transaction whose destructive force, widening impact and long-term effects, whose very reality, consist in such shrouding from view (in the act), from traumatized memory (in the aftermath) and from public notice (in guilt or shame). In "Eveline," Joyce undertakes the tricky narrative task of adducing the now notoriously Irish problem of domestic sexual abuse under a veil of erasure that was itself constitutive of the problem. The paradoxical difficulty confronting Joyce in this effort has been borne out in the critical history of the story: the greater the thoroughness and rigor with which his "highly polished looking glass" captures the obfuscated phenomenology of domestic sexual abuse, the greater the likelihood that his readers would miss the occasioning abuse altogether.[24] We must, as Norris proposes in her reading of the story "Clay," learn to read under a blindfold, a labor demanded in this case by the shadowy offense represented.[25] Perhaps. However, this crux is also where the loose end figures decisively as an interpretive prompt. Joyce's "famous elisions," gaps, and lacunae devices conduce to secrecy in a manner that might well carry the risks cited here, but loose ends, those surface markers inassimilable to the narrative line, announce the fact that they are disguising something without revealing openly *what* they are disguising, without violating the terms of the disguise. Woven together, the loose ends in "Eveline" thus bear a function analogous to Ariadne's thread. They direct the reader to the need to entertain a series of logical possibilities that can lead them to a moment of forensic epiphany, a revelation of the morally outrageous reality in the contours of its concealment.[26]

Once we entertain the contingency that Eveline has suffered sexual trauma by association in the past and as a looming threat for the future, her balked leave taking appears in a different, more complicated motivational light. According to the leading psychoanalytic theory on sexual trauma, "because the victim cannot recall the original traumatogenic event, she is fated to act it out or in other ways imitate it."[27] Eveline may not have suffered the "sheer extremity" of assault that "disables the victim's cognitive and perceptual capacities so that the experience never becomes part of the ordinary memory system."[28] But the family unit, exemplified by the disturbed mother, has undergone an ordeal to this effect, and the dissociated memory of the event has been transmitted to Eveline with (or as) the mandate to 'carry on' in domestic servitude and thereby cement the family crypt. On the "mimetic" paradigm of sexual trauma outlined here, Eveline's painstakingly rational calculation that Norris highlights, her cost–benefit analysis of her impending elopement, also turns out to be a form of rationalization: that is, a ratiocinative translation and misprision of turbulent, unconscious inclinations engendered by her traumatic family history. Enfolded in the calibration of her "right to happiness" versus her recognition of "duty" (*D* 33), of guaranteed "shelter and food" versus the dream of personal safety and respect, lies a more obscure dialectics of desire that cannot be brought to the scales of clear-eyed judgment, and so remains more controlling than controllable.

It seems Eveline's involvement with a prospective sexual miscreant like Frank is more than just bad luck. In him, Eveline has found an objectification of her own dramatic compulsion to repeat the fearful reality she cannot recall or grasp, but desperately wishes to escape. She gravitates to him on that basis. Her only reported affect during their initial courtship, "excitement," resonates of a thrilling agitation in the face of jeopardy no less than arousal in the hopes of gratification. In the theater of Eveline's unconscious, accordingly, Frank is the doppelganger, the reverse mirror image, of her father, the agent of the fearful reality she cannot recall or grasp, desperately wishes to escape, but feels compelled to repeat by remaining. Eveline's effort to "weigh both sides of the issue" (*D* 30) is thwarted by the fact that although Frank and her father seem to pose substantively different if equally weighty hopes and hazards, for Eveline they represent subliminally indistinguishable because emotionally isomorphic options: each is internally striated by cognate stripes of faith and fear. Frank and her father both constitute positive and negative force fields grounded in the traumatic legacy they promise/threaten to extend. At one point in her deliberations, Eveline commits an oft-remarked logical fallacy, which uncannily encapsulates her dilemma of decision: "Then she would be married [...] people would treat her with respect then. She would not be treated as her mother had been" (D 30). Since, as Norris remarks, "It was precisely marriage that visited poor treatment upon Eveline's mother," her thoughts can be seen to insist upon a disparity between her future life "at home" with her father and "another life with Frank" while simultaneously and subliminally registering their probable similitude (*D* 31). Her final state of irresolution is so profoundly immobilizing because it is (like so much of the volume Joyce called "doublingers") doubly articulated. Her more obvious, consciously entertained conflict, predicated upon the different prospects for security and fulfillment posed by staying with father or leaving with Frank, is haunted by an unconscious conflict predicated upon the emotionally fraught aporia at the heart of either course of action, rendering them demoralizingly alike. Such is the profound psychomachia holding Eveline mute and motionless, without voice or effective agency, a psychomachia best explained by reference to those loose ends and the sexual trauma they index.

Coda

Eve Sedgwick would doubtlessly judge my extension of Margot Norris's suspicious reading to be full-on paranoid. I will accept in some measure the designation, if not its pathological implications, with two important provisos. Both draw upon conceptual axioms of the strategic presentism movement of VI 21: the idea that our readings of past literature and culture not only are but *should be* motivated by certain features of the present.

1 Mine is a "paranoia" shared in large part by the child sex scandal Irish literature of recent years, whose authors—Ann Enright (*The Gathering*), Edna O'Brien (*Down by the River*), Keith Ridgeway (*The Long Falling*), Sebastian Barry (*The Secret Scripture*), and Jaime O'Neill (*At Swim Two Boys*)—all allude to Joyce as a founding figure of their own excavation project.

2 Everything from #MeToo to the Catholic Church's cover-up of clerical rape demonstrates that sexual assault and its consequences for all involved parties desperately needs to have been the subject of *more* rather than less paranoia, both in Ireland and here in the United States.

Notes

1 Eve Sedgwick. *Thinking Feeling: Affect, Pedagogy, Performativity.* (Durham: Duke University Press, 2003), 123–51.
2 Ibid., 129, 135–38.
3 Ibid., 144, 147.
4 Stephen Best and Sharon Marcus. "Surface Reading: An Introduction." *Representations* 108 (Fall 2009), 9.
5 Ibid.
6 Ibid., 3.
7 Margot Norris. *Suspicious Readings of Joyce's Dubliners.* (Philadelphia: Penn Press, 2003).
8 Sedgwick, 143. Jacques Lacan. *The Seminar of Jacques Lacan. Book XX, On Feminine Sexuality.* (New York: Norton, 1998), 16–17.
9 Norris, 9.
10 Ibid., 10.
11 Best and Marcus, 13.
12 Norris, 9.
13 Hugh Kenner. "Molly's Masterstroke." James Joyce Quarterly 10.1 (Fall 1972), 20.
14 Katherine Mullin. "'Don't Cry for Me Argentina': 'Eveline' and the Seductions of Anti-Emigration Propaganda" in *Semicolonial Joyce*, ed. D. Attridge and M. Howes (Cambridge: Cambridge University Press, 2000), 171–82.
15 Norris, 60
16 Derek Attridge and Anne Fogarty. "'Eveline' at Home" in *Collaborative Dubliners*, ed. V. Mahaffey (Syracuse: Syracuse University Press, 1012), 105.
17 *The Irish Homestead*, September 10, 1904. "Our Weekly Story," 761
18 Attridge and Fogarty, 95.

19 Norris, 57, 60.
20 Ibid., 2–3.
21 James Joyce. *Ulysses.* (New York: Viking, 1986), 7.
22 Nicolas Abraham and Maria Torok. *The Shell and the Kernel.* (Chicago: University of Chicago Press, 2004), 157–61.
23 Attridge and Fogarty, 107.
24 James Joyce. *The Letters of James Joyce.* Volume I, ed. S. Gilbert. (New York: Viking. 1965), 64.
25 Norris, 146–57.
26 A further clue, noted by Terence Brown, is the allusion in the eponymous title, "Eveline," to a pornographic protagonist who has incestuous intercourse with various family members, her father included. Although Eveline herself would seem too young to be the biological mother, incestuous or otherwise, to school age children, the allusion does "suggest a subterranean theme of sexual abuse" narratively indexed by the loose ends cited here. See James Joyce. *A Portrait of the Artist as a Young Man,* ed. Terence Brown (NY: Penguin, 1967), 253n1.
27 Ruth Leys. *Trauma: A Genealogy.* (Chicago: University of Chicago Press, 2000), 298.
28 Ibid.

Chapter 4

FREE INDIRECT PALAVER

Kezia Whiting

The verbal repetitions that flicker through Joyce's free indirect style in *Dubliners* arouse the interpretive unease that Margot Norris describes as an effect of Joyce's style, and point to the intersubjective and ideological make-up of the narration.[1] Norris's vacillation between personifying the narration of the different stories or "merely endow[ing] it with a function"[2] indicates some of the difficult questions raised by Joyce's narration (which are also questions endemic to free indirect style): where do these particular words come from? Do they (and how do they) give rise to the impression of a unique, cohering mind, of a character? While these questions might prompt us to assign words to *either* a character *or* a separate function of narration, as is the standard critical response to the braid of free indirect style, this kind of textual unravelling entirely misses the point: Joyce's intricate free indirect style entangles narration and character, such that they produce, respond to, and incorporate one another. Joyce's free indirect style both acts in accordance with a character's needs and desires *and* destabilizes their self-conception, but even this threat cannot be severed from the character. The free indirect style of *Dubliners* reveals, and revels in, the textuality of thoughts, such that the characters are produced by a machinery of contagion and repetition that violates any supposed autonomy or self-containment. The culmination of Joyce's repetitions in the final paragraph of "The Dead" highlights what his technique always generates: the simultaneous dissolution and unification of the subject.[3] Like Norris, I consider the narration of *Dubliners* to be either in "collusion or conflict with one or another figure in the story,"[4] but, for me, that collusion or conflict plays out within the subject itself: if the narration bolsters the character, that bolstering is part of their own defensive strategies; if it undermines the character, that undermining cannot be separated from their internalization of being observed.

Norris's approach to *Dubliners* examines its "writerly" (following Barthes) composition, finding that since the 80s "we have more and more the sense that in the process of reading the text we are completing it, producing new versions of it, writing it anew."[5] In this aspect, Norris's implicit forerunner is Hugh Kenner, as her tribute to him shows: she casts him as she had already described herself (in *Suspicious Readings*) as treating Joyce's texts as writerly, filling in their "gaps and void spaces with such powerful, convincing supplements" that they have become a "critical unconscious."[6] In her focus on Joyce's style and strategies of narration, as well as her powerful "speculative counter-narrative" readings of the text, Norris takes up and extends Kenner's approach to Joyce.[7]

Of what is perhaps Kenner's most well-known contribution to Joyce studies, Norris acknowledges that "[w]e could argue over whether Joyce invented free indirect discourse, or whether Hugh Kenner merely discovered its use in Joyce's writing. Kenner's Uncle Charles Principle made this unobtrusive narrative practice audible" ("The Voice and the Void" 485). In fact, Kenner does not necessarily attribute the *invention* of free indirect style to Joyce, but its re-invention. What for Kenner "is apparently something new in fiction, the normally neutral narrative vocabulary pervaded by a little cloud of idioms" is expounded as follows: "which a character might use *if he were managing the narrative*."[8] The constructed and retrospective quality Kenner finds in Joyce's free indirect style is what is new in fiction. The Uncle Charles Principle is often taken as a classic description of the technique of free indirect style, but the emphasis Kenner places on writing in Joyce's use of the technique represents a significant difference from its nineteenth-century predecessor: Kenner tells us the principle involves "*writing* about someone much as that someone would choose to be *written* about."[9] In Joyce, the narration's overtly *written* component entails a new self-reflexivity of character and text, a self-reflexivity that produces a watchfulness at the center of the character, aware of their possible surveillance by others and their presentation in text.

Mechanical descriptions of Joyce's work begin with Joyce himself, as Jean-Michel Rabaté shows when he examines Joyce's own mechanical metaphors to describe *Finnegans Wake*, which Rabaté calls "a word-machine, or a complex machination of meanings, probing and programming the seamy sides of meaning."[10] But this word-machine is already at play in *Dubliners*, where its loosening of traditional conceptions of character and psychology is quietly insistent. The evident challenge *Finnegans Wake* poses to the conception of character (in fiction and social reality), as Derek Attridge finds, is its disintegration of "character as a way of conceptualizing the subject," revealing the "multiplicity and uncertainty [of character] as a culturally produced, historically determined, signifying practice."[11] *Finnegans Wake* does so by "breaking down the boundaries and structures of a word," and "delighting in the multiplicity and uncertainty of meaning normally held at bay by those boundaries, structures, and distinctions," an operation I argue which is already subtly at work in the free indirect style of *Dubliners*, with its strange and generative repetitions.[12] For Norris, reading *Finnegans Wake* through *Dubliners* makes "*Dubliners* much more wild and strange and defamiliarized," a wildness I too wish to foreground.[13] Throughout my essay I rehear a question posed in *Finnegans Wake*—"where did thots come from?" (597.25)—in the narration of *Dubliners*. This child's question, overlaying thinking and children, anticipates the baby coming from some other place (via stork perhaps), and thus attributes to thought the same externality. In particular, the repetitions of *Dubliners* initiate Joyce's articulation of the mechanized production and textuality of "thots."

In Joyce criticism, Kenner turns to the mechanical to describe Joyce's narration and his particular version of free indirect style. The image still holds character and text apart, but their proximity begins to disrupt this distinction: "[Joyce's] words are in such delicate equilibrium, like the components of a sensitive piece of apparatus, that they detect the gravitational field of the nearest person."[14] His simple definition of the Uncle Charles Principle, that "the narrative idiom need not be the narrator's" engenders a whole new perspective on the relation between narration and character, one which, followed to its conclusion, elides the concept of the "narrator" entirely: the motivation, the relation between events and words, the reasons for showing some things and not others, all of these cannot be isolated as simply "the narrator's."[15] Kenner's recognition of Joyce's innovation to free indirect style quickly risks erasing its innovation (its deliberate fuzziness, and thus the intermingling of thought and world it furnishes), in the critical attempt to pinpoint specific words as coming from inside or outside a character. And yet Kenner's description, figuring Joyce's text as the machine which sensitively responds to people, in fact suggests that the "psychology" Joycean free indirect style gives us access to is above all textual, a ghostly effect of one set of words influencing another, a mechanical reproduction. In subsuming the psychological to the mechanical, Joyce's character-effects become products of various discourses caught up in (or inputted to) the narration. These discourses coalesce and disperse, with characters eventually emerging—contingent and unstable—a product of ever-shifting languages.[16] The mechanical does not oppose the psychological, but establishes and unifies it even as it demonstrates its precarious construction.

The narration's incorporation of, engagement with, and resistance to cultural norms and values shows the emerging character, like any subject, to be constituted by their existence in the social world. As Norris's readings demonstrate, narration in *Dubliners* is "not only intersubjective but also social and ideological."[17] Kenner says as much in claiming that "the domain of the interior monologue is actually external," a narrational structuring that heightens Joyce's stylistic disintegration of the self-contained subject (and character) through the enmeshment of narration and character.[18] In showing the cultural and ideological texts that produce and function as thought, Joyce's interior monologue erodes the clear demarcation of character: an articulation of the subject in these terms can only even be its simultaneous disarticulation, in that it is no longer closed-off or self-contained. And it is not just Joyce's interior monologue that demonstrates this external-internal logic of the subject—in fact, it is best articulated through his free indirect style, as Joseph Valente suggests when discussing "Counterparts": Farrington's words are "sufficiently estranged from their author to seem external in origin, but sufficiently proximate to count as his own. In this respect, they represent a perfect correlative to the indirect free style itself, which is usually understood to unfold the characteristically modernist interest in psychic interiority, but only does so while marking the self-alienation of that interiority."[19] As Valente implies, the exteriority of free indirect style does not oppose its presentation of interiority: rather, free indirect style enables Joyce to showcase the self-policing, self-observing, self-concealing operations that are not just within, but that constitute the subject: its otherness from itself.

Indeed, some of the most significant concerns in "The Dead"—haunting, misunderstanding, the transition from Victorian to modern culture, identity, and the politics of borders (specifically nationalist ones: Irish, European, and English)—are all also endemic to free indirect style, making it the perfect narrational counterpart to intensify the story's thematics. "The Dead" begins with one of the most frequently cited examples of Joycean free indirect style, indicating the centrality of this technique to the story: "Lily, the caretaker's daughter, was literally run off her feet" (*D* 138). All that we know about Lily, by the time we get to the "literally" solecism, is her name and her father's occupation. So although her working-class status is evident, it still seems a lot to assume that the word "literally" is literally how Lily would describe her metaphorical state, along with what Michael Mayo calls the "passive-aggression" of the appellative, "the caretaker's daughter" (especially when it is repeated only a few sentences later).[20] Kenner tells us "It is Lily, not the austere author, whose habit it is to say 'literally' when 'figuratively' is meant, and the author is less recounting the front-hall doings than paraphrasing a recounting of hers."[21] But the problem with approaching "literally" as Lily's word is the assumptions we have to make about the existence of characters outside—before and after—the texts in which they exist, as well as about Lily, when we know so little of her ("perhaps illiterate," Kenner proposes, even though she tells Gabriel "I'm done schooling this year and more" [*D* 14]).[22] If, as Norris does, we place importance on the "virgin" reading of "The Dead," then it is difficult to see how one can definitively adduce that the *first* sentence of a story displays a particular character's idiom. Even on re-reading, we are not presented with enough of Lily's words to know her idiom: the only words we actually hear her speak, other than a brief address to Kate Morkan, are to Gabriel, where she shocks him not with solecisms but with her forthrightness (Joyce, *D* 139–40). Indeed, Mayo's reading of the opening paragraphs suggests that on re-reading, it is even more difficult to consider the opening sentence to be inflected by Lily's idiom.

And yet an impression of Lily is there. The sentence demonstrates the textual mechanism of character production in Joyce, whereby one word produces another until a series of repetitions or variations cohere into an idea of a character. Here, the word "literally," which begins with the first syllable of her name and ends with the second "*li*teral*ly*," is called forth by its echo of "Lily." Poor Lily, "sweet-talk[ed] and abandon[ed]" by the narrative, treated by it "as a decorative fixture at the party without inquiring further into her social reality," is forever associated with the misuse of this word, with critical consensus agreeing that this is just the kind of thing she would say.[23] Norris is one of the few critics not to attribute the story's opening directly to Lily. In fact, following Norris's astute observation concerning the "bourgeois agenda of the narrative voice at this moment"—namely that the "social interests of the opening narrative are not Lily's interests but rather Morkan and Conroy interests—perhaps even Morkan and Conroy constructions of what they would *like* Lily's views to be, what Lily *ought* to be saying and thinking about herself and them"—we begin to see that perhaps all of Lily that is on display is her overt *writtenness*, her construction by how another might write her.[24]

Lily's conversation with Gabriel is the first in a series of interactions in which his self-conception is threatened by the way someone else sees him. Joking with Lily about her love life, Gabriel is taken aback by her "bitter and sudden retort": "Gabriel coloured *as if* he felt he had made a mistake and, without looking at her, kicked off his galoshes and flicked actively with his muffler at his patent-leather shoes." (*D* 140; my emphasis). "As if" marks the narration's ambiguous distance from Gabriel's thoughts. The sentence hypothesizes an affect behind Gabriel's blush, moving from his appearance to his feelings, while highlighting the relatively safe assumption—that his coloring signifies he feels he has made a mistake—as only supposition. Presenting Gabriel's feelings as only the vehicle of a simile reminds us that we do not know if this is indeed how Gabriel felt, and that all that is actually described is his appearance. Rhetorically, the sentence inverts the common practice of using appearance to decipher interior feeling, even as it masquerades as such a maneuver.

After this quasi-foray into Gabriel's feelings, the narration retreats into an ostensibly external, objective description of Gabriel, in which his glasses screen his eyes (just as his feelings are screened from us in the description of the face we are given to read). For Pecora, this passage "more accurately reflects what Gabriel sees, or wants others to see, in the mirror of those glistening shoes" (*D* 238):

> He was a stout tallish young man. The high colour of his cheeks pushed upwards even to his forehead where it scattered itself in a few formless patches of pale red; and on his hairless face there scintillated *restlessly* the polished lenses and the bright gilt rims of the glasses which screened his delicate and *restless* eyes. His glossy black hair was parted in the middle and brushed in a long curve behind his ears where it curled slightly beneath the groove left by his hat.
>
> When he had flicked lustre into his shoes he stood up and pulled his waistcoat down more tightly on his plump body. Then he took a coin rapidly from his pocket. (140; my emphasis)

The repetition of restless (in its adjectival and adverbial form) within a sentence confirms that something other than a purely objective narration is at work, an example of the repetitions that come to mark moments of particularly heightened anxiety or emotion for Gabriel. The narration itself restlessly scintillates across the page, flashing its repetitions and alliterations, producing the jittery impression Gabriel conveys. The free indirect style reflects Gabriel's self-consciousness, and in reflecting it, also produces it as the gaze Gabriel constantly postulates. Gabriel needs a moment to collect himself after his blunder, which is why he *actively* flicks his shoes with his muffler, while actively indicating his apparent absorption in the task at hand; but as Norris insists, we should not take the narration of *Dubliners* at its word. It is as though the text responds to Gabriel's need, shielding him from our curiosity about his feelings while he (literally) composes himself. Let us not forget Norris's warning that the narrative voice of "The Dead" is "in league with Gabriel Conroy."[25] Only after Gabriel has regained some control in his relationship to Lily—by forcing the coin on her—does the narration *seem* to get closer to his feelings.[26]

As I've suggested, this textual cover-up is in fact already in sync with Gabriel—to modify Kenner's description of free indirect style, the narration, in shielding him, is influenced by Gabriel's gravitational field, colluding with him even before being "pervaded by a little cloud of [Gabriel's] idioms."[27] Norris touches on this idea when she situates Joyce's narration as a retrospective recounting of events (while diverging from Kenner's analysis, she acknowledges that her "construction of this narrative voice draws on Hugh Kenner's Uncle Charles Principle").[28] Norris proposes that "all narrations could be thought of as *twice-told* events in the sense that they are grounded in a kind of imaginative prior interpretation—an imagined interlocution in which the narrator is an imagined narratee hearing in the mind's ear, as it were, events put together as a story for further retelling."[29] Within the mind's ear the narration eavesdrops on Gabriel's thoughts (prompting him to compose his thoughts and actions with careful dodges) even as it helps him to maintain his pretenses.

The "as if" formulation recurs in relation to Gabriel's feelings multiple times, each highlighting the ambiguity of the knowledge the narration has of Gabriel. In *Dubliners*, Joyce begins experimenting with the relationship between narration and character, with how to narrate the subterfuge familiar to readers of both Gabriel and Leopold Bloom, how to show what is known, what is unsaid, and what is unconscious. The next "as if," in Gabriel's response to Gretta's teasing commentary on the galoshes, again highlights the narration's inability to interpret Gabriel's appearance with certainty, revealing its indeterminate position inside or outside Gabriel's mind: "Gabriel knitted his brows [...] as if he were slightly angered" (*D* 142). "As if" reiterates that the emotion itself is nothing more than one in a series of expected performances. This interaction with Gretta and his aunts is, after all, part of "a standing joke with them" (*D* 142), at "a social event whose participants know their parts virtually by rote."[30]

In fact, one of the habitual gestures constituting Gabriel's role is the above "knitted brows." When Molly Ivors asks "Who is G. C.?," referring to his column in *The Daily Express*, "Gabriel coloured and was about to knit his brows, as if he did not understand" (*D* 147): "as if" now interprets—at a remove—something that never happened, though it may have been expected to happen. The sentence describes both Gabriel's innocent incomprehension of Molly's question and his knowing pretense of that incomprehension. This sentence is strangely placed within and without Gabriel, knowing he is "about to" knit his brows without stating what that unperformed knitting would have signified, and drawing attention to Gabriel's unperformed performance of incomprehension, whether or not it is sincere, all conveyed through the ambiguity of the "as if." With its emphasis on Gabriel's appearance "as if" suggests a simulation (it was *as if* he did not understand *when in fact* ...), but we wait for a revelation that does not arrive. The free indirect style that allows "as if" to pretend to explicate Gabriel's behavior without actually doing so reinforces *and* undermines Gabriel's posturing.

Gabriel is never not posing in some way, and the narration both watches and produces that posturing. His concern that he will "make himself ridiculous" (*D* 140) in his speech already indicates his anxiety how he appears to others, a concern which recurs after the conversation with Molly: "she had no right to call him a West Briton before people, even in joke. She had tried to make him ridiculous before people, heckling him and staring at him with her rabbit's eyes" (*D* 150). The repetition of "before people" and the description of Molly's eyes highlights Gabriel's concern with his appearance, with being made ridiculous less important than it happening "before people." Repeating "before people" at the end of a phrase two sentences in a row produces a stuttering, halting quality, showing the fixed point of Gabriel's thoughts.

The repeated phrases or words of Joyce's free indirect style throughout *Dubliners* introduce into the psychological realism of the nineteenth-century production of character a mechanization both fundamental and corrosive. The repetitions toward the end of "A Little Cloud" attest to this corrosive production of character, which Joyce develops further in "The Dead":

> He looked coldly into the eyes of the photograph and they answered coldly. Certainly they were pretty and the face itself was pretty. But he found something mean in it. Why was it so unconscious and lady-like? The composure of the eyes irritated him. They repelled him and defied him: there was no passion in them, no rapture. He thought of what Gallaher had said about rich Jewesses. Those dark Oriental eyes, he thought, how full they are of passion, of voluptuous longing! [...] Why had he married the eyes in the photograph?
>
> He caught himself up at the question and glanced nervously round the room. He found something mean in the pretty furniture which he had bought for his house on the hire system. Annie had chosen it herself and it reminded him of her. It too was prim and pretty. A dull resentment against his life awoke within him. (*D* 63)

The first sentence is a primer in the way Joyce's text functions mechanically, with the communication between Little Chandler's eyes and those of his wife, Annie, paralleling the text's reflection of the word "coldly." Do her eyes reflect his eyes, does he only see his own reflection in the surface of the glass, or do they answer coldly simply as a textual echo, a repetition through which we postulate character? The paired repetitions of pretty (describing Annie's eyes and face in the second sentence and the furniture in the second paragraph) further develop this effect of textual mirroring, so that what we eventually find "mean" is the look that can "find something mean" in eyes and furniture alike. Like the free indirect style, Little Chandler blurs distinctions. The parallel between the furniture and Annie is reiterated in the next sentence that superfluously tells us "it reminded him of her." The periphrasis is Little Chandler's, his thoughts circuiting through the mechanical repetition of adjectives that come to link Annie to the furniture. Little Chandler reduces his wife to a pair of eyes, which, in reflecting his cold look both do and do not have their own agency. They are capable of answering, but only to mirror his look, with his omnipresent sense of being seen materialized in his wife's eyes. As the desire to escape his life builds in this passage, he wishes for another pair of eyes—foreign, exotic eyes—to see him and define him through their look. The repeating adjectives—coldly, pretty, and mean—suggest the circular mechanism of Little Chandler's thoughts, with a word entangling itself into other thoughts once it has been used. The eyes pervading the ending of the story indicate how thoroughly Little Chandler feels himself observed, and indeed his being seen is folded back into the text itself in the free indirect style which sees him seeing his wife. The passage's preoccupation with eyes self-reflexively thematizes the watchfulness at the heart of Joyce's protagonists, always aware of their possible surveillance by others and their presentation in text. In this case, Little Chandler's thoroughly dissatisfied reflections on his own life are knitted to the text's scrutiny of him.

It is not quite, as Kenner claims of Gerty MacDowell, that the characters are "caught up into the narrative machinery," but that they are produced by this narrative machinery, by the textual logic of contagion and repetition.[31] And yet, in "The Dead," Gabriel is not just produced by this textual contagion; he begets it. More than a "little cloud of idioms," it is a stylistic tic that betrays Gabriel's sway over the narration.[32] A number of Joyce's Dubliners, including Little Chandler and Gabriel, rely on writing for their self-conception: none more so than James Duffy, with his "odd autobiographical habit which led him to compose in his mind from time to time a short sentence about himself containing a subject in the third person and a predicate in the past tense" (*D* 83).[33] Duffy's habit is a perfect example of "writing about someone much as that someone would choose to be written about."[34] This single sentence makes possible a shift of authorship from Joyce to Duffy, the whole story produced by Duffy's "odd autobiographical habit," with the distance and apparent externality of the third person, and not the first, what marks it as belonging to him. The external vision afforded by the third person allows Duffy to *compose* himself, reminding himself that he is seen by others. And there is a similar effect throughout "The Dead": Gabriel's watchfulness and care not to give too much of himself away incentivizes the story's apparently objective passages, in which free indirect style shows Gabriel everywhere he appears not to be. John Paul Riquelme thinks that the story's free indirect style invites the reader "to stand in two places at once as the recipient of what may be the character's private language, addressed to no one except himself, and as the recipient of the narrator's public language, addressed to us."[35] But thoughts are never addressed to only their thinker.

There is no "private language" for Gabriel, or for any of Joyce's protagonists—their thoughts are always guarded, self-reflexive, infused with conceptions of propriety, and very much aware of their "public" reception. The "public language" of the narration is intrinsic to Gabriel's experience. As Norris notes, Gabriel "postures not only in his words and speeches but even in his most intimate thoughts."[36] Free indirect style is the perfect vehicle for Joyce to convey the public construction of our thoughts and their habitual deceptions to ourselves and others.

Gabriel's awareness of the public nature of thought does not lessen his self-absorption, but intensifies it. After hearing Gretta's story, he reflects that "[w]hile he had been full of memories of their secret life together, full of tenderness and joy and desire, she had been comparing him in her mind with another" (*D* 173). In his self-pity Gabriel is no more correct in thinking Gretta has been comparing him in her mind with another than he was earlier when he assumed he knew what she was thinking—indeed, thinking that she has been comparing him with Michael Furey, when all we know is that she has been thinking of Michael Furey, shows the tenacity of his solipsism.

Pecora suggests that in the ending of the story Gabriel "turns his life into a text, he mythologizes his existence in a literary emancipation that can in fact only repeat the contradictions and anxieties he longs to overcome."[37] Indeed, Gabriel's tendency to self-authorship is evident in the repetitions of this sentence, where his perhaps fictional memories inform and bolster his self-conception in this moment of revelation through decidedly textual operations. The repetitions of "secret life" and "tenderness" make explicit Gabriel's pointed re-visioning of the moment when he and Gretta are walking back with the others along the Liffey, when these phrases are first used:

> He longed to defend [Gretta] against something and then to be alone with her. Moments of their secret life together burst like stars upon his memory. [...] He was standing with her in the cold, looking in through a grated window at a man making bottles in a roaring furnace. It was very cold. Her face, fragrant in the cold air, was quite close to his; and suddenly she called out to the man at the furnace:
>
> —Is the fire hot, sir?
>
> [...] A wave of yet more tender joy escaped from his heart and went coursing in warm flood along his arteries. Like the tender fires of stars moments of their life together, that no one knew of or would ever know of, broke upon and illumined his memory. He longed to recall to her those moments, to make her forget the years of their dull existence together and remember only their moments of ecstasy. For the years, he felt, had

> not quite quenched his soul or hers. Their children, his writing, her household cares had not quenched all their souls' tender fire. In one letter he had written to her then he had said: *Why is it that words like these seem to me so dull and cold? Is it because there is no word tender enough to be your name?* (*D* 168)

The six times Joyce uses the word "tender" in *Dubliners* all occur in "The Dead," five on the same page—and four in this paragraph. The repetitions create a wave-like effect, repeating and building on previous images, like the waves of tender joy that course through Gabriel. "Tender" radiates through the passage, orienting and framing Gabriel's romanticized description of his and Gretta's relationship. These images are repeated and reworked later when it begins to dawn on Gabriel that Gretta has not been thinking of him: "A dull anger began to gather again at the back of his mind and the dull fires of his lust began to glow angrily in his veins (*D* 172). In this sentence, Gabriel's "tender fire" is rebranded as "dull" while his "tenderness" is explicitly named "lust." The adjective "dull" is recycled from both the "dull slumber" described in Joyce's letter and Gabriel's characterization of his and Gretta's "dull existence together." The dullness of the sentence itself, with the doubling of dull and angry, is the result of Gabriel's snuffed out desire. His passion runs its course via a cycle of fire imagery, which intensifies from what he thinks of as his and Gretta's mutual "souls' tender fire," to his "fever of rage and desire" as he longs to overmaster her, then ends in this dull glow. Norris implies that the text's propensity to repetition stems from Gabriel when she suggests that "[t]he text's obsession with the phrase [Gabriel's description of Browning's poetry], like Gabriel's, is with its quotability, the aesthetic ring that invites reiteration and repetition. Indeed, Gabriel rhetorically asks permission from himself to borrow part of his own phrase for his after-dinner speech."[38] In fact, we can read all the repetitions of the story, its touchstone phrases, as marking Gabriel's inseparability from the narration, displaying his infatuation with "the quotability and lyricism of his own phrase" and his literary posturing and habit of seeing himself from the outside, as if in the third person.[39]

But if all these repetitions are productions of Gabriel and his different emotional states, then what do we do with the last paragraphs of the story: are the repetitions there Gabriel's, or are they, with their chiasmatic crescendo, the erasure of Gabriel, the marker of his absence as his "identity was fading out into a grey impalpable world" (*D* 176)? Even as it describes a loss of identity, the syntax of this phrase points to Gabriel through its repetitions of words already used to describe Gabriel's thoughts and feelings. "Fading" takes us back to "fade" in the previous paragraph, in which Gabriel reckons it better to "pass boldly into that other world [...] than fade and wither dismally with age" (*D* 176). With this dismissal of ageing in mind, the recurrence of "fade" begins to feel quite familiar, especially since "grey," repeatedly used in the story to refer to his aunts' old age, accompanies it. Ageing itself requires an overhauling of one's self-conception, is its own kind of identity loss—just not the plaintive, sacrificial dissolution Gabriel ascribes to himself. The sentence also recycles "impalpable," used earlier to describe the "impalpable and vindictive being" Gabriel feels opposing him:

> A vague terror seized Gabriel at this answer as if, at that hour when he had hoped to triumph, some impalpable and vindictive being was coming against him, gathering forces against him in its vague world. But he shook himself free of it with an effort of reason and continued to caress her hand. He did not question her again for he felt that she would tell him of herself. Her hand was warm and moist: it did not respond to his touch but he continued to caress it just as he had caressed her first letter to him that spring morning. (*D* 174)

This paragraph, and its play with the word "vague," initiates the juxtaposition and nebulous relationship between the solidity and the impalpability of the world taken up in the penultimate paragraph where "impalpable" is repeated, which likewise presents character itself as both solid and indistinct. The movement of the descriptor "vague" from Gabriel's terror to the vindictive being's world suggests that whatever gathers forces against Gabriel is already part of him, highlighting the connection between himself and Furey. Gabriel's vague terror can be read either as unspecified or as a specific terror of vagueness, vagueness which is ironically embodied in Furey's ghostliness and is also the effect of the free indirect style from which Gabriel emerges.

In the first words of the penultimate paragraph—"Generous tears filled Gabriel's eyes" (*D* 176)—Joyce's free indirect style irradiates their uncertain proprietorship. Gretta bestows the adjective "generous" on Gabriel a few pages earlier in response to his story of pecuniary circuity, an apparent ploy to disguise Gabriel's desire to possess Gretta by parading his solvency. It is while telling Gretta about the pound he lent to Malins that his "desire to seize her" peaks, entwining his (in)ability "to overmaster her" with his generosity, and his desire to dominate with his affluence (*D* 170). A similar entanglement between his self-imaged generosity and arousal occurs earlier in Gabriel's attempt to give Lily the coin, which Norris reads as following his possible "repressed sexual interest" in Lily.[40] When "generous" re-surfaces in the story's ending it mocks Gabriel's eagerness and presumptuousness, but I would suggest it is his own self-pity that produces this mockery, and which nonetheless returns to an image of Gabriel as a possessive individual. "Generous," following Kenner's principle, is how Gabriel would describe his weeping retrospectively, creating a sense of both proximity to Gabriel's feelings and ironic distance from them.[41] The mechanical memory of the text churns up "generous" to characterize Gabriel, generous in its appellations and the multiplicitous meanings created. Riquelme suggests that the word could be "the narrator's judgment about Gabriel's feelings rather than a description or rendering of them unless we maintain that in the midst of crying he is aware of the size of his own tears"[42]: well, the story is not told in the present tense so we do not have to assume the narration is simultaneous with the events, but Riquelme actually gives us a fitting description of Gabriel's pretensions and self-romanticization. Of course he would be aware of the size of his own tears as he cries.[43]

The story's ending does not mark a shift away from Gabriel into a "seemingly objective narrator" as Johnson suggests.[44] Nor does he experience "a dissolution of the self," and if he does give "up *something*, his deluded sense of control, superiority, and knowledge" this is only to replace it with an exaggerated debasement that is merely an inversion of his self-importance.[45] We find Gabriel in the midst of the narration's seeming objectivity, in the midst of this dissolution, contemplating his own self-dispossession (and therefore as much in possession of it as ever): "His own identity was fading out into a grey impalpable world: the solid world itself which these dead had one time reared and lived in was dissolving and dwindling" (*D* 176). The confusion between an impalpable world and a solid one, and between a world that is reared while being lived in, is passed over as the sentence ends with the lessening of the world it describes. But, as with all those times "when a narration can be caught in a confusion, disjunction, contradiction, or even a lie" (Norris, *Suspicious Readings* 7), these inconsistencies indicate the narration's lack of objectivity even as Gabriel is supposedly dwindling in the text—they hint at the "blizzard of palaver" Norris scents out in these final paragraphs.[46]

The text's penchant for repetition culminates in the final paragraph, and, as elsewhere, displays Gabriel's orchestration.[47] The paragraph recycles Mary Jane's observation, itself quoted from the newspaper, that "snow was general all over Ireland" (*D* 176), and along with the repetitive descriptions of the falling snow, continues the dulling effect initiated by earlier repetitions and chiasmatic constructions. It also returns to Molly Ivors and Gretta's entreaty to go to the west of Ireland, and now yields: "The time had come for him to set out on his journey westward" (*D* 176). The possessive, extraneous "his journey," (rather than just "the time had come to go westward") is Gabriel's inflection, along with the protracted opening clause ("the time had come") that imbues the journey with predestination, aggrandizing Gabriel's drawn-out acquiescence to Gretta and Molly's suggestion. "The time had come" positions Gabriel as passive to time itself, yet even this lack of agency is presented with the grammatical flourish of the past perfect, poeticizing and valorizing what amounts to a visit to his wife's childhood home. Indeed, the persistence with which the narration romanticizes Gabriel, even including his self-loss, finally invalidates that supposed subjective dissolution. Earlier in the story we hear the palaver with which Gabriel celebrates himself through his celebration of his aunts; now we discern his palaver as he is forced to reassess his self-conception, and morosely exaggerates the "fading" of his identity.

Even if Gabriel's identity did fade out into the world ("The Dead," according to Gabriel), that would still only be to recognize that it has always been congruent with it, and that both world and character are congruent with the text in which they occur. The subject position emerges in its very dispossession; the borders of the character are erased as they are created. The illusion of the integrity of the subject is necessary to the invalidating mechanisms of social construction in the first place.

Throughout the story the narration not just colludes, but merges with Gabriel, which means that throughout the story the narration is protective of Gabriel even as it shows up an understanding of him as self-contained and unique: it shares, produces, and protects his interests; it romanticizes his successes and his failures; it props him up when his self-conception is challenged; but it also displays Gabriel's existence as based upon an entirely fallacious account of himself and of subjectivity. If "the dissolution of the character's self is communicated and transferred through free indirect style," then so too is its defense.[48] Both these forces—of dissolution and of fortification—are within Gabriel, and both continue in the final paragraphs. The repetitions of "The Dead" are the hallmark of Gabriel's enmeshment in the narration: his (de)composition is founded upon a textual mechanics that gathers and disperses him through patterns of repetition.

Notes

1 Margot Norris, *Suspicious Readings of Joyce's* Dubliners (Philadelphia: University of Pennsylvania Press, 2003), 8.
2 Ibid., 7.
3 For John Paul Riquelme, who notes not just the verbal, but the stylistic, thematic, and event repetitions of "The Dead," these repetitions show "the story's heterogeneous, dissonant character" and multiplicity of meanings. "For Whom the Snow Taps: Style and Repetition in 'The Dead.'" *The Dead: Complete, Authoritative Text with Biographical and Historical Contexts, Critical History, and Essays from Five Contemporary Critical Perspectives*, ed. Daniel R. Shwarz (Boston: Bedford Books of St Martin's Press, 1994) 219–33, 221.

4 *Suspicious Readings*, 7.
5 Ibid., 6.
6 Norris, "The Voice and the Void: Hugh Kenner's Joyce." *Modernism/modernity* 3 (2005): 483–86, 484.
7 *Suspicious Readings*, 6.
8 Hugh Kenner. *Joyce's Voices* (Rochester: Dalkey Archive Press, 2007), 17; my emphasis.
9 Ibid., 21; my emphasis. As I will later discuss, Kenner hypothesizes Lily's act of "recounting" in the solecism in the first sentence of "The Dead" and argues that in "Eumaeus" in *Ulysses* "we find Bloom written about as he would choose" (16, 35).
10 Rabaté, Jean-Michel. "Lapsus ex machina." *Post-Structuralist Joyce: Essays from the French*, ed. Derek Attridge and Daniel Ferrer (Cambridge: Cambridge University Press, 1985) 79–101, 79. Rabaté refers to Joyce calling himself an engineer to both August Suter and Harriet Weaver, with the *Wake* as his engine, and calling the book "my old flying machine." The book refers to itself as a "vicociclometer" (qtd in Rabaté 80–81).
11 Derek Attridge, *Joyce Effects: On Language, Theory, and History* (Cambridge: Cambridge University Press, 2003), 57.
12 Ibid., 57.
13 Norris, *Suspicious Readings*, 6.
14 Kenner, *Joyce's Voices*, 16.
15 Ibid., 18.
16 As Valente argues, "the subjectivity of his characters takes shape under and through the pressure of a series of interpellative discourses [...]. The subject [...] emerges at the point of [these discourses'] intersection and conflict," "Between Resistance and Complicity: Metro-Colonial Tactics in Joyce's *Dubliners*." *Narrative* 6.3 (1998): 325–40, 331.
17 Norris, *Suspicious Readings*, 8.
18 Kenner, *Joyce's Voices*, 32.
19 Joseph Valente, *The Myth of Manliness in Irish National Culture, 1880–1922* (Urbana: University of Illinois Press, 2011), 210.
20 Michael Mayo, "Beyond the Uncle Charles Principle." *James Joyce Quarterly*. 56.3–4 (2019): 245–66, 247.
21 Kenner, *Joyce's Voices*, 16.
22 Ibid., 17.
23 Norris, *Suspicious Readings*, 230.
24 Norris, "Stifled Back Answers: The Gender Politics of Art in Joyce's 'The Dead.'" *Modern Fiction Studies* 35.3 (1989): 479–503, 479.
25 Norris, *Suspicious Readings*, 9.
26 Vincent Pecora also reads this description of Gabriel as performing a "psychological function": "it reinscribes Gabriel's equanimity, reclothing him in the princely attitude he celebrates later," "'The Dead' and the Generosity of the Word." PMLA 101.2 (1986): 233–45, 239.
27 Kenner, *Joyce's Voices*, 16–17.
28 Norris, *Suspicious Readings*, 261n1.
29 Ibid., 11.
30 "For Whom the Snow Taps: Style and Repetition in 'The Dead.'" *The Dead: Complete, Authoritative Text with Biographical and Historical Contexts, Critical History, and Essays from Five Contemporary Critical Perspectives*, ed. Daniel R. Shwarz (Boston: Bedford Books of St Martin's Press, 1994) 219–33, 228.

31 Kenner, *Joyce's Voices*, 17.
32 Ibid., 17.
33 According to Karen Lawrence, "Mr Duffy in 'A Painful Case,' in fact, represents all the Dubliners who consciously or unconsciously have 'an odd autobiographical habit [...]' (p. 108). Like Don Quixote, who literally attempts to chronicle his own exploits, these characters wish to 'write' their own stories." *The Odyssey of Style in* Ulysses (Princeton: Princeton University Press, 1981), 22–23.
34 Kenner, *Joyce's Voices*, 20.
35 Riquelme, "Style and Repetition," 223.
36 Norris, Margot and Vincent P. Pecora. "Dead Again." *Collaborative Dubliners*, ed. Vicki Mahaffey. Syracuse: Syracuse University Press, 2012. 343–75, 367.
37 " 'The Dead' and the Generosity of the Word." PMLA 101.2 (1986): 233–45, 234.
38 Norris, *Suspicious Readings*, 220.
39 Ibid., 220.
40 Norris, *Suspicious Readings*, 229–30.
41 Johnson spells out the ambiguity of this one word, and the interpretive crisis it instigates for the final two paragraphs: "Is Gabriel weeping copiously, weeping in sympathy with his fellow human beings, weeping in the manner in which he wants to be seen to be weeping because his wife has so generously so described him? Is the word Gabriel's (appropriated from Gretta's description of him) or is it the narrator's?" Introduction to *Dubliners* by James Joyce (Oxford: Oxford University Press, 2000) vii–xl, xxxviii.
42 Riquelme, "Joyce's 'The Dead': The Dissolution of the Self and the Police." *ReJoycing: New Readings of Dubliners*, ed. Rosa M. Bollettieri Bosinelli and Harold F. Mosher (Lexington: University Press of Kentucky, 1998) 123–41, 138.
43 Pecora finds a similar self-reflexivity in the word "generous," suggesting that "it is precisely the way Gabriel, as well as many of those around him, would see these tears—as an expression of Gabriel's sincere and selfless sympathy for Gretta, for Malins and Aunt Julia, for Michael Furey" (242).
44 Jeri Johnson, Introduction to *Dubliners* by James Joyce (Oxford: Oxford University Press, 2000) vii–xl, xxxvii.
45 Riquelme, "Dissolution," 124–25.
46 Norris, "Dead Again," 371.
47 Riquelme meticulously analyzes the many repetitions of this paragraph, including the semantic linkage of "softly," "faintly," and "swoon" ("Style and Repetition" 225).
48 Riquelme, "Dissolution," 139.

Chapter 5

"BUT WHO WAS GERTY?": "NAUSICAA," *THE LAMPLIGHTER* AND THE STYLES OF MODERNISM

Anne Fogarty

The woman reader and the conventions of women's sentimental and romance fiction are at the nub of "Nausicaa," at once determining and skewing interpretations of this interlude which takes place at twilight on Sandymount strand. Since Gerty MacDowell's reading is conspicuously on display in the narrativization of her inner thoughts, she is destined as a character always to be measured in accordance with the values assigned to her cultural choices, whether enforced or imagined. Joyce's well-known comments on his artistic purposes for this episode, though decked out with bravado, are contradictory and opaque. His bold announcement of the "specially new fizzing style" of "Nausicaa" in a letter to Frank Budgen in late 1919 is somewhat undercut by a further declaration to him in January 1920 that the episode will be "written in a namby- pamby jammy marmaledy drawersy (alto là) style with effects of incense, mariolatry, masturbation, stewed cockles, painter's palette, chitchat, circumlocutions, etc. etc."

This catalogue suggests not only that "Nausicaa" is a pastiche pieced together from heterogeneous sources, but also that it hinges on the appropriation and mimicry of a feminine style that is viewed as cloying, comic, and childish.[1] Yet, this dismissive stance is belied by the recognition that, as Jed Deppman has revealingly contended, Joyce relished the linguistic experimentation in "Nausicaa" and its exercise in overblown intertextuality and flamboyantly mocking portrayal of femininity to such a degree that he conspicuously mined it in the composition of the *Tristan and Isolde* passages in *Finnegans Wake*, modelling Isolde in particular on aspects of Gerty.[2] The style of "Nausicaa" became, in sum, an abiding part of his toolkit as an innovating modernist. His breezy insouciance about his undertaking in episode thirteen masks a serious intent.

Notoriously, the much beset serialization of *Ulysses* in *The Little Review* was brought lastingly to a halt in 1920 when objections were made to the section of "Nausicaa" in which Bloom masturbates.[3] Not only was Bloom's immorality found offensive, but so too was Gerty's sexual knowingness. The complaint against the July–August 1920 issue was initiated by the young daughter of a New York lawyer who had fortuitously read it; he referred the matter to John S. Sumner, Secretary of the New York Society for the Suppression of Vice. In 1921, the New York Court of Special Sessions found Jane Heap and Margaret Anderson guilty of publishing obscenity. Ironically, an episode that purposefully foregrounds the reading habits of a young Dublin woman and plays stylistically and conceptually with the idea of the woman writer was itself deemed unsuitable for a young female readership in the United States by a woman reader. Walter Kendrick noted the circularity of these presuppositions, observing that Gerty "is a classic Young Person, acting as if she had already been debauched by reading 'Nausicaa'."[4]

Tellingly, the policing of what women read and the corrupting influence of unsuitable material on a female audience framed the debates about the scandalous nature of *Ulysses* and "Nausicaa" in particular. To a degree, the issue of the inadmissibility of women's reading has not vanished, but it is now inflected in other ways in interpretations of this episode and centers on concerns not with morality, but with cultural capital and deficits in female education. Although routinely condemned, and certainly not academic, Gerty's reading is, in fact, eclectic and up-to-date, encompassing popular poetry and mass-market penny magazines targeted at a female audience, such as *The Princess's Novelette* and *The Lady's Pictorial*. Recent research has shown that, far from being the solely trivial, consumerist outlets they are regularly presumed to be, these journals were contributed to by all of the major Victorian and Edwardian female writers and often included Irish correspondents. Kathryn Ledbetter has argued that these publications provided "a closed space that valued and expanded women's interests."[5] These magazines gave visibility to women. Their mixed offerings of fashion and beauty advice, columns on health, reports on weddings and society events, and fiction, Gerry Beegan has demonstrated, enabled women to become visible and freely to cross-associate in a public arena in ways which had not been possible before.[6]

Gerty's espousal of a crucial nineteenth-century woman's novel is of a piece with her interest in an enlivening female cultural sphere. In musing about the street-lights in Sandymount at the approach of evening, she self-consciously invokes "*The Lamplighter* by Miss Cummins, author of *Mabel Vaughan* and other tales" (*U* 13.633–4). Her punctilious citation of the title page of Maria Cummins's best-selling novel, first published in 1854, grants it a conspicuous position and, as a consequence, it has been fastened upon by critics as a means at once of assessing the limits and parameters of her literary taste and of circumscribing and determining the nature of Joyce's stylistic experiments in this episode.[7] In a contradictory and highly gendered maneuver, the novel often is cursorily cast as a prototypical work of nineteenth-century sentimental fiction, and held to bear out the debased values defining and impoverishing Gerty, while at the same time serving as a valid and suggestive intertext for Joyce's purposes as author. A text that is, on the one hand, deplored if merely seen as part of women's reading agendas is, on the other, given an elevated status if conceived of as part of the materials alluded to and deconstructed by the male, modernist author.

In taking issue with such assumptions, the purpose of this essay is threefold: first, briefly to survey how Cummins's text has regularly been set up as an interpretive key to "Nausicaa" but in the process short-circuited, dismissed, or patchily read; second, to revisit *The Lamplighter*, to examine its publication history and to scrutinize the complex and knotted themes addressed by Cummins especially with regard to female desire and self-determination, and the problematic roles of ethnicity and class in the pursuit of social betterment in antebellum America; and, third, to consider in the light of feminist re-evaluations of this text how it might be seen to reverberate in "Nausicaa," at once cutting across and interconnecting with its themes and motifs and also supplying a canvas for the development of a transgendered modernist style. Cummins's novel is more pertinent, weighty, and challenging than has hitherto been recognized in analyses of "Nausicaa." Moreover, it operates as a dynamic intertext and not just as a convenient source that yields itself up for easy pilfering and parodying. "Nausicaa" and *The Lamplighter* may be viewed not only in tandem but as inter-animating each other. The idea of the woman writer and her putative idioms and linguistic tics haunt the episode and propel Joyce's production of a style that mimics and worries at gender oppositions and eventually blurs the boundaries between the concerns of supposedly separate areas: the female domain of sentimental fiction, the eclectic borrowings and brash styles of a *soi-disant* masculine modernism, and the levelling, down-to-earth perspectives of realism, utilized in the initial chapters of *Ulysses*, and still contouring aspects of the later, more experimental episodes. A revisiting of *The Lamplighter* and the issues it raises about female *Bildung* and the values of white colonial societies allows us to interrogate "Nausicaa" afresh and to assess its vexed intermingling and clashing of female and male points of view and registers.

Until recently, Gerty MacDowell was one of the most denigrated and negatively construed of Joyce's problematic female figures. Estimations of her as shallow and negligible, in part, are linked with assumptions about the sentimental novel and women's writing overall. Hugh Kenner's views of Gerty and the style used to depict her are the most rebarbative. In *Dublin's Joyce*, he contended that "she is a massive epiphany of second-hand living,"[8] In his study of *Ulysses*, he opined that "the first half of 'Nausicaa' is narrated by the Arranger imitating a Victorian lady novelist" and that it was composed in a "notably degenerate nineteenth-century idiom."[9] Homing in more closely on Maria Cummins, he concluded that the style of this opening section, which he assumed derived from *The Lamplighter*, created a new Bloom in unfamiliar guise as a romantic hero. Overall, he adduced that Joyce deliberately imitated a defective style and that narrative skills in this episode were at "a conspicuous ebb" like the tide.[10] Damningly, he pronounced that the interlude on Sandymount strand "kills an hour, also a sexual edginess" for Leopold Bloom, thereby cancelling out Gerty's role.[11] Karen Lawrence also declared unease with Gerty whom she found "less interesting" than other characters in *Ulysses;* she attributed this lack to Joyce's recycling of previously employed parodic techniques that had a flattening effect in this episode.[12] Fritz Senn's account of Gerty was more measured. While he adjudged that she was "almost incapable of recognizing an identity" and that her thoughts depended on "pre-existing classification[s]," he declared her ultimately to be "a triumph of indirect characterization."[13] He resorted to similarly paradoxical formulations to describe the episode as a whole: although he held that the clichéd style of the first half of "Nausicaa" was limited and capable only of reflecting "its own vacuity," he nonetheless discerned a "protean quality" to the episode overall.[14] Denis Donoghue also proposed a contradictory take on "Nausicaa" in that he held the sentimentalities voiced by Gerty to be close to those Joyce himself enjoyed, but yet averred, borrowing a Yeatsian distinction, that she was more "a character rather than a personality" and "more the result of her cultural conditions than the self-willed author of new experience."[15] In this view, a clichéd style, if given an authorial fundament, is of value but not if attached to the novelistic invention of a female figure seen as inherently wanting.

This essay takes its bearings from pioneering assessments of "Nausicaa" by Suzette Henke and Kimberly Devlin that connected it with *The Lamplighter* and set out to recuperate Gerty as a character and the discourses that mediated her. Yet, even their readings found it difficult fully to accommodate Cummins's novel, which served always as a negative index of femininity, the woman's novel, and women's educational opportunities. Positing that "Gerty McDowell is James Joyce's Emma Bovary," Henke argued that Gerty fashioned herself on Cummins's heroine, despite the parodying of the saccharine prose and pious religiosity of *The Lamplighter.* [16] She held that Cummins's novel as well as contemporary magazines and advertisements served a compensatory function for Gerty who drew on them to offset the shortcomings of her own existence and to patch together an account of her appearance, behavior, and demeanor. Kimberly Devlin neatly inverted this argument while still deeming *The Lamplighter* to be a negative measure of femininity and a counter-text for the modernist writer. She proposed that Joyce, in depicting Gerty's fantasy of playing the heroine in Cummins's text, upturned its formulaic aspects and sentimentalism.[17] The two texts are diametrically opposed in Devlin's reading: where Gerty Flint in *The Lamplighter* changed from "a temperamental heroine" into "an animated cliché, an exemplar of female martyrdom," in "Nausicaa" Gerty mutates from a generic type into a temperamental heroine, "dissatisfied with her lot."[18]

The premise of this essay is that *The Lamplighter* functions as a dynamic intertext for "Nausicaa." We may instructively juxtapose but also read across the two works, rather than holding them simply as oppositional. Citations of popular texts in *Ulysses* are rarely inert embellishments; they frequently signal sociopolitical points of contestation, knotted cultural nexuses, as well as playfully mischievous textual transpositions and deformations. Above all, they are heterodox and deliberately cut across traditional hierarchies and scruples about carefully policed and loftily upheld lines of distinction between high and low forms of art. Cummins's *The Lamplighter* was linked with a vogue for domestic fiction and sentimental narratives initiated by Susan Warner's *The Wide, Wide World*, published in 1850. On appearance, it was the biggest bestseller in the US in 1854, second only to Harriet Beecher Stowe's *Uncle Tom's Cabin*. Both novels were published by John P. Jewett who cannily marketed them, exploited their popularity, and cross-linked them.[19] He produced Cummins's novel in several different formats from inexpensive to deluxe and, after initial sales, worked to widen its readership, commissioning an abridged, illustrated children's edition which recast it as an abolitionist allegory, drawing overt links between Gerty's plight and that of slaves.[20] Thus, the novel was actively imbricated in political debates in the period, especially about the freeing of slaves and the oppression of women, and targeted at a wide readership extending far beyond the niche female audience with which it is commonly tied. The dissemination of *The Lamplighter* in the UK was aimed also at a variegated readership with no fewer than thirteen different firms involved in producing editions between 1854 and 1893. Summarizing its publication history, Susan S. Williams notes, the readers of the novel "were as likely to be foreign as American [...] to be children as adults, and men as women."[21] Further, the publication of Cummins's novel well into the twentieth century attests to its continuing popularity. Gerty's taste is thus not old-fashioned but vogueish and contemporary. Joyce's appropriation likewise capitalizes on the currency of Cummins's bestseller and exploits

its variable pedigrees as a specifically woman's novel, a quintessentially American work, a transatlantic book, and a text with an enduringly broad-scale popular appeal.

Formally too, *The Lamplighter* unites several different genres. It may be categorized as a romance, a sentimental fiction, a Dickensian story about the fortunes of an orphan and outcast, a feminist *Bildungsroman*, a domestic fiction, a melodrama, and a colonial narrative that is particularly concerned with the virtues and values of an emergent white middle class in the United States. In addition to all of these cross-affiliations, its status as an urban fiction, still a nascent mode in the latter half of the nineteenth century, depicting aspects of life in Boston in working class and upper middle-class milieus, must also have been a point of attraction for Joyce. In what follows, my focus will be on links and tensions in *The Lamplighter* in its aspects as a feminist *Bildungsroman* and as an American colonial novel,[22] conflicts which are taken up by and played with in "Nausicaa." The processes of female Bildung in *The Lamplighter* are more complex than often discerned. Set in Boston, it tells the story of an abandoned, uneducated orphan, initially called Gerty but later Gertrude, rescued as a child by the elderly Trueman Flint, a lamplighter, who houses her in his spartan rooms. She is subsequently adopted by the upper middle-class Mr. Graham and his blind daughter, Emily. Contrary to unexamined presuppositions in Joycean criticism, the text, while certainly couched in a sentimental discourse, is crisply controlled and does not provide the model for the narratorial voice who espouses a romantic, effusive, and flamboyantly feminine prose in *Ulysses.*

Surprisingly, readings of *The Lamplighter* have so far ignored its Irish subtexts which are germane to its portrayal of both a reformed and purposeful femininity and a new discourse of American national identity. Indeed, names and identity are central cruxes in the plot. The orphaned Gertrude is frequently questioned about who she is, as in her first conversation with Emily Graham in which she laments the fact that she does not have "any other name" (53). The identity of her parents remains a mystery until the end of the novel. Though Gertrude has to be schooled by those who befriend her and learn the virtues of humility and self-sacrifice, she also asserts her independence and her right to choose the family whom she wants to live with and care for. Reading is central to Gertrude's transformation. The blind Emily introduces her to a range of works and trains her to read books aloud for both of them to enjoy. This education concentrates on the inculcation of feminine virtues of empathy and humility but also involves a feminist assumption of independence as Emily underlines in arguments with her father. Thus, Gertrude insists on the right to earn her own living and trains as a school teacher in order to ensure that she will be financially autonomous.

Hence, even though women's roles are shown to be largely domestic, the caretaking functions they fulfil come about in Cummins's text by choice and not imposition, and active not passive virtue is prized.

A strangely muffled set of references to a panoply of Irish figures, generally female servants and housemaids, strews the text. Due to waves of emigration in the eighteenth and nineteenth centuries, there was a largescale Irish emigrant population in Boston from both Protestant and Catholic backgrounds. It was divided on sectarian lines and also viewed with suspicion by the native Yankee inhabitants.[23] These schisms are registered in Cummins's text which, in general, renders the Irish as peripheral or erased presences.[24] However, it is noteworthy that they are part of all of the households to which Gertrude is attached. Indeed, her education and transformation from an uncouth child with an uncontrollable temper and ignorant of religion into a morally upright woman who is self-possessed and domesticated takes place initially at the expense of these figures. The Christian virtues that Gertrude painstakingly acquires are counterpoised by the endemic traits of Irish servants. Her initial teachers and mentors are Trueman Flint and his neighbor Mrs. Sullivan, a Protestant whose Irishness goes unremarked. She educates Gertrude emotionally and practically, teaching her how to be orderly and to keep house for Trueman. Willie, her son, becomes a surrogate brother for Gertrude, but is also destined to be her ideal soulmate and future spouse. Sexual desire is always mediated and rendered safe by family connections in Cummins. It is telling, hence, that the reformation of Gertrude is taken in hand by a woman whose dead husband was presumably an Irish immigrant, and that she marries Willie Sullivan at the end of the novel. These Irish figures enable her rags to riches story and her transformation from a penniless orphan to a well-endowed married woman.

Gertrude's abiding link with the Sullivans initiates a pattern of ambivalent depictions of Irishness in the novel. On the one hand, the Irish enable personal change and bolster the qualities that Cummins endorses for living a good life but, on the other, they are seen through a racist lens as different, dirty, and disruptive. Several of the chief trials that Gertrude faces revolve around these servants. The calamitous burning of her carefully preserved keepsakes by the Irish maid Bridget, "a remarkably stupid specimen" (117), causes her much pain. Yet, the occasion is used by Gertrude as an opportunity for developing her powers of self-abnegation and forbearance, thus transmuting Irish obtuseness into moral wisdom. She therefore never berates Bridget and hides her pain.

One of the most prominent moments of feminist defiance in the novel occurs when she makes a stand against Mr. Graham by insisting on leaving his household—where she has been accepted as a companion and ersatz daughter for Emily—to nurse Mrs. Sullivan's dying father. Although Graham's objection to her decision is patriarchal and classist, Gertrude's case for nursing the dying Mr. Cooper is not entirely at odds with his views. She explains that Mrs. Sullivan "is exceedingly neat and particular in all her arrangements and has always done her work herself, and declares she would sooner admit a wild beast into her family than an Irish girl" (131). Gertrude thus interposes herself between her self-chosen family and the specter of encroaching Irish servants and the wildness they embody. In part, she deflects this feared debasement, but in part she harnesses it.

Yet, ironically, she takes leave of "Irish Katy" (148), one of the maidservants in the Graham household, before departing, reinforcing the view that she is at once in league with and opposed to the Otherness that the Irish female servant represents. Indeed, in the novel we only hear these servants' particular idiom when they are in conversation with her. Thus, "Irish Katy's" halting, differently accented English is captured when she bids farewell to Gerty: "'Sure, Miss Gairthrude [...] and it's right gude in you to be afther comin' to bid us good-by. I don't see how you gets memory to think of us all, and I'm shure yer'll never be betther off than what I wish her'" (148–49). Another episode cross-connecting but delimiting Gertrude from Irish servants occurs in Chapter XXXIII after she has returned to the Graham household to nurse Emily who has been unwell. Mrs. Prime, the housekeeper, is perturbed to find her ironing Emily's dresses and exclaims "'but what should you be doin' Bridget's work for, I want to know?'" (245). Gertrude takes on Bridget's role to spare her female friends from close association with social inferiors who are stigmatized and held apart. She subsumes their function as carers but also absorbs and repurposes their wildness.[25]

The rehabilitation of the male figures, her lost father, Philip Amory, and Willie Sullivan, involves a counterbalancing of colonial values and the ethos of sentimental love. Willie Sullivan leaves Boston for six years to take up a post in India where he proves himself and earns a fortune. However, he only befits himself as Gertrude's husband after he has confirmed his love for her on the grounds of the purity and perfection that she embodies: "a young girl [...] without family, wealth or beauty; but with a spirit so elevated as to make her great, a heart so noble as to make her rich, a soul so pure as to make her beautiful" (349). In so doing, he also clears up a misapprehension that he is in love with the wealthy but flighty Isabel (Belle) Clinton to whom Gertrude believes he is engaged. The fact that he eschews the values of fashionable society recommend him further to Gertrude; the qualities that define him—he is described as "open-hearted, generous, manly and affectionate" (369)—comport with the attributes prized by a philosophy of sentimental love.

In the latter half of the novel, the mysterious stranger, using the alias of Mr. Philips, who woos Gertrude during a sojourn at Saratoga Springs transpires to be her father and onetime lover of Emily Graham. In the past, he is falsely accused of forgery by Mr. Graham and banished from his home. In a blazing row with Graham on that occasion, Amory tragically blinds Emily, who has fainted, when he mistakes a bottle of acid for water and dashes her face with its contents to revive her. Gertrude's mother, we learn, was Lucy Grey, the daughter of a sea captain whom Amory got to know when he fled the United States for Brazil. They marry there but Amory gets separated from her during an outbreak of malaria. Gertrude's mother subsequently dies of the disease when she returns to Boston leaving her an orphan. Crucially, Amory also has amassed a fortune as a result of gold prospecting in California and he too remains loyal to his first love, Emily, whom he marries at the end of the novel. Like Willie, he has to earn his re-entry into Gertrude's life and begs her to accept him first as a "trusted friend" (391). But, as Nina Baym has contended, the restoration of her father is gratuitous, as Gerty has "exceeded her mentors" and is not in need of paternal guidance even if his reappearance does relieve her of the necessity of nursing Emily.[26] However, the renovated family units that emerge at the end of the novel are necessary to its philosophical core which ties sentimental, feminist, and national goals. *The Lamplighter* aligns the possibility of female self-determination and quest for moral rectitude with the pursuit of a white American racial destiny which is nonetheless murkily rooted in hidden ethnic affiliations with an immigrant culture such as that of the Irish in Boston and with capitalist, colonial enterprises in California, Brazil, and India. Laura Wexler has argued that sentimentalism is inherently associated with an expansive, imperial project and that its energies "were intended as a tool for the control of others, not merely as aid to the conquest of self."[27] The effect of what Wexler calls the "tender violence" of the sentimental novel is evident in the exploitation and suppression of others (including women, servants, and the foreign associates of the entrepreneurial American businessman), which form the hidden subtexts of Cummins's text.

Joyce's hibernicization of Cummins's female protagonist not only transposes *The Lamplighter* to an Irish setting, it somewhat redresses its deep-seated anxiety and prejudices about Irish female savagery. It does so by replacing the obstreperous Irish servant girl, who fuses civilized and wild values, with a recalcitrant modern Irish woman, Gerty MacDowell, who, albeit "as fair a specimen of winsome Irish girlhood as one could wish to see" (*U* 13.80–1), conceals a knowing sexuality under her prim demeanor and rejects traditional aspects of women's roles. On Sandymount strand at twilight she meets with her friends, Cissy Caffrey and Edy Boardman, who are engaged in looking after young brothers, the twins, Tommy and Jacky Caffrey, and the infant Boardman. Symbolically, these women devote their attentions to male siblings who already incorporate and enact crushingly patriarchal imperatives, fighting with each other, commandeering the women's attention, and cutting across their mutual bonds. Gerty accompanies them, but distances herself from the caretaking roles expected of her, pointedly advertising the anti-maternal current in her emotions by lamenting the presence of the "squalling baby" (*U* 13.404) and the "snottynosed twins" (*U* 13.529). Hence, "Nausicaa" problematizes the symbolic nexus between women and servant roles in *The Lamplighter* and between maternity and femininity in Irish nationalist discourses. It is thus caught up in the very issues about women's role in modernity and the forging of the contemporary nation that Cummins's novel posed in a US context. Irish colonial identity is also at stake in "Nausicaa," as the triad of female friends represents not just aspects of modern femininity but also of the Irish subaltern state. In this latter regard, Gerty particularly embodies Irish whiteness with her "waxen pallor," "ivorylike purity" (*U* 13.87–8), and hands of "finely veined alabaster" (*U* 13.89), while Cissy Caffrey with her "golliwog curls" and penchant for cross-dressing "in her father's suit and burned cork moustache" (*U* 13.276–7) is seen in terms of her gender transgressiveness and blackness.[28] The cross-association of Irish subalternity with black identity at once suggests parallels between forms of oppression and the links forged by feminists and suffragettes with slaves, but it also points up a problematic conflation in the pejorative discourses and oppositional movements of the period.

Just as Cummins spliced together a number of different genres to tell the story of Gertrude Flint, so too Joyce assembles a wide and eclectic array of discourses to describe Gerty MacDowell and to give us not only a sense of her vantage point on the world but also to deconstruct it. Because of this, our view of Gerty is vitiated; she is depicted obliquely through indirect discourse and is composed from an assemblage of traditional, stereotypical views of women, religious sentiments and tropes particularly linked with the Virgin Mary, images from and allusions to women's romances, advertisements, and magazines, baby talk, and sporadic injections of everyday realism and Dublin demotic, chiming with the initial style of *Ulysses*. Indeed, a central question that has exercised critics is whether Gerty may be considered to be a delimited figure at all rather than merely a projection produced by the discourses in which she is entwined and which script her. Countering such views and stressing the function of female agency in the narrative, Margot Norris has winningly argued that the voice that speaks in the first half of the episode may be conceived of as a "phantom narrator constructed by Gerty's imagination to produce the language of her desire, the hypothetical discourse of her praises that she fears no one will ever utter."[29] Importantly, too, Norris advanced the view that critique in the episode is directed not so much against aspects of modern life but rather "modernism's own desire" and its "blind eye to the cruelties of its own elitism."[30]

The first half of "Nausicaa" is stylistically more fragmented and less unitary than often presupposed. The Gerty-narrator occasionally affects omniscience as in the opening lines, sometimes a putatively feminine style that is anachronistic, strives for an unreachably refined, elevated register, and wheels out truisms and sentimental comments, and often defaults to a more naturalistic, ironized view of the world. The narration at once offers a pastiche of femininity and of the cultural horizons of Gerty and a parody of the male author's attempt to mimic a female style and to commandeer the disparate reading material of a young, contemporary woman. The "specially new fizzing style" that Joyce invents depicts Gerty as a naturalistic figure, trapped by poverty and lack of opportunity in an unhappy home where she has witnessed "deeds of violence" (*U* 13.298) sparked by her father's alcoholism, a modern woman who follows fashion and wears a "neat blouse of electric blue selftinted by dolly dyes (because it was expected in the *Lady's Pictorial* that electric blue would be worn)," a romance heroine who yearns for "a manly man with a strong quiet face" (*U* 13.210), a moral paragon who embodies stereotypically feminine virtues as "a sterling good daughter [...] a second mother in the house, a ministering angel" (*U* 13.325–6), a jaded commentator on life who wishes someone would give the "little brats of twins" (*U* 13.466) "a good hiding for themselves" (*U* 13.469), and a proactive, sexually aware adult whose "woman's instinct told her that she had raised the devil" (*U* 13.517–8) in Bloom, the "gentleman in black" (*U* 13.349). Putting into effect Samuel Butler's theory that Nausicaa was, in fact, the authoress of the *Odyssey*, a composite, tessellated woman-author made up of various versions of Gerty and the Gerty-narrator piece together the first half of episode thirteen, which offers rare insight into Joyce's youthful female figure, while simultaneously deconstructing her.[31] "Nausicaa" also continues and upturns *The Lamplighter* especially in its redeployment of central images in Cummins's work, the stars and urban streetlamps, which are beloved of Gertrude Flint and become symbolic of her moral and emotional transformation. These images are replicated in episode thirteen of *Ulysses*, but mischievously superseded by the climactic fireworks which transpose and accompany the orgasmic climaxes of Gerty and Bloom.

The devastating and startling caesura, "Tight boots? No. She's lame! O!" (*U* 13.771), apparently effects a sharp breakage between female and male narrators and abandons the discourses linked with the woman author and her fictional personae and the male author's orchestration of them. However, as many have contended, most prominently and eloquently John Bishop, "Nausicaa" is not as divided and dichotomized as it appears.[32] The shift from the Gerty-narrator and from Gerty to Bloom, while it returns us to the point of view of a figure with whom we are acquainted, also defamiliarizes him as his initial flow of thoughts is unexpectedly cruel and foregrounds female difference in sexist, racist, and ableist views.[33] Bloom assumes that Gerty's disability is an obstacle and that this is why "she's left on the shelf" (*U* 13.773), he singles out female oddities, "a nun or negress or a girl with glasses" (*U* 13.776–7), as apt subjects of erotic titillation, and recalls Cissy Caffrey denigratingly as "the dark one with the mop head and nigger mouth" (*U* 13.898). The tender violence that is an underlay of sentimental fiction thus infiltrates and colors Bloom's interior monologue. Joyce courts the twilight and encroaching darkness to broach vexed issues about the political position of the colonial subject and the equivalence between varying forms of subjection as well as to think about sexism and the roles women in a patriarchal society.

Other aspects of the woman's novel and of the activity of the female reader carry over into the second part of "Nausicaa." Suzanne Clarke has argued that modernism cast the sentimental as an "unwarranted discourse" and defined itself as superior to the banal concerns and emotional preoccupations of women's fiction.[34] These lines of demarcation, however, are blurred throughout episode 13 of *Ulysses*, in the first part of which the Gerty-narrator betrays an intimate knowledge of the texts read and produced by women which are referenced and endorsed as well as parodied. One effect of the optics provided by *The Lamplighter* is to raise Bloom from disparaged outsider to all-commanding romantic hero; he becomes "her all in all, the only man in the world" (*U* 13.671–2) for Gerty. This romantic rhetoric is deconstructed but also reinstated as are Bloom and Gerty as sentimental hero and heroine in the course of Joyce's playful reworking of Cummins's text. It is Bloom rather than Gerty who undergoes a moral transformation in the latter half of the episode and he is as concerned with the everyday and with sentiment as she. Just as Gerty was taken up with her conflicted relations with Edy and Cissy, so too Bloom contemplates the tensions surrounding the women in his life, Molly, Milly, and Martha Clifford. His emotions oscillate as he shifts between guilt, "I'm all clean come and dirty me" (*U* 13.797), deflation "[a]ftereffect not pleasant" (*U* 13.852), accusatory surmises about women's petty rivalries, "[w]ouldn't lend each other a pinch of salt" (*U* 13.819–20), and sexist presumptions about female behavior "[e]yes all over them [...] [s]harp as needles they are" (*U* 13.912–13). But a mitigation of his cutting assessments of women takes place as he muses on sensual memories of Molly, "know her smell in a thousand" (*U* 13.1024). The lights and stars, insignia of female desire in *The Lamplighter*, perform a similar function in "Nausicaa." But they also allow male and female viewpoints to converge and inform each other. Thus, as Bloom contemplates Howth, the night sky, the Bailey lighthouse, and the Kish lightship, his attitudes soften and take on a more melancholic complexion. In step with this, he becomes more tender toward Gerty and thinks of her sentimentally: "O sweet little, you don't know how nice you looked" (*U* 13.1085).

Like Gerty who dreams about becoming a poet, he fantasizes about producing a *Titbits*-style story, *The Mystery Man on the Beach*, written, however, in the style of a woman's romance. Male and female viewpoints and styles, after sharp divergence, come together in Bloom's initially anti-sentimental monologue. Some of the idiom of the Gerty-narrator, who often uses baby language, for example, enters into his wording: "Lovers: yum yum" (*U* 13.1100). In contemplating writing a message in the sand for Gerty he continues this prospect of a transgendered textuality, informed and reshaped by the woman reader and author. The sentence he commences is broken off: "I [...]. AM. A." (*U* 13.1258–64). It has been variously completed, but may be seen as crossing the male and female styles of the episode, containing as it does the root of the Latin verb *amare* (to love) and the surname of Gertrude Flint's lost father, Amory.

If Bloom takes on aspects of the sentimental fiction writer, then Gerty becomes a confederate of the modernist author with his mocking deformations, word play, and allusive indirection. The bat that emerges at twilight insinuates the suppressed and unfinished story of female desire into the ending of "Nausicaa" and also captures the labile nature of a narrative that floats between, clashes and connects gendered identities and writing styles. The closing lines of the episode are voiced from the ambiguous vantage point of Gerty, endowing her with a forlorn purchase on the narrative, despite her truncated story. Her mocking call of cuckoo is directed at "that foreign gentleman that was sitting on the rocks looking" (*U* 13.1302–3), a position she had occupied earlier. Unlike the heroine of *The Lamplighter*, Gerty's story does not achieve resolution, least of all the supposed closure of marriage, but she is conferred with the moral authority not only to accuse Bloom but to call out the pretensions and elitism of modernist style with regard to those women's genres (such as the sentimental novel and the female *Bildungsroman*) that it feeds off while denigrating them.

The Lamplighter and "Nausicaa" are not divergent but intertwined fictions that resonate suggestively with each other. Through foregrounding women's reading and prejudicial assumptions about the woman author in the depiction of Gerty MacDowell, Joyce raises needling questions about the value of genres, the legitimacy of different modes of gendered discourse, and the difficulty of authentically voicing the Other. The mimicry of women's fiction and styles couched from the point of view of the woman author and reader enable him to destabilize the authority of the male writer and also to produce crossover modes that interfuse male and female viewpoints. The sentimental novel is absorbed and continued in the modernist epic, not rejected out of hand. However, the problem of difference troubles the margins of both works, the largely silent Irish Bridgets who are displaced by the heroine of *The Lamplighter* and the women of color whose plight is falsely conflated with that of subaltern white Dublin women in "Nausicaa," even if a tentative set of connections between Bloom and Gerty can be forged. Attentive readings of Cummins and Joyce at once attest to the lasting centrality of sentimental discourses and to their radical emphasis on the banal and everyday, but also to their unwarranted aspects in shoring up sexist and racist ideologies.

Notes

1 *LI*, p.132 and *LI*, 135.

2 Jed Deppman, "The Return of Medievalism: Joyce in 1923," *Medieval Joyce*, ed. Lucia Boldrini (Amsterdam: Rodopi, 2002), 45–78 (75).

3 For details of the legal proceedings against *The Little Review*, see Paul Vanderham, *James Joyce and Censorship: The Trials of "Ulysses"* (New York: New York University Press, 1998), 39–56, Robert Spoo, *Without Copyrights: Piracy, Publishing and the Public Domain* (New York: Oxford University Press, 2013), 156–59, and Joseph M. Hassett, *The "Ulysses" Trials: Beauty and Truth Meet the Law* (Dublin: Lilliput Press, 2016), 71–93.

4 Walter Kendrick, *The Secret Museum: Pornography in Modern Culture* (New York: Viking Penguin, 1987), 183.

5 Kathryn Ledbetter, "Periodicals for Women," *The Routledge Handbook to Nineteenth-Century British Periodicals and Newspapers*, eds. Andrew King, Alexis Easley, and John Morton (London: Routledge, 2016), 260–75 (260).

6 Gerry Beegan, "Women of the World: *The Lady's Pictorial* and Its Sister Papers," *Women, Periodicals and Print Culture in Britain, 1830s–1900s*, eds. Alexis Easley, Clare Gill, and Beth Rodgers (Edinburgh: Edinburgh University Press, 2019), 232–55.

7 Maria Susanna Cummins, *The Lamplighter*, ed. Nina Baym (New Brunswick: Rutgers University Press, 1988). All references will be to this edition and will be noted in parentheses.

8 Hugh Kenner, *Dublin's Joyce* (London: Chatto and Windus, 1955), 257.

9 Hugh Kenner, *Ulysses*. Revised Edition (Baltimore: Johns Hopkins University Press, 1987), 101 and 106.

10 Kenner, *Ulysses*, 104.

11 Ibid., 105.

12 Karen Lawrence, *The Odyssey of Style in "Ulysses"* (Princeton: Princeton University Press, 1981), 119–23.

13 Fritz Senn, "Nausicaa," *James Joyce's "Ulysses": Critical Essays*, eds. Clive Hart and David Hayman (Berkeley: University of California Press, 1974), 277–311 (296, 320).

14 Senn, 309, 310.

15 Denis Donoghue, "On a Chapter of *Ulysses*," *The Practice of Reading* (New Haven: Yale University Press, 1998), 222–35 (232).

16 Suzette Henke, "Gerty MacDowell: Joyce's Sentimental Heroine," *Women in Joyce*, eds. Suzette Henke and Elaine Unkeless (Urbana: University of Illinois Press, 1982), 132–49 (133).

17 Kimberly Devlin, "The Romance Heroine Exposed: 'Nausicaa' and *The Lamplighter*," *James Joyce Quarterly* 22, 4 (1985): 383–96.

18 Devlin, 385.

19 Susan S. Williams cogently argues that the canny marketing and varying formats deployed played a crucial role in responses to *The Lamplighter*. See "'Promoting an Extensive Sale': The Production and Reception of *The Lamplighter*," *The New England Quarterly* 69, 2 (1996): 179–200.

20 Maria S. Cummins, *The Lamplighter Picture Book* (Boston, 1856).

21 Williams, 200.

22 For an examination of the ambivalent values of the colonial *Bildungsroman* in *The Lamplighter* and episode 13 of *Ulysses*, see Gregory Castle, "Colonial Discourse and the Subject of Empire in Joyce's 'Nausicaa'," *Joyce: Feminism/Post/Colonialism, European Joyce Studies 8*, ed. Ellen Carol Jones (Rodopi: Amsterdam, 1998), 115–44.

23 For a history of the Irish in Boston, see Thomas H. O'Connor, *The Boston Irish: A Political History* (Boston: Black Bay Books, 1995) and for an account of the Irish women who worked in service in US households, see Margaret Lynch-Brennan, *The Irish Bridget: Irish Immigrant Women in Domestic Service in America, 1840–1930* (New York: Syracuse University Press, 2009).

24 William Kupinse notes the presence of these servants in a footnote but does not analyse their symbolic role. See "Household Trash: Domesticity and National Identity in *The Lamplighter* and the 'Nausicaa' Episode of *Ulysses*," *South Carolina Review* 23, 1 (1999): 81–87.

25 Though she does not address the Irish figures, Lydia Fisher argues that Gertrude is depicted as having a combination of native American goodness and wildness and that a domesticity that is crossed with savagery is seen as advantageous. See "The Savage in the House," *The Arizona Quarterly* 64.1 (2008): 49–75. On the malleability of the family in Cummins's text, see Cindy Weinstein, "'A Sort of Adopted Daughter': Family Relations in *The Lamplighter*," *English Literary History* 68, 4 (2001): 1023–47.

26 Nina Baym, *Woman's Fiction: A Guide to Novels by and About Women in America, 1820–1870* (Ithaca: Cornell University Press, 1978), 169.

27 Laura Wexler, "Tender Violence: Literary Eavesdropping, Domestic Fiction and Educational Reform," *The Culture of Sentiment: Race, Gender, and Sentimentality in Nineteenth-Century America*, ed. Shirley Samuels (Oxford: Oxford University Press, 1992), 9–36 (15).

28 On the problematic depiction of Cissy Caffrey, see Casey Lawrence, "'The Link between Nations and Generations': Cissy Caffrey as Racialized and Sexualized Other in James Joyce's *Ulysses*," *Joyce Studies Annual* (2018): 108–21.

29 Margot Norris, "Modernism, Myth, and Desire in 'Nausicaa'," *James Joyce Quarterly* 26, 1 (1988): 31–50 (39).

30 Norris, 38, 49.

31 Samuel Butler, *The Authoress of the Odyssey Where and When She Wrote, Who She Was, the Use She Made of the Iliad, and How the Poem Grew under Her Hands* (London: Longmans, 1897).

32 John Bishop, "A Metaphysics of Coitus in 'Nausicaa'," *"Ulysses"—En-Gendered Perspectives: Eighteen New Essays on the Episodes*, eds. Kimberly J. Devlin and Marilyn Reizbaum (Columbia: University of South Carolina Press, 1999), 185–209.

33 Angela Lea Nemeck argues by contrast that Gerty and Bloom share a physical stigma. See "Reading the Disabled Woman: Gerty MacDowell and the Stigmaphilic Space of 'Nausicaa'," *Joyce Studies Annual* 10 (2010): 173–202.

34 Suzanne Clarke, *Sentimental Modernism: Women Writers and the Revolution of the Word* (Bloomington: Indiana University Press, 1991), 1.

Part IV

Joyce's Webs

Chapter 6

ULYSSES: THOUGHTS IN ISOLATION

Michael Groden

I

I write in isolation, confined like other Joyce scholars because of the spring 2020 COVID-19 pandemic. Gone for now is my usual mixture of private concerns and other public, sometimes Joyce-related, events. Gone, too, is the biggest annual Joyce occasion, the International James Joyce Foundation's Bloomsday conference scheduled this year for Trieste, as are smaller events, including the New York James Joyce Society's meeting in late March to celebrate the publication of my new book, *The Necessary Fiction: Life with James Joyce's "Ulysses."*[1]

Writing that memoir made me think a great deal about the effect of reading *Ulysses* in the first place and then rereading it, in my case many times. I think about that again in these unusual circumstances—with particular attention to Margot Norris' groundbreaking book on reading and rereading Joyce's novel, *Virgin and Veteran Readings of "Ulysses"*—and also about the larger Joycean scholarly community that provides an elaborate context for the vast "veteran readings" of the book. Now, with much time available but without any chance to walk much around my community, I can still accompany Leopold Bloom on his journey through Dublin.

Virgin and Veteran Readings contrasts an imagined first reading of *Ulysses* with subsequent rereadings. When I first encountered *Ulysses*, I qualified in many ways as Norris' "virgin reader."[2] I read the book only because it was the first one in a fall-term 1966 undergraduate course on the modern European novel. I knew nothing about James Joyce and hadn't read *Dubliners* or *A Portrait of the Artist as a Young Man* or, for that matter, *The Odyssey*. I was unaware of what was coming in the book regarding Stephen Dedalus, Leopold Bloom, or Molly Bloom. But in other ways, because of the course's structure and my growing interest in *Ulysses*, I slid into a kind of quasi-veteran reader long before

I finished the book. The class included twelve hours of lectures by Professor Peter Bien; about a hundred pages of mimeographed notes (only readers of a certain age will know what this means); and two secondary books, Stuart Gilbert's *James Joyce's "Ulysses"* (from 1930) and Frank Budgen's *James Joyce and the Making of "Ulysses"* (1934).[3]

My reading of the book with its excitement over what I was encountering provided an unexpectedly delightful first run through *Ulysses*. Through a second reading as an undergraduate and then two more as a graduate student, my understanding grew, as did my sense of some ways the book might be talked about and also studied. The subsequent readings provided what Norris calls "a veteran reading shadowing" the first one that "makes the significance of what is withheld" from the original reading "available to us."[4] Patricia Meyer Spacks calls this process a "palimpsest": "The layers of experience accruing from early readings, partly erased, remain partly discernible. Each new layer both adds to and subtracts from what has gone before."[5]

In isolation, as my sense of time and the pre-pandemic past became distorted, I focused on those topics in *Ulysses*, often recalling details from my virgin reading, and the isolation the pandemic brought about led me to the communities in *Ulysses*, both who is in them and who is not.

II

As Leopold Bloom walks along the streets of Dublin just before he eats lunch, he reflects on himself and Molly in the early years of their sixteen-year marriage and now in the present. "I was happier then," he asks himself. "Or was that I? Or am I now I?"[6] His subsequent thought leads to another question: "Can't bring back time. Like holding water in your hand. Would you go back to then? Just beginning then. Would you?" (8:610–12). Despite, or maybe because of, his worries about Molly and her likely assignation with Blazes Boylan on this day, he doesn't answer his own question.

On his day of uncertainty, Bloom's mind returns many, many times to Molly. He tries to avoid thinking about her and Boylan, even though Dubliners he meets bring "the conquering hero" up to him over and over again. Two men separately inquire about Molly's upcoming concert tour with Boylan by asking him, "Who's getting it up?" (*U* 5:153, 8:773), and he finds himself near Boylan more than once. His thoughts about Molly are anything but insecure, morose, or depressed, though. Instead, they are overwhelmingly tender and loving. "Must have been that morning in Raymond terrace she was at the window watching the two dogs at it," he thinks while riding to Dignam's funeral in "Hades" after he recalls the probable moment Rudy was conceived. "Give us a touch, Poldy. God, I'm dying for it. How life begins"

(*U* 6:77–81). Sometimes he revels in the pure sensuality of the memory; at other times, recollections of the past remind him how different things were before Rudy died.

Bloom is aware all day of Boylan's impending visit to his wife. Why doesn't he return home before 4:00 p.m. to stop it? Is he too passive or paralyzed, or just resigned to what he considers fate? Does a masochistic part of him accept and even desire the betrayal? The ending of *Ulysses* adds new puzzles. Along with Bloom, Norris' "virgin readers" learn in the last two episodes that Boylan did indeed visit and have sex with Molly. And yet when Bloom returns in the middle of the night to his and Molly's bed ("the bed of conception and of birth, of consummation of marriage and of breach of marriage" [*U* 17:2119–20]) and lies next to Molly's warm body, he considers himself to be truly back home. His reasons for apparently accepting her infidelity are presented as a muddle of possibilities—resignation, responsibility—only some of which are spelled out and none of which can be a sole explanation.

His thoughts combine sensuality and wistfulness. As he drinks a lunchtime glass of burgundy and eats a gorgonzola sandwich, he notices two flies copulating on the pub's windowpane and remembers every detail and sensation of a magical afternoon with Molly among rhododendrons on the hill on Howth, overlooking Dublin to the north. Lying on the ground with her was an unforgettable experience for him—and, we learn at the novel's end, equally for her, especially since he proposed to her that day and she accepted. But the memory provokes him to make another comparison: "Me. And me now" (*U* 8:904–17).

This thought, which is probably accompanied by a mental sigh, is one of many in which Bloom thinks about returns. He tends to consider them a bad idea. In the cabman's shelter in "Eumaeus" late in the evening, he talks about Parnell with Stephen Dedalus and says that "coming back was the worst thing you ever did because it went without saying you would feel out of place as things always moved with the times" (*U* 16:1402–03). If Parnell's return were possible, it would be "highly inadvisable, all things considered" (*U* 16:1311–12) because "You were a lucky dog if they didn't set the terrier at you directly you got back" (*U* 16:1339–40). Odysseus wasn't attacked by his faithful dog Argos when he returned to Ithaca, although he did have to deal with the small matter of the hundred suitors, and Bloom's thought "Returning not the same" probably acknowledges his own suitor-invaded home. He once made the mistake of bringing home an injured canine (*U* 16:1606–10), an indiscretion that still rankles Molly—"the night he walked home with a dog if you please that might have been mad," she complains (*U* 18:1086–87). Now this unlucky dog doesn't face a dangerous terrier, but he does encounter repositioned furniture against which he bumps his head, flakes of potted meat in his bed, and the imprint of another man there.

Returns in the mind, though, appeal to Bloom. Before falling asleep, the "Ithaca" narrator tells us, he likes to fantasize about unlikely possibilities, such as sudden wealth, or to revisit events from his past: "It was one of his axioms that similar meditations or the automatic relation to himself of a narrative concerning himself or tranquil recollection of the past when practiced habitually before retiring for the night alleviated fatigue and produced as a result sound repose and renovated vitality" (*U* 17:1755–58). Soon after this axiom about mental pleasures is reported, he faces both the desired and the dreaded actual return to Molly in their bed.

In their different ways, Molly Bloom and Stephen Dedalus also ponder the passage of time and the present's relationship to the past. "Lord its just like yesterday to me," Molly says about her early life in Gibraltar and the first man who kissed her there (*U* 18:821), and in a different key, as she mentally relives her afternoon of sex with Boylan, she complains that "its only the first time after that its just the ordinary" (*U* 18:101). Most dramatically, though, as she ends her monologue, and the novel, by repeating her words of acceptance to Bloom's marriage proposal, past and present merge. Stephen, as is his wont, addresses such issues much more abstractly. "Molecules all change. I am other I now," but, on the other hand, the "I" of the self is "I by memory because under everchanging forms." He sums up this paradoxical condition—constantly changing, constant amid the changes—in his playful mental observation as he thinks about himself as a young student at Clongowes Wood College, as a man who has incurred various financial debts at different times, and as he is now: "I, I and I. I" (*U* 9:212). He seems to wonder whether the first-person pronoun denotes a self that remains constant or rather a group of discrete "I"s who add up to a collective self. Certainly the latter, since he states aloud that "In the intense instant of imagination, when the mind, Shelley says, is a fading coal, that which I was is that which I am and that which in possibility I may come to be. So in the future, the sister of the past, I may see myself as I sit here now but by reflection from that which then I shall be" (*U* 9:381–85).

Bloom may be correct regarding returns. Youth never comes back; perhaps trying to repeat an earlier experience can be dangerous. But returning is not always a bad idea, as he knows, especially since it leads to experience that is other than perfection. I appreciated philosopher Martha Nussbaum's analysis of *Ulysses* in terms of Bloom's embrace of "the flawed particular," "the mercy and tenderness" of Molly's assent at the end "that really do embrace the inconstancy and imperfection of the real-life reader and real-life love," and the novel's humor and joy: "since [*Ulysses*] is so obviously having so much more fun being flawed than it would have had being perfect and classical, the reader is seduced into taking pleasure in the flawed and excessive, into thinking that perhaps it is in this world where things are not perfect and jokes go on a little too long that real heroism is to be found."[7]

III

Within the broad community of Dublin, Bloom is often isolated. In the newspaper offices in "Aeolus," for instance, he speaks with Red Murray about a short paragraph to accompany an ad for his client, Alexander J. Keyes, tea, wine, and spirit merchant. In his response, Murray places himself within the group of people who work to put the paper together:

> — Of course, if he wants a par, Red Murray said earnestly, a pen behind his ear, we can do him one.
> — Right, Mr Bloom said with a nod. I'll rub that in.
> We. (7:34–37)

For Murray, "we" includes his group. When Bloom cites it, he knows that it cannot include him.

Stephen finds himself in a similar situation. In "Wandering Rocks" a few hours later, he encounters his sister Dilly at a used-book stand and notices that she has purchased a second-hand French-language textbook. As he responds to her question about the quality of the book, he repeats the "we" that she uses for the broken-down remnants of the Dedalus family led by the shiftless alcoholic Simon, a "we" that doesn't include him:

> — Here, Stephen said. It's all right. Mind Maggy doesn't pawn it on you. I suppose all my books are gone.
> — Some, Dilly said. We had to.
> She is drowning. Agenbite. Save her. Agenbite. All against us. She will drown me with her, eyes and hair. Lank coils of seaweed hair around me, my heart, my soul. Salt green death.
> We. (*U* 10:872–78)

For her part, Molly complains that men "have friends they can talk to weve none" (*U* 18:1456–57). Her friends seem to exist only in her memories of her Gibraltar childhood and adolescence. Her monologue that closes *Ulysses* is almost entirely devoid of Dublin friends.

All three of *Ulysses*' main characters are isolated individuals. Their apartness practically defines them. At breakfast in the Martello tower, Stephen feels isolated when the milkwoman favors Buck Mulligan and the Irish-speaking Englishman, Haines. As he talks to Deasy after his class in "Nestor," his headmaster lectures him that "We are a generous people but we must also be just," prompting Stephen's response, "I fear those big words [...] which make us so unhappy" (2.262-64). As Robert Spoo points out, Deasy's "we" refers to the Irish Protestant Ascendancy, while Stephen's "us" aligns himself with the Irish Catholic majority that Deasy trivializes.[8] Perhaps most painfully, he is aware as he talks about Shakespeare in the National Library of Ireland that novelist George Moore will be hosting a party that evening to which Stephen isn't invited and that George Russell will be editing a volume of young poets' works, also ignoring Stephen. His mental reaction: "See this. Remember" (*U* 9:294).

Bloom, for his part, encounters several groups during his day, but they all deny him entry, giving him no chance to say or even think "we." Early on, the trio of men, including Simon Dedalus, who share his carriage to Paddy Dignam's funeral in "Hades" resists his attempts to ingratiate himself, and the group that Red Murray identifies with doesn't include him. Nor, it seems, do the men he meets in the *Freeman's Journal* offices in "Aeolus" or those in Davy Byrne's pub in "Lestrygonians." He has individual friends, such as Josie Breen, and Gerty MacDowell sees him positively through a romantic haze, but his only "we" involves his family. He remembers, for instance, an old pianist who used to accompany Molly while she sang and who used to amuse Milly: "All we laughed" (*U* 4:294–95). His personal escape from his condition is his family of three, and his memories of his son.

Stephen's separation is less complete than Bloom's, and in some ways it is willed. In *A Portrait of the Artist as a Young Man* he made isolation a badge of honor, a major part of the grand gesture of his solo flight from Ireland: "When the soul of a man is born in this country there are nets flung at it to hold it back from flight. You talk to me of nationality, language, religion. I shall try to fly by those nets."[9] And he defiantly proclaimed that "I do not fear to be alone or to be spurned for another or to leave whatever I have to leave."[10] In *Ulysses*, he is beginning to realize implications of what he proclaimed, what being alone might mean, as in his conversation with Deasy and after speaking during his Shakespeare talk about Ann Hathaway seducing young Will. He thinks then, "And my turn? When?" (*U* 9:261). As it is, Stephen gets included in groups when he is useful to Buck Mulligan or when he offers to buy drinks in "Aeolus," but rarely elsewhere.

As someone assumed to be a Jew, Bloom is never an insider. Men gather together throughout the novel, but he is always excluded. He is occasionally welcomed into groups but only when he isn't around to hear, as when Myles Crawford, the newspaper editor, mentions "all the talents" represented by the men in the office and professor MacHugh chips in that "If Bloom were here," the collection would include "the gentle art of advertisement" (*U*7:605, 7:608). In "Wandering Rocks," as Lenehan and M'Coy walk together, they notice Bloom at an outdoor book cart and, after Lenehan reminisces about riding in a car with Bloom and Molly following a dinner at which he was a dishwasher and Bloom talked obliviously to a fourth passenger as Molly's breasts bounced against Lenehan, he praises him as "a cultured allroundman" and "not one of your common or garden [...]" with "a touch of the artist" about him (*U* 10:581–82; Joyce's ellipsis). But Bloom is too far away to hear.

Bloom doesn't even acknowledge possible connections with fellow Jews. Moses Dlugacz, the butcher he buys pork from in "Calypso," is probably a Jew despite the meat he sells, but, with Bloom's connection with Jewish culture so thin, he makes no mention of this. And he tries to tell the story of the stinginess of Reuben J. Dodd, assumed by all the men in the carriage ride to Paddy Dignam's funeral in "Hades" to be Jewish, but he is thwarted by Martin Cunningham (*U* 6:262–91). (One puzzling detail contradicts this pattern of Bloom's isolation from groups: he is a Mason. The fact is mentioned several times,[11] but Bloom never thinks about the organization and its significance to him.)

It isn't just that the characters are isolated from groups. Throughout *Ulysses*, "us" and "we" denote groups that are unpleasant, not very desirable, sometimes even dangerous. Most directly, Bloom's presence in Barney Kiernan's pub in the "Cyclops" provokes a steady stream of remarks about "us" and "them," with "them" sometimes denoting the British, more often Jews. Fritz Senn has noted that Bloom is invited in by the Citizen—the most hostile, belligerent, and anti-Semitic of the men in Barney Kiernan's pub:[12]

> Old Garryowen started growling again at Bloom that was skeezing round the door.
>
> —Come in, come on, says the citizen. He won't eat you.
>
> So Bloom slopes in with his cod's eye on the dog and he asks Terry was Martin Cunningham there. (12:407–11)

With its Homeric echo—"He won't eat you"—this is quite an invitation. Once Bloom is inside, some of the demeaning comments are spoken in his presence: "The friends we love are by our side and the foes we hate before us" (*U*12:523–24); "We want no more strangers in our house" (*U* 12:1150–51); "The strangers, says the citizen. Our own fault. We let them come in. We brought them in" (*U* 12:1156–57). When he is away from the pub, his exclusion is made explicit when one of the men, a Protestant in this otherwise homogenously Catholic group, declares directly, "We don't want him" (*U* 12:1634).

Bloom repeatedly exacerbates the situation in the pub by saying the wrong thing or talking when he should keep quiet, but he's in a tough situation, in the presence of drunken, hostile men who unquestioningly see themselves as "we" in contrast to his "I." Except in the abstract—"I belong to a race too, says Bloom, that is hated and persecuted. Also now. This very moment. This very instant" and "Robbed, says he. Plundered. Insulted. Persecuted. Taking what belongs to us by right" (*U* 12:1467–71)—he has no recourse to any "we."

One of the *Ulysses* notebooks available at National Library of Ireland includes a group of quotes from Otto Weininger's *Über die letzten Dinge* (1904; On Last Things). As Wim Van Mierlo points out, Weininger has been cited as a source of Bloom's appellation in "Circe" as "the new womanly man" (*U* 15:1978–99). Joyce took notes here on such topics as morality, mass psychology, sado-masochism, murder, and other topics.[13] One of his notes is "Personen die in einem Raum beisammen sind bilden eine Gemeinschaft gegen Neu-Eintretender" (People who are in a space together always form a community against newcomers).[14] It isn't clear whether Joyce had Bloom in mind as he wrote the quote (Van Mierlo suggests that it might have been related to Stephen's performance on Shakespeare in "Scylla and Charybdis"), but maybe Joyce was thinking about Barney Kiernan's pub. It is there that Bloom is an outsider more than anywhere else in the book.

In the drafts for "Cyclops," Stephen Dedalus is part of that community in the pub. He seems to enjoy the camaraderie of the men in the bar as he buys them drinks. It is quite a crowd: with one misstep, such as not buying a round of drinks (the mistake Bloom makes), the Citizen or the narrator could instantly ostracize him. And he is not really in the group, as the narrator indicates when he points out Stephen's failure to live up to father: "Bit of a shaper that fellow, son of Si Dedalus. He was in Paris in the quartier latin and he came back an atheist. He'll never be as good a man as his father anyhow."[15]

In the published *Ulysses*, Stephen memorably says two very different things about Jews, one near the beginning of the novel and one near the end. In "Nestor," his employer Deasy comments that "England is in the hands of the jews. In all the highest places: her finance, her press. And they are the signs of a nation's decay. Wherever they gather they eat up the nation's vital strength." As a response, a "merchant, Stephen said, is one who buys cheap and sells dear, jew or gentile, is he not?" (*U* 2:346–49; 2:359–60). But in the second-last episode, "Ithaca," as he drinks cocoa in Bloom's kitchen, Stephen responds to his host's request for a "strange legend" by singing a medieval ballad about a young Christian boy who accidentally kicks a ball over a Jew's wall and through his windows. When the man's daughter goes outside and sees the boy, she invites him into her house and then kills him: "She took a penknife out of her pocket / And cut off his little head. / And now he'll play his ball no more / For he lies among the dead" (*U* 17:825–28, Joyce italicizes all the words). Is the song a direct insult to a man he considers a Jew and a rejection of a presumed invitation to join a family with a Jewish man at its head? Or is Stephen preparing for his polite decline of Bloom's invitation to spend the night in his house by rejecting the "we" of a family more generally?

In the notorious dialogue from "Cyclops," when Bloom leaves the pub to try to find Cunningham to join him on their mission to help the Dignam family, one of the men in the pub, John Wyse Nolan, asks, "why can't a jew love his country like the next fellow?" J. J. O'Molloy asks in response, "Why not?" and quips, "when he's quite sure which country it is" (*U* 12:1628–30). In two early "Cyclops" drafts, Joyce upped the ante. The remark is there, somewhat reworded, but in it O'Molloy asks the original question, and Stephen provides the answer.[16] Ever since I first saw the drafts in the early 1970s, I've wondered why Joyce put Stephen in the episode and how he thought the novel would proceed after Stephen made these remarks and then went on to meet and be rescued by Bloom. Would he have been there while Bloom was in the pub? (The fragmentary drafts don't say.) I also wonder what Joyce was thinking when he took him out. Maybe he removed him because of the incredible narrative difficulties of leaving him in. (I suggested this when I wrote about this passage in *"Ulysses" in Progress*.[17]) But also, in writing him out, Joyce changed Stephen's relationship to "inside" groups by eliminating him from this especially heinous one. My sense of Stephen's general isolation in *Ulysses* grew even more powerful after I became aware that he was once inside this group in "Cyclops."

In his book about manuscript study, *Riding with Rilke*, Ted Bishop has written that "Part of the reason we work in archives is, I'm convinced, for the archival jolt, a portal to knowledge and, in itself, an assurance that we have connected with something real."[18] "Cyclops," that most inhospitable of Homeric episodes (one-eyed giants eating Odysseus' men) and of *Ulysses* episodes, at least to Leopold Bloom (xenophobia, anti-Semitism), proved very hospitable to a genetic critic. Genetic criticism, manuscript study, puts the writing at the center of those activities and foregrounds the writing along with the published text. As Stephen speculates in "Nestor": "Had Pyrrhus not fallen by a beldam's hand in Argos or Julius Caesar not been knifed to death. They are not to be thought away. Time has branded them and fettered they are lodged in the room of the infinite possibilities they have ousted. But can those have been possible seeing that they never were? Or was that only possible which came to pass?" (*U* 2:48–52). In taking Stephen out of "Cyclops," Joyce removed him from the book from "Wandering

Rocks" until "Oxen of the Sun," leaving him more isolated than in the drafts. In writing him out, Joyce changes Stephen's relationship to "inside" groups.

Over and over again, *Ulysses* puts its main value on an individual isolated within a community. Throughout the novel, Bloom resists and withstands all kinds of Homeric-type temptations. Also, both he and Stephen, partly reluctantly and partly willingly, resist the temptation to belong, especially to an inside group. Bloom has little choice. As a Jew, or as someone everyone thinks of as a Jew, this native-born Irishman faces questions like "What is your nation?" (*U* 12:1430). In some major ways, even though Bloom has been inside Ireland his entire life, the door to the country is closed to him.

The real 7 Eccles Street was demolished in the 1960s, but its front door was rescued from the building's facade in 1967 during the night before the demolition. The door is now in the city's James Joyce Centre. Robert Nicholson has noted that when poet Patrick Kavanagh unveiled the rescued door at the pub on Bloomsday 1967, he pronounced, "I hereby declare this door shut."[19] The fictional 7 Eccles Street in *Ulysses* is not closed to us as readers, but we can never really walk through its door. We are in the kitchen twice and the bedroom twice, as well as in the house regularly in Bloom's and Molly's thoughts, and we even accompany Bloom to his outhouse. But we aren't really inside. At best, the door is ajar, even if quite widely. Like any work of art, *Ulysses* is partly an open door and partly a closed one. It remains mostly or entirely closed to many of its readers, while it somewhat or substantially opens to others.

Philosopher Gaston Bachelard has made some tantalizing remarks on open and closed doors. In *The Poetics of Space*, he includes a small section on the dialectics of open and closed and especially on "open" and "closed" as metaphors. He asks, "Shall we harden or soften the metaphor? Shall we repeat with the logicians that a door must be open or closed?" Not surprisingly, he answers "no": "The door is an entire cosmos of the Half-open," just as humans are "half-open beings."[20] *Ulysses* itself is open for readers who are entranced by the half-open door of 7 Eccles Street, by the half-open characters of Leopold Bloom, Molly Bloom, and Stephen Dedalus, and by the half-open novel itself, opening as it does onto human minds and onto many and varied aspects of life and of culture. The novel opens enough both to let readers in and then (for some, although not for all of us) to let them out.

At the end of his brief consideration of doors, Bachelard asks, "Onto what, toward what, do doors open? Do they open for the world of men, or for the world of solitude?"[21] *Ulysses* balances these alternatives, or plays them off in relation to each other, in terms of "us" and "them," or "we" and "I." The novel offers a welcoming opening door to solitude, that almost magical realm for Bachelard where imagination and poetry come alive and thrive.

IV

My dedication in *The Necessary Fiction* is to "Joyceans and *Ulysses* readers everywhere."[22] Margot Norris dedicates *Virgin and Veteran Readings of "Ulysses"* to "the wonderful community of Joyce scholars who have made the study of his work a life-long pleasure for me."[23] Like many other similar tributes, these recognitions gratefully acknowledge a group we have happily chosen to associate ourselves with, one that accepted both of us early in our careers and has sustained each of us for close to half a century. I wrote that, for me, the word "Joycean" can stand for "a congenial group of individuals, diverse in many ways but linked by a common interest in one writer's works."[24]

This leads to a final aspect of time and returns, and to the inside groups in *Ulysses*: the "we" of Joyce scholarship, the so-called "Joyce Industry," the Joyce community, Joyceans. Even as a group standing outside a text that only partly lets us in, we're a kind of inside group. We often try to deny or deflect insider status by saying proudly that we are open to all newcomers and to everyone, including professional scholars, independent scholars, enthusiasts, and dazzled or puzzled readers from all over the world, and by insisting that we impose no viewpoint or position regarding Joyce and his works. But we *are* insiders, since Joyceans appear to understand *Ulysses* better than most people, or at least we seem to talk convincingly as if we do. We go to nice places for conferences (in normal times), and we are an inside group all to ourselves. We are like Leopold and Molly Blooms who have found each other. We even have our own anthem: "Love's Old Sweet Song," a song that Morris Beja has called the international anthem of Joyceans.[25]

I've gotten myself into a bind between "inside" groups—presented as so unappealing in *Ulysses*—and the (differently?) inside group that we outsider-Joyceans have created for ourselves. I can't resolve this dilemma. I don't know how, and I'm not sure I want to. It points to one of many contradictions within *Ulysses*. We are inside as Joyceans, facing the text from the outside. Maybe we suffer from tunnel vision. Is there a light at the end? Maybe, maybe not, but if there is, it is partial, and we can't find it alone. As long as we get to read and talk about *Ulysses*, whether virtually or again in the future when (unlike Leopold Bloom) we're released from our isolation, that tunnel is, I repeatedly find, a quite nice place to be.

Notes

1 Michael Groden, *The Necessary Fiction: Life with James Joyce's "Ulysses"* (Brighton, UK: Edward Everett Root, 2019).

2 Margot Norris, *Virgin and Veteran Readers of "Ulysses"* (New York: Palgrave Macmillan, 2011), 1.

3 Stuart Gilbert, *James Joyce's "Ulysses": A Study* (1930; reprinted with new preface, New York: Vintage, 1952); Frank Budgen, *James Joyce and the Making of "Ulysses,"* introduction by Hugh Kenner (1934; reprinted, Bloomington: Indiana University Press, 1960).
4 Norris, *Virgin and Veteran Readings of "Ulysses"*, 3.
5 Patricia Meyer Spacks, *On Rereading* (Cambridge, MA: Harvard University Press, 2011). 274.
6 James Joyce, *Ulysses*, ed. Hans Walter Gabler with Wolfhard Steppe and Claus Melchior, Afterword by Michael Groden (New York: Random-Vintage, 1986), episode 8, line 608. Subsequent references will be cited parenthetically in the text by episode and line number.
7 Martha C. Nussbaum, *Upheavals of Thought: The Intelligence of Emotions* (Cambridge, UK: Cambridge University Press, 2001), 709, 707, 690–91.
8 Robert Spoo, "Nestor," in Catherine Flynn, ed., *New Joyce Studies: Twenty-First Century Critical Revisions* (Cambridge, UK: Cambridge University Press, forthcoming).
9 James Joyce, *A Portrait of the Artist as a Young Man* (1916; ed. Chester G. Anderson, New York: Viking, 1964), 203.
10 Joyce, *A Portrait of the Artist as a Young Man*, 247.
11 Especially in "Lestrygonians" (8:184, 8:960–63) and "Circe" (15:450–51, 15:758–60, 15:770, 15:2724, 15:2854–55, 15:4298–99, 15:4951–56).
12 Fritz Senn, "Kyklonomastics," *James Joyce Quarterly*, 36, no.3 (Spring 1999): 501.
13 Wim Van Mierlo, "The Subject Notebook: A Nexus in the Composition History of *Ulysses*—A Preliminary Analysis," *Genetic Joyce Studies* 7 (Spring 2007) <https://www.geneticjoycestudies.org/articles/GJS7/GJS7_MierloSubject>.
14 National Library of Ireland MS 36,639/3, 29, citing Otto Weininger, *Über die letzten Dinge* (1904).
15 Buffalo MS V.A.6, 2r-2v; transcribed in Phillip F. Herring, ed., *Joyce's Notes and Early Drafts for "Ulysses": Selections from the Buffalo Collection* (Charlottesville: University Press of Virginia, 1977), 181.
16 Buffalo MS V.A.8, 22 and Buffalo MS V.A.6, 2r; transcribed in Herring, *Joyce's Notes and Early Drafts for "Ulysses,"* 170, 181.
17 Michael Groden, *"Ulysses" in Progress* (Princeton, NJ: Princeton University Press, 1977), 135–37.
18 Ted Bishop, *Riding with Rilke: Reflections on Motorcycles and Books* (Toronto: Viking, 2005; New York: Norton, 2006), 36.
19 Robert Nicholson, *The James Joyce Daybook: A Companion for 1990* (Dublin: Anna Livia Press, 1989), entry for June 16.
20 Gaston Bachelard, *The Poetics of Space* (1958; trans. Maria Jolas, 1964; rpt. Boston: Beacon, 1994), 221, 222.
21 Bachelard, *Poetics of Space*, 224.
22 Groden, *Necessary Fiction*, vi.
23 Norris, *Virgin and Veteran Readings of "Ulysses"*, [v].
24 Groden, *Necessary Fiction*, 171–72.
25 Morris Beja, "'Even today [...]': In Memory of Zack Bowen," The James Joyce Society Tributes to Zack Bowen <http://joycesociety.org/Zacktributes.htm>.

Chapter 7

INORGANIC FORM FROM JAMES JOYCE TO ELEANOR CATTON

Derek Attridge

I

Among the many strengths of Margot Norris's extensive writing on Joyce is her concern for the reader's experience of the text. Whether peering through the surface textures of *Dubliners* to detect the subtle play of power and desire,[1] imagining the first-time reader of *Ulysses* enjoying its surprises and tessellations,[2] or drawing on recent theoretical movements to illuminate the workings of *Finnegans Wake*,[3] her critical writing does ample justice to the unique way an encounter with the Joycean text challenges, puzzles, disconcerts, but always rewards. In this essay I will explore one aspect of Joyce's formal innovation, taking my cue from this characteristic of Margot Norris's writing by examining the contribution it makes to the reader's experience of *Ulysses*, and consider some writers who followed in Joyce's footsteps.

Of course, "the reader" is not an unproblematic concept. In the first instance, the reader is inevitably myself, but I will do my best to exclude what might be idiosyncratic about my responses. The value of a community of critical readers, such as Joyce is lucky to have, is that idiosyncrasies—as likely to be a feature of "veteran" as of "virgin" readings, to use Norris's terms—can be spotted and ironed out. "Experience," too, is a complex term. It figures centrally in several philosophical schools, notably empiricism, with its assumption that knowledge derives from sensory experience, phenomenology, sometimes labelled the "philosophy of experience," and existentialism, which emphasizes personal decisions. I propose to use the term in a fairly colloquial sense to refer to what happens, mentally, emotionally, and physically, in the process of literary reading. What I don't want to imply by using the term is that a theory of the literary work as experienced event is primarily an empirical—that is to say, a psychological or neurological—theory interested in what goes on in reader's brain (or, for that matter, a physiological theory interested in what goes on in the rest of the body), even though any conclusions that might be drawn about the reader's experience might be mappable onto these domains.

Literary form is usually discussed in terms of the dictum that form and meaning are inseparable, a dictum that goes back at least to the Romantics. The notion of "organic form," introduced most influentially into English literary criticism by Coleridge (following A. W. Schlegel), continues to surface right up to the present. A recent work of literary theory states: "[T]here is no moment, not even a theoretical one, at which it is possible to isolate a purely formal property—at least without turning the literary work into something else."[4] Similar comments could be culled from a wide range of critical and theoretical texts, ranging from introductions for students to philosophical tomes. The hugely influential model of interpretation favored by the founders and proselytizers of "close reading" in Britain and the USA—T. S. Eliot, I. A. Richards, William Empson, F. R. Leavis, W. K. Wimsatt, Reuben Brower, and many others—took the inseparability of form and content as a fundamental axiom.

Yet, there is also an ancient—more ancient, in fact—tradition of proposing form alone as a source of aesthetic pleasure, without being the subsidiary partner in a form-content marriage. Music and the visual arts are obvious domains in which this tradition flourishes, and some lyric poems might be said to possess formal arrangements that please in a manner independent of the content. It's a tradition that links form with *beauty*, a topic I don't propose to pursue here; beauty of form plays only a small part in the experience of Joyce's work, which might be more accurately thought of as a challenge to this idea. I do, however, wish to follow up the thought that form—sonic, visual, structural, rhetorical—can operate in ways other than as a reflection, or enhancement, of the content established by the referential function of the words.

Before going any further, it's necessary to clarify what exactly is meant by these two terms, *content* and *form*, in the argument I am making. I take content to be the world which the words of the text bring into being for the reader, including the dictionary meanings of words, the referents of proper names (where these are nonfictional), the images conjured up by both literal and metaphorical verbal collocations, and the characters, narrator(s), places and events in a narrative sequence. Form, by contrast, comprises all those features of the text that do not point to the extra-verbal world of people, things, events, and places: its material properties (such as sounds and rhythmic movement), its repetitions and patterns, its deviations from established patterns, its structural articulations, and its lexical and syntactic characteristics. What is termed "style" is the consistent use of certain formal properties, say the employment of arcane vocabulary, the preference for short sentences, or the repetition of particular grammatical structures.

The use of rhetorical figures is an aspect of form, some (traditionally called *figures of speech*) involving the verbal surface, such as alliteration, anaphora, or archaism, others (*figures of thought* or *tropes*) having a more direct relation to the content, such as metaphor, personification, or bathos. In making this distinction, it's helpful to think in terms of the reader's experience: a rhetorical figure is a moment of disturbance in the smooth processing of language, whether it's a linguistic feature (like a rhyme) that momentarily makes one aware of the words' material composition or an eddy in the seamless passage from language to meaning (as when a metaphor requires an act of interpretation). In the case of figures of thought, the result is a modification of the content; in the case of figures of speech, the relation to content is less obvious.

Although my concern in this essay is not with poetry, we can turn to the features of regular verse to challenge the idea that form always relates to content. Does every metrical line forge a union between form and content? Can every rhyme be justified as contributing to the meaning of the poem? Although much critical ingenuity has been deployed in making such connections, the vast majority of lines don't exhibit close unity of form and content. The history of Western poetry in the twentieth century illustrates the abiding impact of the doctrine of organic form at the same time as it highlights the inorganic nature of traditional verse form: poets who threw off what they saw as the shackles of meter and rhyme often did so in the name of an increased organicism. In doing so, however, they removed one of the sources of readerly pleasure. As children, we enjoyed rhyme and meter for their own sakes, or perhaps for their assault on the semantic operation of language; as adults, we should not pretend we have lost that ability to enjoy the patterned dance of words.[5]

To make this point is not to devalue the power of form as a component of the meaning of the literary work. I've argued elsewhere that we ought to think of "meaning" in the reader's experience as a verb, not a noun, and of the operation of meaning as itself an aspect of form—or, rather, of forming.[6] Nevertheless, I want to suggest that to appreciate fully the revolution in literary fiction carried out by Joyce we need to raise the question of what I'm calling "inorganic form": that is, the contribution made to the reader's experience (and, I would add, pleasurable experience) by formal properties operating with a degree of independence, without, that is, playing second fiddle to content.

II

Joyce's early work shows him to be a devotee of organic form. While the poems of *Chamber Music* employ traditional forms, prioritizing their contribution to lyrical grace over their other functions, the stories of *Dubliners* eschew obvious formal devices to create the sense of a slice of unmediated life. (That Joyce in doing so makes subtle use of the formal properties of prose and the generic properties of the short story has not passed critics like Margot Norris by.) It's in *A Portrait of the Artist* that formal innovation becomes a major feature: the opening pages create for the reader a quite different experience from that of the novels written during the previous two centuries.[7] But although form is foregrounded in those pages, it's still operating in an organic relation to meaning: by departing from the norms of the written language to generate the impression of a child's thought processes, Joyce is fusing form and content in a manner that was to prove highly influential on later writers.

The technique of interior monologue, developed so skillfully in *Ulysses*, takes this innovation further. By fragmenting the regular configurations of language, Joyce conveys a vivid sense of his characters' mental world, and had he written the entire work in the "initial style" of the opening chapters it would have been received, for all its formal innovations, as a major breakthrough in the tradition of the realist novel, a book to set beside the several volumes of Dorothy Richardson's *Pilgrimage*—with their stream-of consciousness technique—that had already appeared by 1922.[8] But of course Joyce's play with formal devices soon went in a different direction. In introducing headlines into the "Aeolus" episode of *Ulysses*—quite literally, as the earlier version of the chapter published in the *Little Review* in 1918 was a continuous narrative in the same style as the previous episodes—Joyce demonstrated that formal devices could operate without contributing to the representation of his characters' mental worlds.

The headlines in "Aeolus," like all the stylistic innovations that follow in the book, can of course be related to the content of the chapter, which takes place in the office and printing works of a newspaper. But if we think in terms of the reader's experience, it's clear that this connection is something we make at a remove from our direct apprehension of the fictional narrative; that's to say, we register it consciously once we see what is going on, but our awareness of it doesn't feed into our ongoing engagement with the lives of Stephen Dedalus, Leopold Bloom, and the newspapermen. In a similar manner, the play with sound in "Sirens" can be connected to the musical performances in the Ormond Hotel, the inflated parodic interpolations in "Cyclops" can be seen as a comment on the exaggerations of the barflies, the parade of English styles in "Oxen of the Sun" can be matched to the months of gestation, and so on.[9] In every case, the reader, once she has discovered the relationship (or been informed of it in a critical work), can accept it as proof that there is a purposiveness to this formal feature, and go on to enjoy the stylistic adventures—whether the increasingly unlikely headlines, the hilarious parodies poking fun at various kinds of rhetoric, the brilliant pastiches of prose styles that impede rather than enhance the referential capacity of the language, and so on. Form can be said to enhance content, but only via an intellectual operation.[10] It is still meaningful, but its relation to content is no longer organic.

This loosening of the connection between form and content means that there is a degree of arbitrariness in the choice of the particular style for each chapter.[11] The goings-on in Bella Cohen's brothel *could* have been related in the initial style, or with parodic interpolations, or in a continuous unpunctuated flow; the reader's experience would have been very different in each case, but an argument could have—and no doubt would have—been made for the appropriateness of each. (It's harder to imagine a different style for the child's experiences at the start of *Portrait*, or an alternative to the initial style to capture the fragmented run of thoughts.) And what goes for individual episodes goes for the Homeric structure as a whole. Detecting parallels between events in the narrative and episodes in the *Odyssey*—noting the shape-shifting in "Proteus" or the seductive arts of the barmaids in "Sirens," for example—is an enjoyable aspect of an engagement with the novel, and can lead to reflections on the nature of epic, the figure of the hero, or the vicissitudes of history, but it doesn't emerge immediately from the words on the page. It's easy to forget that the familiar episode titles aren't present in the book, and it's hard to say how many of them might have become part of the standard commentary if Joyce hadn't circulated them to friends. Indeed, if Joyce had called his novel *Hamnet*, there would no doubt exist a mountain of exegesis tracing the parallels with both Shakespeare's life and his most famous play.

Without Joyce's tabulating of each episode's title, "technic," organ, etc. in the famous schemata given to Valéry Larbaud and Carlo Linati, then, much of what we take for granted in our commentaries would probably never have emerged. Certain recurrent features of the chapters might still have been detectable, however. A careful reader of the chapter we know as "Lotus-Eaters," for instance, might notice a recurring motif. Hugh Kenner lists some of them: "the warmth, the directionless walk, the gelded horses munching in their nosebags, the communicants in the church Bloom passes through, the chemist's chloroform and poppysyrup, the lemony smell of the soap, the anticipated warm bath."[12] Without external guidance, such a reader would be unlikely to think of a specific episode in the *Odyssey*, but would certainly sense that the events and objects in the chapter were obeying some rule external to the fictional world. And in introducing this list Kenner puts his finger on the most revolutionary aspect of Joyce's use of formal devices in *Ulysses*: "[T]he episode's Homeric parallel, Lotos-Eaters, appears to take charge of much of its random detail" (22). It's not, in other words, just a question of formal features operating independently of content and being associated by the conscious interpretive action of the reader; the content is to some extent experienced as being *determined* by the form (although the connection still requires a conscious mental act). Kenner suggests, for instance, that the discovery by Bloom in "Nausicaa" that his watch has stopped at 4.30 p.m., and his immediate assumption that this must have been the exact moment of his wife's adultery, is just the sort of coincidence that would happen in the kind of novel whose sentimental style has dominated the first part of the episode. It wouldn't, he argues, have occurred in any other episode of the novel.[13] Whether or not we make a connection with the *Odyssey*, we are aware that the things that happen, and the language in which they are related, follow a pattern in excess of the fictional world itself. Once detected, they form part of the reader's experience, a pleasure derived not from the content the language is bringing into being but from the writer's brilliance in making language conform to a predetermined schema.

The pleasure we take in noting Joyce's successful implementation of his self-imposed rules is in part an appreciation of what we may call his *craft*. The element of craft is something works of art share with other well-made artefacts; it doesn't elicit the same kind of response as the artwork, and thus doesn't have the potential to change the reader's grasp on the world, but it does provide real enjoyment coupled with admiration for the artist's skill. Once we notice the flower words in "Lotus-Eaters" or the musical terms in "Sirens" we are likely to smile inwardly as they occur; they are a kind of pun, and puns are, potentially at least, a pleasurable linguistic effect. There may be more to this aspect of *Ulysses*, however; to say that these features operate independently of the work's content is not to say that they have no significance other than as entertainment. To find external imperatives governing content is to have the assumptions on the basis of which we usually read fiction challenged: it is to be reminded that the words we are engaging with are all the result of deliberate choices, and that there are rules governing even the most transparent realism that the writer has to follow in order to achieve the effects desired. There are also more specific rewards: the word-choices in *Ulysses* and the matches between Joyce's novel and the *Odyssey*, for instance, function to fuse elements of the perceived world normally kept apart: we see new patterns and new alignments, just as we do in a successful metaphor.

Other chapters offer similar pleasures. In "Hades," for instance, Bloom remembers Molly saying "I'm dying for it," notes the "[d]ead side of the street," reflects on the "dead weight" of the coffin, refers to the "dead letter office," and observes that priests are "dead against" cremation. If it's possible to explain these verbal allusions as unconscious reflections of the funeral in progress (and hence, again, obviating any need to refer to Homer), the same explanation won't do for the many references to the organ Joyce allotted to the chapter: "He took it to heart," "Wear the heart out of a stone," "Vain in her hearts of hearts," "That touches a man's inmost heart," and so on. Equally separate from any character's consciousness, and easy to overlook without external prodding, are the shape-shifting terms in "Proteus," the flower-names in "Lotus-Eaters," and the windy words in "Aeolus." The frequent references to music in "Sirens" would perhaps be more obvious to an uninstructed reader; it would be hard to remain unaware that the episode is awash not only with actual examples of musical performance but words with a musical resonance, even when music is not being referred to: "Miss Kennedy [...] *transposed* the teatray" (92); "If he doesn't *conduct* himself I'll *wring* his *ear* for him" (104–5); "Miss Douce *chimed* in" (147); "they urged each each to *peal* after *peal*, *ringing in changes*" (174–5); "Must be a great *tonic*" (219–20); and so on.[14] The device is particularly striking when characters choose to speak, or think, in words that reflect the episode's governing trope, revealing themselves to be innocent victims of an imperative outside their ken.

The enjoyment we derive from noticing how the Odyssean correlation or the nominated category in the schema determines the thought and speech of the characters in a given chapter isn't derived from enhanced realism; on the contrary, it's enjoyment of the formal device itself as it colors the narrative content. (At the same time, attending to this aspect of *Ulysses* doesn't involve any diminishment of the astonishing detail of its content.) There is still an element of arbitrariness—"Hades" could have been studded with words relating to earth or "Sirens" with references to water[15]—and the exercise of relating form to content, or, rather, content to form, still has to be consciously carried out, perhaps with the help of a critical commentary or Joyce's schema. Though in using this technique Joyce tightens the connection between form and content that, in examples like the headlines of "Aeolus," he had loosened, it can't be said to be an organic relationship.[16]

III

We could describe these Joycean effects as the operation of rules, chosen with a degree of arbitrariness, upon the style and other formal properties of the text, over and above those of grammar, genre, and sense. *Ulysses* as a whole, for instance, is subject to such rules as "relate each chapter to an episode in Homer's *Odyssey*; give the main characters Homeric equivalents; make every chapter correspond to an organ, an art, a 'technic', etc." (In some cases, however, it's likely that Joyce decided on the correspondence after having written the chapter.) Individual chapters are subject to other rules: "Where there is a choice of terms, choose the one that suggests a death/the heart/flowers/wind/music [...] etc." Although some commentators have sought to attribute these rules to the work of a hidden originator,[17] there's no need to invoke a human figure—except that we are aware of Joyce's own presence behind the verbal games, smiling rather than paring his fingernails (a point I shall return to at the end of this essay).

Ulysses changed the realm of possibility for later writers of fiction, and one of the choices that became available was that between sticking to the old method of making form subservient to content or following Joyce's new path by creating works in which content is determined, to some degree at least, by form. (Not everyone appreciated the nature and extent of Joyce's revolution: B. S. Johnson, for instance, boasted that in his novel *Travelling People* he had outdone his forebear by making the distinctive style of each of his chapters appropriate to the content.)[18] One writer who took up the challenge was Samuel Beckett, most prominently in *Lessness* (1970), a work of 120 sentences in which the first 60 sentences are repeated, but in a different order. In a further self-imposed constraint, he also allowed himself only 166 different words.[19] Film also furnishes examples: in Peter Greenaway's *Drowning by Numbers* (1988), for instance, each of the numbers from 1 to 100 either appears visually or is spoken by a character, mostly in the correct sequence—a structure, notes Greenaway, "independent of any internal plot, story or narrative."[20]

The most extensive body of literary works written in obedience to arbitrarily chosen rules is that associated with the *Ouvroir de littérature potentielle* (Workshop of Potential Literature), or Oulipo. Founded by Raymond Queneau and François Le Lionnais in 1960, Oulipo fostered a huge variety of literary writing in which the normal generic rules were supplemented (or contradicted) by additional constraints. The most famous Oulipian works are Queneau's 1947 *Exercices de style*, in which the same short anecdote is given in ninety-nine different stylistic versions,[21] and Georges Perec's 1969 *La Disparition*, a 300-page novel in which the letter *e* is missing.[22] Perec was influenced by the less readable *Gadsby* (1939), by Ernest Vincent Wright, subtitled *A Story of Over 50,000 Words Without Using the Letter "E."*[23] There exist many anthologies and surveys of Oulipian writing, in both prose and verse (in the latter field, such writing is sometimes called "procedural poetry"), and writers continue to create new constrained texts and to invent new constraints.[24] To take one remarkable recent instance, Christian Bök's 2001 book *Eunoia* consists of five chapters, each of which is composed of words that use only one vowel, in the sequence *a, e, i, o,u*; moreover, each chapter—made up of from five to nineteen 12-line sections, describes "a culinary banquet, a prurient debauch, a pastoral tableau and a nautical voyage"—a sequence that could be read as alluding to the *Odyssey*.[25]

Some anthologies include examples of "anticipatory plagiarism"—works (like Queneau's *Exercises de Style*) that pre-date Oulipo but display similar characteristics.[26] One of many specimens is the tradition of the cento, a poem made up solely of quotations from other poems. An early instance of this genre is the fourth-century poet Ausonius's "Nuptial Cento," a sexually explicit description of a wedding day—and night—made up entirely of lines and half-lines from Virgil. *Ulysses*, with its Homeric framework and its episode-appropriate events and vocabulary, undoubtedly deserves a place as an anticipatory Oulipian work. The compendium of rhetorical figures in "Aeolus," for instance, operates very like an Oulipian text,[27] as do the various rewritings in particular styles—the parodies in "Cyclops," the pastiches in "Oxen of the Sun," and the distinctive uses of language in episodes like "Circe," "Eumaeus" and "Ithaca." *Finnegans Wake* is less obviously Oulipian on account its free-ranging linguistic inventiveness, but—as with the river names in the ALP chapter—there are numerous local examples of the application of transformation rules that turn normal language into a comic echo-chamber.

IV

As a worthy successor to *Ulysses* in its use of an autonomous formal structure, and to demonstrate that this fictional mode is still a fruitful resource, I turn now to Eleanor Catton's 2013 novel *The Luminaries* (2013).[28] My own experience of this work was determined by the fact that I first encountered it as an audiobook. Having enjoyed Catton's first novel, *The Rehearsal*, I downloaded the new work as soon as it was available, knowing very little about it—though I could see I was in for a long listen.[29] As the book unfolded, each of its parts began with the announcement of a title, a date (until near the end these were all in 1866), and a grid reference. The chapter headings within those parts were intriguing but puzzling; such phrases as "Mercury in Sagittarius," "Saturn in Libra" and "Sun in Capricorn" meant very little to me other than to signal a connection to astrology. It was quickly clear, however, that what I was hearing was a pastiche of a Victorian novel, including brief summaries at the start of each chapter. A feature of the novel that became very noticeable as the recording went on was that the parts became shorter and shorter, and that toward the end the chapters within the parts also diminished in length. This formal device certainly contributed to the experience of the narrative content: a sense of the speeding up of the action and of the revelations that explained some of the earlier mysteries. The most condensed account of the major events of the narrative occurred as the lengthy preliminary summary to the very last chapter, which itself consisted of just a few lines of dialogue. Another formal device, a time-shift that allowed the book to end at a moment just before the beginning, added to the revelatory character of the closing. And the intricacy of the plotting, as nuggets of information passed from character to character and were thus revealed to the listener, was certainly part of my pleasure in the novel's formal properties.

It was only when I bought a hard copy of the book that I realized how complex and determining of the action the astrological structure is.[30] The decreasing length of the parts could now be seen as a carefully calculated construction: each of the twelve parts is about half the length of the previous one, and each part is made up of a diminishing number of chapters, from twelve to one. Part One is 360 pages long; Part Twelve just over a page. Seen on the page, the character chart at the start of the book is easier to make sense of than when heard in a recording: twelve characters under the heading "STELLAR," each with a "related house"; seven characters under the heading "PLANETARY," each with a "related influence"; and one character headed "TERRA FIRMA" with the note "*deceased.*" Thus, for example, the first stellar character is "Te Rau Tauwhare, *a greenstone hunter*," whose related house is "The Wells Cottage (Arahura Valley)," while the first planetary character is "Walter Moody," whose related influence is "Reason."

What the audiobook couldn't reproduce, and what explained these categories, was the astrological chart prefacing each of the book's parts, showing the position of the seven planets (including sun and moon) identified with the seven planetary characters in relation to the twelve signs of the zodiac (or "houses") identified with the twelve stellar characters. Figure 7.1 gives the first chart in the book, showing the planetary positions in relation to the signs of the zodiac on January 27, 1866 when seen from the small gold-prospecting town of Hokitika on the West coast of New Zealand's South Island, whose precise geographical co-ordinates are indicated.[31] Each of the twenty major characters, that is, is identified either with a zodiacal constellation (these twelve characters are named around the outside of the circular chart) or a planet (indicated on the chart by signs of the zodiac) apart from one, who is dead when the book begins; and their interactions are governed by the placing of the planets within the zodiacal houses on the particular date and at the particular locality of the chapter in question. Furthermore, the personalities and occupations of the characters reflect the supposed qualities of their astrological equivalents.

To give one example: the opening chapter is titled "Mercury in Sagittarius," and the chart indeed shows the symbol for Mercury sitting within the slice of zodiacal pie labelled with the sign for Sagittarius and the name of the character, Thomas Balfour, the Sagittarian. It's not difficult to work out that the character represented by Mercury is Walter Moody, a lawyer, just off the boat in Hokitika, whose conversation with the aforesaid Balfour

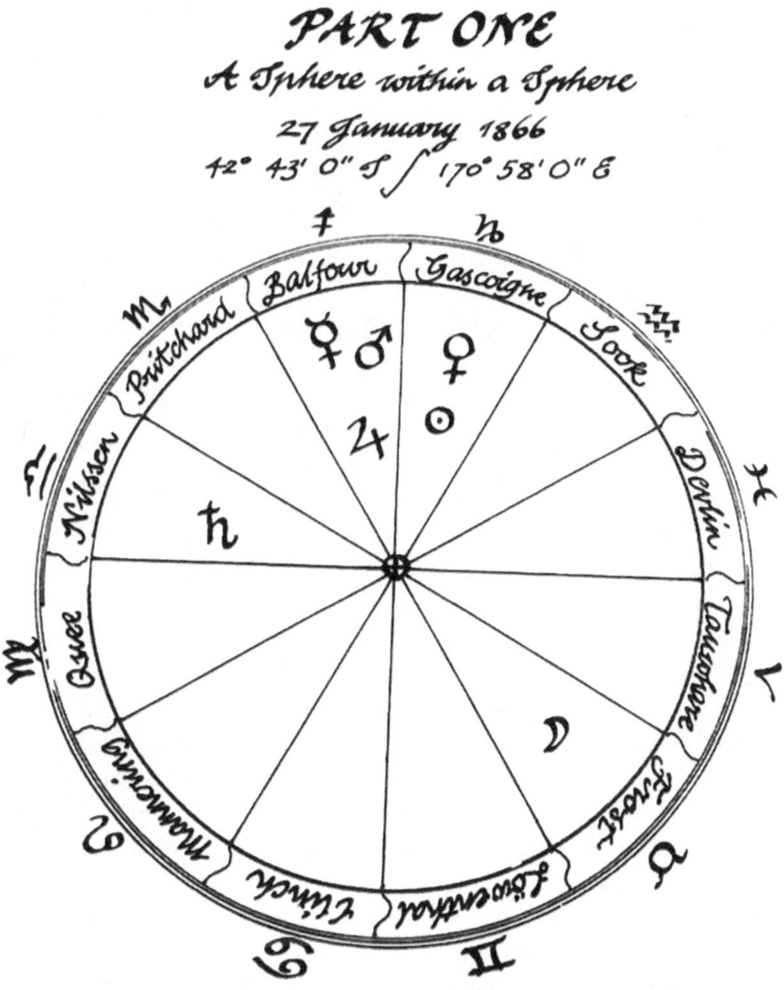

Figure 7.1 Astrological chart prefacing Part One of Eleanor Catton, *The Luminaries*.

takes up much of this first chapter. The opening scene also relates to the chart: the twelve men associated with the twelve zodiacal signs are all in the smoking room of the Crown Hotel, and as the chapters of this part proceed, they reveal their own knowledge of the events that have brought them together in conclave: the discovery of the dead man (Crosbie Wells), the disappearance of another man (Emery Staines), and the apparent attempted suicide of a woman (Anna Wetherell), all occurring on the same evening two weeks earlier and all involving one or more of the characters identified with the planets. These events remain at the heart of the narrative, among the many mysteries with which the reader is tantalized.

The question I want to ask is this: what does the complex structural apparatus contribute to the reader's experience of the novel? What kind of pleasure does it offer? I enjoyed the audiobook immensely, as an intricately woven mystery story in which the competing impulses of greed and love energize and twist human behavior, in which the desire for gold, sex, and opium drive the diverse characters to different ends, and in which the distinction between truth and fabrication remains unresolved to the end. It would seem, then, that knowledge of the astrological armature is unnecessary, however useful it might have been to the author in writing the novel. Yet my feeling is that my second experience of the novel, in which I was aware of that armature and during which I could turn back to the information at the beginning of the book or part in order to check parallels and conjunctions, was richer, and did fuller justice to Catton's achievement.

Like Joyce's Homeric parallels, Catton's astrological armature is an example of inorganic form. As with Joyce's Homeric allusions, there's no limit to the connections we can draw between that armature and the book's content—I've already mentioned the mapping of the characters onto the Zodiac—but this is not a matter of the form as a secondary element enriching the primary meaning. That Moody's encounter with Balfour mirrors the appearance of Mercury in the sector of Sagittarius in the Hokitika sky on that particular night doesn't enter into our experience of the narrative, as the audiobook version demonstrates; rather, like those words for death in "Hades" and wind in "Aeolus," it's the formal conditions that necessitate the encounter.[32] Likewise, the lengths of the parts are determined not by the content but by an external scheme, which we can relate to the waning of the moon, but which doesn't in itself contribute to the content.[33] We enjoy the formal arrangements for their ingenuity, their playfulness, the reminder they provide that we are reading a fiction, not a historical report. They are part of our sense of what I have called elsewhere the *authoredness* of the work: the knowledge that it's the product of the inventive labor of an artist, to whom, as readers, we owe a degree of responsibility.

V

I have argued in the past that form and meaning in most works of literature are not two separate properties of the work, but rather that, in the experience of reading, the sequence of formal events produces a mobilization and staging of meaning. Literary meaning, that is, is not simply a matter of a verbal sequence that sends the reader to a series of referents (there's nothing wrong with reading a literary work in this way, but it would not be treating it as literature); it's an *enactment* of referring, a process in which the work's formal properties play a crucial role. What I have been calling inorganic form, however, doesn't participate directly in this staging of meaning. The relation between Joyce's Homeric schema or Catton's zodiacal patterning and the meanings of the text can be thought of as one of *layering*, an additional stratum that the creative reader can treat in a number of ways (or ignore). Think of the relation between a painting and its title, or between a programmatic musical work and the verbal program: these elements of the work have to be taken in separately by the mind, and the manner in which they are used by the viewer or listener in enriching the experience of the work is not usually prescribed in advance. (There are, however, traditions in which formal elements contribute to the reader's experience in a predetermined way—some types of medieval number-symbolism, for instance.)

Although there's no necessity for formal arrangements of this kind to mirror content, there's a definite satisfaction to be had when such mirroring can be detected. The content of writing associated with Oulipo often reflects the constraint it observes: for instance, the narrative of the *e*-less *La Disparition* concerns the disappearance of a character by the name of Anton Voyl. (In the English translation he is Anton Vowl.) The chapters of Bök's *Eunoia* not only obey a rule that requires them to deal with the four topics enumerated earlier, but "must allude to the art of writing" (103). I've already mentioned the familiar strategy of linking Joyce's chosen style to the content of the episode, and it could be argued that the use of the zodiac in *The Luminaries* reflects the characters' helplessness in the face of the fates that ensnare them. Such parallels are not necessary to the operation of inorganic form, however, and are sometimes the product of critical ingenuity after the fact rather than a genuine report on the reader's experience. And when form appears to influence content, the familiar illusion of unmediated reference to an existing world is profoundly disturbed.

Of course, from the point of view of the writer, these constraints often function effectively as generative principles rather than limitations, just as a requirement to rhyme can be a spur to creativity in verse. But from the reader's point of view, it's not clear how aware of a formal feature of this type one needs to be in order for it to be effective. For the most part, Oulipean texts wear their constraints on their sleeves, and it's impossible to avoid the zodiacal charts in the printed version of *The Luminaries.* But without Bök's note explaining the additional constraints of *Eunoia*, few readers would appreciate them, and, as I noted earlier, without Joyce's schemata we might still be in ignorance of some of the formal features of *Ulysses.* Do readers unaware that the organ of "Hades" is *heart* or that of "Sirens" is *ear* nevertheless subliminally register their frequent occurrence? I suspect not—and in any case, to the extent that this unconscious effect does take place, the feature is no longer operating inorganically.

Inorganic form, then, complicates the idea of the literary work as a linear temporal experience in which all aspects are geared toward the representation of a single world, however complex. But it is still part of the literary experience: it contributes importantly to the pleasure to be gained and has the potential, as an important contributor to the work's singularity, to alter, however slightly, the reader's apprehension of their own world. It's not as if formal devices can operate without any meaningful effects at all; even a resistance to interpretation carries meaning of a kind.[34] One aspect of the reader's experience of inorganic form is enjoyment of the author's wit (if I may resurrect an older critical term), a quality especially evident when formal arrangements can be seen as influencing content. The apparently mechanical operation of many Oulipian procedures masks their human origin; but to attend fully to the Homeric parallels or the zodiacal framework of the novels I've been considering is to enrich one's reading by entering, as it were, the workshop of the writer, a place of mental delight and verbal creativity, and thus to augment one's engagement with the work's human dimension. To close with a quotation from Margot Norris, in one of her fine introductions to Joyce, "It may be in this domain of style and language that the manifestation of the human achieves its greatest poignancy in Joyce's work."[35]

Notes

1 Margot Norris, *Joyce's Web: The Social Unraveling of Modernism* (Austin: University of Texas Press, 1992); *Suspicious Readings of Joyce's* Dubliners (Philadelphia: University of Pennsylvania Press, 2003).

2 Margot Norris, *Virgin and Veteran Readings of* Ulysses (New York: Palgrave Macmillan, 2011). Of course, Norris's virgin reader is imagined from the point of view of a very experienced veteran, and thus unlikely to perpetrate significantly idiosyncratic responses.

3 Margot Norris, *The Decentered Universe of* Finnegans Wake: *A Structuralist Analysis* (Baltimore: Johns Hopkins University Press, 1974). See also Norris's use of Possible Worlds Theory in *Virgin and Veteran Readings.*

4 Derek Attridge, *The Singularity of Literature* (London: Routledge, 2017), 166–67. This essay constitutes a rethinking of my earlier position.

5 A recent assertion of the importance of recognizing that the formal properties of verse don't necessarily contribute to meaning is by Jonathan Culler: "Rhythm, repetition, sound patterning [are] independent elements that need not be subordinated to meaning and whose significance may even lie in a resistance to semantic recuperation" (*Theory of the Lyric* (Cambridge: Harvard University Press, 2017), 8). For an even more obvious indication of the capabilities of form divorced from semantic content, we need think only of the power of non-verbal music.

6 Attridge, *Singularity*, 152–53.

7 For a discussion of the revolutionary nature of these pages, see Derek Attridge, *Joyce Effects: On Language, Theory, and History* (Cambridge: Cambridge University Press, 2000), 59–77.

8 These volumes were *Pointed Roofs* (1915), *Backwater* (1916), *Honeycomb* (1917), *The Tunnel* (1919), *Interim* (1920), and *Deadlock* (1921).

9 One of the few critics to set aside these links is Patrick Parrinder, who regards them as belonging to "the time-honoured category of Irish Bulls." *James Joyce* (Cambridge: Cambridge University Press, 1984), 163.

10 In a discussion of the functions of poetic rhythm in an earlier work, I distinguished between "mimetic" and "emblematic" iconic devices, a distinction that has relevance here: "Mimetic devices take effect as an immediate part of the reading activity, and need not reach consciousness as a separate semantic mechanism; they contribute to that sense of heightened meaning which we can experience even when we cannot explain it. Emblematic devices, on the other hand, provide relations between the linguistic substance and the larger world only by means of a conscious intellectual act" (*The Rhythms of English Poetry* (London: Longman, 1982), 288). An early version of this distinction was proposed by Alexander Baumgarten: in aesthetic judgments, sensible properties can be either "intuitive" or "symbolic" (see Paul Guyer, *A History of Modern Aesthetics*, vol. 1, The Eighteenth Century (Cambridge: Cambridge University Press, 2014), 326).

11 Karen Lawrence puts it more strongly in what remains the best account of this aspect of *Ulysses*: "As the narrative norm is abandoned during the course of the book and is replaced by a series of styles, we see the arbitrariness of all styles" (*The Odyssey of Style in "Ulysses"* (Princeton: Princeton University Press, 1981), 9). One critic who attempts to justify the styles in organic terms is Charles Peake (*James Joyce: The Citizen and the Artist* (London: Edward Arnold, 1977)). Some other critics, such as F. R. Leavis, S. L. Goldberg and Leo Bersani, acknowledge this aspect of Joyce's writing only to deprecate it (see Attridge, *Joyce Effects*, 175–85).

12 Hugh Kenner, *Ulysses* (London: George Allen & Unwin, 1980), 22.

13 Ibid., 105.

14 Emphases added. References are to line numbers in the Gabler *Ulysses*.

15 Daniel Ferrer, in "Echo or Narcissus," demonstrates that it's possible to find some of Joyce's stylistic categories working for chapters other than those designated in the schemata (*James Joyce: The Centennial Symposium*, ed. Morris Beja et al. (Urbana: University of Illinois Press, 1986) 70–75).

16 *Finnegans Wake* is awash with formal devices that are not organically related to any fictional content; that a huge number of phrases, names and titles begin with the letters HCE or ALP, for instance, is not a reflection of the lives or inner experiences of the characters.

17 The best-known of these suggestions is David Hayman's "Arranger" (Ulysses: *The Mechanics of Meaning*, revised edition (Madison: University of Wisconsin Press, 1982), 88–104). Hayman's Arranger has human agency; for instance, he refers to the "intrusive and puckish arranging impulse" (125).

18 "Joyce used this device in ULYSSES, of course, but by allowing the nature of the subject matter of each particular series of events which form one chapter to determine organically the style chosen, I seem to have avoided the contrivance to which Joyce was sometimes reduced" (B. S. Johnson, Letter to George Greenfield, October 18, 1961; quoted in Jonathan Coe, *Like a Fiery Elephant: The Story of B. S. Johnson* (London: Pan Macmillan, 2004), 115).

19 I take this figure from an essay by another novelist who was fascinated by numbers: J. M. Coetzee, "Samuel Beckett's 'Lessness': An Exercise in Decomposition," *Computers and the Humanities* 7 (1973): 195–98.

20 *Expose*, https://exepose.com/2018/10/05/30-years-of-drowning-by-numbers-a-qa-with-peter-greenaway/. Musical forms, of course, depend on the observation of rules, such as those of Western harmony or those of twelve-tone serialism.

21 Raymond Queneau, *Exercices de style* (Paris: Gallimard, 1947), translated by Barbara Wright as *Exercises in Style* (London: Gaberbocchus, 1958). As the date of publication indicates, the work was Oulipian *avant le lettre*. Queneau explicitly declared the importance for him of Joyce's work; see Dennis Duncan, "'Joyce, un pornographe': *Ulysses, A Portrait of the Artist as a Young Man*, and the Sally Mara Novels of Raymond Queneau," *James Joyce Quarterly* 52 (2015): 351–68 (352).

22 Georges Perec, *La Disparition: Roman* (Paris: Denoël, 1969), translated by Gilbert Adair as *A Void* (London: Harvill Press, 1994).

23 Ernest Vincent Wright, *Gadsby: A Story of Over 50,000 Words Without Using the Letter "E"* (Amazon Books on Demand, 2015).

24 Some examples of anthologies are *Oulipo: A Primer of Potential Literature* (Normal, IL: Dalkey Archive Press, 1998); *Oulipo Compendium*, revised edition, ed. Alastair Brotchie and Harry Mathews (London: Atlas Press, 2005); *All that Is Evident Is Suspect: Readings from the Oulipo 1963–2018*, ed. Ian Monk and Daniel Levin Becker (San Francisco: McSweeny's Publishing, 2018); and *The Penguin Book of Oulipo*, ed. Philip Terry (London: Penguin, 2019). For a spirited defense of procedural poetry, see Marjorie Perloff, "The Oulipo Factor: The Procedural Poetics of Christian Bök and Caroline Bergvall," *Textual Practice*, 18 (2004): 23–45. Terry, in *The Penguin Book*, lists over seventy-five different Oulipian constraints (515–20).

25 Christian Bök, *Eunoia* (Toronto: CoachHouse Press, 2001), 103. Additional constraints observed by Bök include the use of at least 98% of the available vocabulary for each letter and the total exclusion of the letter *y*. I have not been able to locate a copy of another extraordinary Oulipean fiction of recent times: Doug Nufer's *Never Again* (2004), a 40,000-word novel whose every word is used only once. See Jonah Katz, "Exercises in Wile," *Cultures and Traditions of Wordplay and Wordplay Research*, ed. Esme Winter-Froemel and Verena Thaler (Berlin: De Gruyter, 2018), 137–64 (157–58).

26 See, for instance, Terry, *Penguin Book*, xvii–xviii and *passim*.

27 As an appendix to their annotations to *Ulysses*, Gifford and Seidman provide a listing of well over a hundred figures of rhetoric in "Aeolus" (Don Gifford and Robert J. Seidman, "Ulysses" Annotated: Notes for James Joyce's "Ulysses", revised edition (Berkeley: University of California Press, 1974), 635–43).

28 Eleanor Catton, *The Luminaries* (London: Granta, 2013). Other recent novels that are structured according to a formal decision made by the author include Donal Ryan's *The Spinning Heart* (2012) with its 21 chapters each voiced by a different character, Kamila Shamsie's *Home Fire* (2017) with its Joycean use of *Antigone* as a template and its five sections from the point of view of the five central characters, and Damon Galgut's *The Promise* (2021), in which the four sections are constructed on the basis of four funerals.

29 Audiobook read by Mark Meadows (Audible, 2013).

30 The audiobook does present the "character chart" at the start, but this passes the ear very quickly, and, in any case, provides only limited information.

31 Catton, *The Luminaries*, 1. In her acknowledgments, Catton refers to the website www.astro.com, which generates a zodiacal chart for any date, time, and place that the user provides. I'm not sure what to make of the fact that when I enter the details given in the book the chart generated is somewhat different from that printed. If it turns

out that the novel's charts are not accurate, would this matter? Perhaps no more than whether Joyce wrote the invented name "Thrift" or the name of a real Dubliner, "Shrift," in *Ulysses*: the writer of fiction is free to alter the documented world at any point. Nevertheless, so much in both novels *is* taken directly from life that one might justifiably feel a little cheated to discover discrepancies.

32 The mapping of the night sky onto the relations among characters is not mechanically carried through, however; it is done selectively and judiciously.

33 The lengths of the parts and chapters don't, in fact, correspond to the actual phases of the moon on these dates, as can be verified at www.moonpage.com.

34 If I were to attempt a defense of my earlier statement quoted in the third paragraph of this essay, it would be by emphasizing the word "purely": because there is always some significance in a formal choice, there is no such as thing as a purely formal property.

35 Margot Norris, *The Value of James Joyce* (Cambridge: Cambridge University Press, 2016), 7.

Chapter 8

JOYCE'S "THE DEAD" AND SHAKESPEARE'S *ROMEO AND JULIET*: A READING OF MEMORY, ADAPTATION, AND AFTERLIFE

Beryl Schlossman

Possibly the turning point in Joyce's portrayal of passion, eroticism, and poetics, "The Dead" alludes to Shakespeare's "*The Most Lamentable and Excellent Tragedy of Romeo and Juliet*."[1] My essay will engage with the particular uses of betrayal, adultery, commodification, and romantic love that prolong the effects of this tragedy through Joyce's modernity. The rhetorical strategy of citation, adaptation, and afterlife engages the Freudian (and Lacanian) "return of the repressed," an essential element of the plot and the narrative of Joyce's novella.[2] It is a vector leading the reader through the fragments of discourse and distracted consciousness interspersed in the narrative all the way to the suspicious silence at its end.

Margot Norris's "The Politics of Gender and Art in 'The Dead'."[3] and a later essay, "'Not the Girl She Was at All': Women in 'The Dead'"[4] respond to earlier critics' approaches to ideology, feminism, and psychoanalysis in Joyce's novella with a study of narration and the "stifled back answer," a compromise between the silence of submission and an irresistible urge to talk back. Norris investigates Joyce's use of an anti-Romeo and Juliet supported by his allusions to Ibsen's radicalism. This path into "The Dead" shows the underside of a Dublin holiday party with many conversations, music, dancing, elaborate drinks and food, and Gabriel's speech. Several women at the edges implicitly question the festivity and its hospitality: Lily is a mere servant, Molly abruptly refuses the meal, and Gretta's intensely emotional response to hearing an Irish song narrated by a young woman betrayed and abandoned by a Lord, "The Lass of Aughrim," acts out the return of the repressed and evokes the violence of history.

Among the solitary disempowered figures of celibates, drinkers, children, and painful aspirants to self-domination or pleasure who appear in the colonial world of *Dubliners*, Joyce's portrayal of Gabriel Conroy is unusual in its focus on marital love and an unexpected ghostly lovers' triangle in "The Dead." Gabriel is the center of narrative interest; Gretta, one of Joyce's sympathetic and attractive women characters, is presented from without; her role is limited to her husband's perceptions of her. She is as far from Shakespeare's Juliet as Gabriel is from the passion of Romeo—except perhaps for a few moments of Gabriel's memory and imagination. These few moments nonetheless allow Shakespeare's text to resonate powerfully between the lines. Because of its ongoing impact and prestige on the stage, its unparalleled poetic language, and its iconic power to represent the baroque drama of love and mourning, Romeo and Juliet lives on in the poetics of adaptation.

The thematic intertwining of love and death reaches all the way from Sappho through modernism. In Sappho's poetry, the goddess of love, Aphrodite, is accompanied by the young boy, Eros; the familiar Latin names, invoked in Shakespeare, are Venus and Cupid. Venus has shifting eyes, for Sappho, and the young boy with his arrows is described as Eros the bitter sweet. The Renaissance pursues this oxymoron and adds to it the allegorical oppositions of Love and War, Pleasure and Pain, and Life and Death. (Eros himself is the offspring of Poros, Plenty and Penia, Poverty.) The oppositions are summarized in the notion of love-melancholy: it is at the core of Shakespeare's *Romeo and Juliet.*

The Morkans' annual party—at Twelfth Night, which marks the end of the Christmas season and the feast of the Epiphany—echoes the feast of the Capulets, but only in retrospect. Lily is bitter, but Gabriel is happy as he looks at his wife Gretta, and their love is not star-crossed. No longer young, Gabriel Conroy is a writer and a teacher, and weary of Ireland. His thoughts wander: framed and hanging on a wall over the piano, a stitched illustration of Shakespeare's balcony scene appears as a signal to the reader, as if an image borrowed from Shakespeare shaped Gabriel's sense of his own life, his mother's impact, and his love for Gretta. Shakespeare's balcony scene is evoked two more times: on the stairway in the discreet fever of Gabriel's desire, and in Gretta's confession. Its effect is intensified by the counter-scene of the "Lass of Aughrim" kept outside by Lord Gregory. Michael Furey sang the song to Gretta in her youth.

Poetry first enters the novella from Gabriel's book reviews for the conservative *Daily Express.* Molly Ivors challenges his Irish loyalty and his interest in other languages: she cries scandal, teases him, flirts with him, and tries to enlist him for a trip west. Aunt Julia's name and her performance suggestively echo the name of Shakespeare's Juliet and her identity as a bride, an essential topic of discussion through the play, from Paris as the chosen bridegroom to Paris as rival, mourner, challenger, and finally, victim of his own righteousness as a desperate Romeo adds his corpse to the others in the Capulet crypt. Joyce uses the signifier of Julia/Juliet to echo Shakespeare's allusions to the politically doomed star-crossed love: "Gabriel recognized the prelude. It was that of an old song of Aunt Julia's—*Arrayed for the Bridal*" (193). Juliet is first buried in her wedding clothes. While Shakespeare's lovers are unusually young, Aunt Julia is shown as old and decrepit except for her vocal art. Unmarried women, "old maids" waiting forever for a bridegroom, are not uncommon in Joyce's Dublin. Interestingly, there are none in Shakespeare's Italian setting.

Gabriel Conroy is an intellectual and the authority of his family, but he is also jealous, vain, and insecure. He worries about the effect of his speech and thinks that "Some quotation that they could recognise from Shakespeare or from the Melodies would be better" (179). Contemporary English poetry appears to him to be out of the intellectual range or the sympathies of his aunts and their guests. Gabriel dances only once, with Molly, nor does he notice his wife dancing. This blindness is not Cupid's, and ironically recalls the importance of Capulet's feast for the lovers who fall in love and seal their fate in the dance, without knowing each other's name. Romeo and his clan are masked enemies who leave the feast before old Capulet's banquet. Perhaps Molly's "discourteous" departure echoes the political discord that Shakespeare's Friar seeks to end. But the Friar's plot misfires, and no bride can put an end to Ireland's colonial woes.

At the moment before their departure, Gabriel sees Gretta above him, in an echo of the balcony scene: "Gabriel had not gone to the door with the others. He was in a dark part of the hall gazing up the staircase. A woman was standing near the top of the first flight, in the shadow also. He could not see her face but he could see the terracotta and salmon pink panels of her skirt which the shadow made appear black and white. It was his wife. She was leaning on the banisters, listening to something. [...] There was grace and mystery in her attitude as if she were a symbol of something" (210–11). Gabriel's standard Catholic references to the sacred coincide with a bizarre vagueness about Gretta as a symbolic figure. Throughout the portrayal of perhaps the only lively couple in *Dubliners*, there is a creeping sense of Victorian and Irish repression blamed on women. Most of the feminine figures in the novella appear as debased and desexualized objects, and Gabriel's "symbol of something" threatens to turn his wife into a statue. But beyond his happy admiration of Gretta at the beginning, and notwithstanding their "dull existence together," Gabriel's desire for a night of love at the Gresham Hotel evokes moments of youth and courtship marked by the stars that Joyce takes from Shakespeare: "Moments of their secret life together burst like stars upon his memory. [...] Like the tender fires of stars moments of their life together, that no one knew of or would ever know of, broke upon and illumined his memory. He longed to recall to her those moments, to make her forget the years of their dull existence together, and remember only their moments of ecstasy. For the years, he felt, had not quenched his soul or hers" (214–15).

Gabriel's romantic intention and his erotic passion go awry, as his wife suddenly reveals her own emotion linked to a set of Irish contexts. The ghost of love and melancholy takes on an identity as Gretta's first love. The first balcony scene hides a second one, as an Irish song about betrayal and sexual violence, "The Lass of Aughrim," impels Gretta to reveal her (carefully hidden?) early romance with a poor young man who came to her garden in Galway and threw pebbles up to her window. This scene recalls Philip Sidney's unhappy lovers as well as the balcony scenes in Shakespeare. When Gretta admits in her humble way that the young man died for love of her, Gabriel's angry jealous reaction further distances him from his tearful wife, who has confessed only to an innocent youthful attachment. But there his terror begins: he feels upstaged by a dead boy because he realizes that he is incapable of true love: "She was fast asleep. [...] So she had had that romance in her life: a man had died for her sake" (223).

After the suggestive representations of the balcony scene and the Shakespearean echoes of the lovers' happiness, another borrowing from Shakespeare's play occurs in a rhetorical flourish that seems to be a final epiphany. But from the beginning of the novella, until Gabriel's moment of resignation in the final paragraphs, his wife's Galway background—and perhaps the feminine itself, as shown by a series of discordant moments—conflicts with Gabriel's longing to escape Irish realities of culture and power. In the unlit room at night, alone with his wife, Gabriel Conroy finds himself lost in the world of the dead and impelled to leave the markers and boundaries of known life in an ambiguous surge of emotion that ends *Dubliners*. Romance is invoked and then abandoned, and the star-crossed lovers are forgotten in the final snow scene.

The tradition of love poetry that informs Shakespeare's play and that originates in the writing of Sappho gives some insight into the experience that Gabriel observes from the outside. The poet Sappho refers frequently to the gods in poems about the depths and heights of love. She wrote:

> It seems to me that he is similar to the gods, that man who is sitting next to you, and who, close to you, listens to the sweet sound of your voice, and how you, full of charm, smile toward him: but in my chest,

> this has taken away the calmness of my heart when I look at you, it happens suddenly that I become mute, for my tongue lies motionless, a subtle fire instantly trickles through my skin, with my eyes I see nothing, there is a dull thunder that rushes in my ears, and sweat breaks out, a trembling seizes all my limbs, I am more pale than dry grass, and I seem to myself no longer far away from having died. But one must bear everything.[5].

Simultaneously analytic and intimate, Sappho's account of desire presents the form of Eros as both bitter and sweet; it includes the shining-forth of beauty and the suffering of passion.

The Renaissance associates Sappho's figure of bittersweet Eros with Plato: the intuition that shapes the currents of Neoplatonic thought seems to indicate that the identity of Sappho was unknown to Marsilio Ficino and his followers. Renaissance confusion over the Platonic identity of the Sapphic Eros (bitter and sweet, "dulce amarem") has lingered into modernity. In indirect tribute to Sappho, the ambivalence of suffering and bliss that she evokes appears as compelling to present-day readers as it did to Ficino, Lorenzo de' Medici, and Michelangelo.

In his studies of Renaissance art, Edgar Wind highlights a tradition derived from antiquity that emphasizes the love of a god for a mortal. In its most extreme forms, Amor is presented as a god of Death on Roman sarcophagi, in Italian Renaissance painting, and in Renaissance emblems. Wind suggests that Shakespeare draws on the background of Eros as the love of a god slips toward the representation of mortality.[6]

The literature of courtly love and the products of Renaissance Neoplatonism preserve Sappho's bittersweet Eros until the modern period rediscovers her and uncovers the translated texts and fragments. Sappho's Eros is violent, shaking, and driven; Eros, she says, is the servant like herself, of Aphrodite. In fragment 31, Sappho's most famous poem, Eros is 'inside' the desiring narrator (or speaking I). Eros brings this speaker close to death. The voice of the Poet is transformed in the framework of modernism, but Eros the bittersweet takes on modern shapes that echo its lyrical origins.

Anchored in the literary and visual arts of Greco-Roman antiquity, the intertwining of love and death that permeates Renaissance culture is central to *Romeo and Juliet*. Love and death (or love and melancholy) permeate the play with their oppositional power, in images of simultaneous tenderness, beauty, and violence. These images of an experience that transforms the characters of Romeo and Juliet and sets them apart from their feuding families also transform views of love in modernity. From the star-crossed encounter at Capulet's feast soaring to the balcony scenes where Juliet speaks some of the most moving and beautiful poetry of love and descending to the depths of the Capulet family tomb, the lovers move along a meteoric trajectory. The obstacles imposed by the feud on the secret intrigues of their love allow free rein to the forbidden language of love exchanged between Juliet and Romeo. Translated or adapted from Sappho's poetry, the lovers' language also implies a process of fragmentation and dismemberment. In this context, dismemberment becomes an image of the opposition faced by the lovers in the play. It also serves as an image of modernist adaptation, across genres and forms of expression. Adapting and interpreting Shakespeare's play (aside from its own layers of translation and adaptation) can be understood as a dialectical process of dismemberment and re-membering (as per the French origin of the literal terms).

Dismemberment is a brutal form of dispersion, fragmentation, and destruction that is archaically evoked in the revenge of Dionysos against Pentheus and Orpheus, but also in the love poetry of Sappho, whose destroyed manuscripts are also, literally, dismembered. In contrast to the serene images of bodies restored to wholeness, the Sapphic subject of love is under attack from within. This interiority filters aspects of Sappho's antiquity through Shakespeare's iconic tragedy of love. Dismemberment turns into a form of adaptation when it is paired with memory: in this theoretical context, dismemberment (and remembering) offers a way to repair the violence, to restore, disseminate, revive, or translate the dramatic text and its range of performance.

The play evokes the feud throughout its references to sexuality, magic, madness, and military prowess, but the dangers that the lovers face and the threat of uncontrollable violence that arises in response to their transgression initially distance them from these ambient discourses. Shakespeare uses them as contrast to reinforce the virtue and innocence of the precocious heroine. The portrayal of Romeo is less consistent, more diverse, and increasingly hyperbolic as the play advances through its tragic effects.

The fate of the lovers, however, is implacably marked by three images of dismemberment. The first is veiled, even opaque. It appears in the enigmatic passage of the "Gallop apace" speech when "come, night" is repeated several times. Juliet invokes the night and Romeo, but suddenly switches to a poetic formality as she imagines the afterlife with Romeo in a kind of paper-doll vision of shared love. The switch is thrown perhaps by the threatening figure of Night, allegorized as the feud itself in these lines:

> Come, civil night,
> Thou sober-suited matron all in black (3.2.10–11)

The repetitions of "come, gentle night" lead into the abrupt vision of Romeo in the heavens:

> Give me my Romeo, and when I shall die,
> Take him and cut him out in little stars (3.2.20 ff.)

Shakespeare smooths the non sequitur with the repetitions, and the mysterious tone of Juliet's invocation is deliberately suspenseful within the terms of the play even as it also protects her from the full understanding of their gruesome star-crossed fate. The threatening figure of night is allegorical, almost as if she came from Juliet's unconscious knowledge.

Juliet imagines Romeo's dismembered body projected into the sky; either he is dispersed in many starry fragments or else the form of his body is outlined in a constellation. Romeo's afterlife, then, is conjured as heavenly, like the gods evoked in classical poetry, although the adaptation of Romeo to the skies and heavens of Juliet's love adds a dark reminder of the star-crossed quality and the obstacles imposed by civil discord. The threat of the night, as Juliet personifies it, recalls the feud and uncannily echoes her mother's recent demand for Romeo's death.

But the innocence and opacity of Juliet's image of her lover among the constellations fade before the rhetorical term of dismemberment as Romeo's desperate state brings him to the Friar, who chides him for his surrender to madness. "Thy wit," says the Friar,

> Is set afire by thine own ignorance,
> And Thou dismembered in thine own defense (3.3.129–133).

Tumbling from the heaven of love and the balcony world to the hell of banishment, confusion, and the news of Juliet's death that leads him to the Capulet crypt, Romeo again kills a man, this time with only half-hearted seeking to avoid violence. This recalls the Friar's judgment of Romeo's love-madness—dangerous passion, ignorance, and loss of his wit. Perhaps in baroque drama, so obsessively enamored of violence, Romeo's impassioned sense of rivalry and the madness of his desperate love justify the murder of the impossibly lightweight Paris, who echoes the feuding youths and gets himself killed. Desperate, murderous, and suicidal, Romeo is absolved (forever after, it seems) as if he were some kind of god of love in the terms of the play. If there is a hint of *sparagmos*, the "ritual" and magical cannibalistic murder caused by Dionysos seeking revenge, it is given to Romeo to express it. His literal threat of dismemberment uttered shortly before the end of the play clarifies the earlier images of Romeo's own dismemberment with its brutality, and reveals the veiled, screened menace of matronly Night in Juliet's self-consoling thoughts about the lover's image among the stars. Romeo bids his man stay away from the tomb in these words:

> But if thou, jealous, dost return to pry
> In what I farther shall intend to do,
> By heaven, I will tear thee joint by joint
> And strew this hungry churchyard with thy limbs (5.3.33–36)

From Dionysos to Sappho, whose fragmented poetry shaped a long tradition and our current understanding of love, adaptation bestows new life (an afterlife) on a work potentially threatened with various forms of effacement and destruction. The effects of Dionysos—his masks, his magical possession of subjects, and his powers to dominate the heights of love-madness and violence—are poignantly evoked in the intimate interior dismembering experience of love that Sappho's Fragment 31 portrays as a near death experience that deprives her narrator of language, vision, hearing, and other sensory effects. Sweating, trembling, and paleness—all the effects of the beloved's charms—reveal the narrator's passion as a deadly but intimate and interiorized dismemberment.

Shakespeare's play recalls the afterlife of Sappho's vision of love, its translation into baroque dramatic esthetics, and even the translational power of its prolonged cultural memory. It is as if Sappho's vision, through its own refashioning of Dionysian passion, enters the unconscious of classically infused literature. The feudal conflicts that block love add a political dimension that classical literature did not require: civil strife is enemy to the savage wild love that appears, in Shakespeare, as a doomed passion that cannot bend to the forces of convention.

In Shakespeare's play, love and melancholy first combine in the figure of Romeo. He enters the play in 1.1, following a Prologue in sonnet-form, a brief comic interlude, and a fight scene opposing Capulets to Montagues. The lovesick Romeo and his Juliet are announced in the Prologue as "A pair of star-crossed lovers" (P 6). "The fearful passage of their death'marked love" is announced as the subject of the play (P 8). The rich background of textual sources of *Romeo and Juliet* includes Greek romances, European folklore, a single line in Dante, and the *novelle*, or short stories, of several Italian writers. In 1562, Arthur Brooke's first rendering in English appeared, a definite source for Shakespeare.

It is thought that Sir Philip Sidney's sonnet sequence, "Astrophil and Stella" (1591), is an important contemporary source for Shakespeare. Perhaps its most important influence is in the extended leitmotif of stars, taken up from Shakespeare through modernism: the character of the lover, also the narrator, whose name alludes to Sidney's first name and to the star that is the name of the beloved. In both cases, there is a sense of the star and the star-lover as screened identities. Sidney's poetry connects Renaissance poetic practice with the screens that modernism and post-modernism use to elude censorship and to transform autobiographical impulses into fiction.

As is often the case, Shakespeare's sources come from across the genres of poetry, prose, and drama, but the explicit topic of love and death allows particular emphasis on the literary traditions of love poetry, including themes from his sonnets and the strategic use of sonnet form within the play. The play builds on the contrast between rhymed verse, used to indicate conventional love, including the first encounter between the lovers, at Capulet's feast, and blank verse that conveys the stark drama of emotion and a newly infused lyric intensity that marks the play after Romeo and Juliet fall in love.

For Shakespeare, Cupid is blind. Derived from the Greek Eros, Cupid becomes the Renaissance agent of love. In Sappho's poems, the lover succumbs to the blinding power of love itself, but Shakespeare's Cupid is the cherubic figure wearing a blindfold that we see in Renaissance iconography. The blindness of Cupid resonates throughout the play and enters the lovers' understanding of the obstacles they face, before and after Tybalt's death.

A line in canto 6 of Dante's *Purgatorio* that mentions the Montecchi family of Verona and the Capelletti party of Cremona as examples of civil dissent is a distant source of the horrified discovery that each lover makes of the other's family when it is already too late to alter the course of their love.[7] (Dante, *Purgatorio* VI: 106). The canto might return to haunt a modern writer who had studied Dante in Italian, and certainly it was known to the Italian Renaissance writers whose stories influenced Shakespeare's predecessors in French and English. In that sense, Dante is an unconscious source for Shakespeare. Sir Philip Sidney's sonnet sequence on unhappy love, "Astrophil and Stella," is, by contrast, a work that Shakespeare seems to have used freely, especially for paired images of dark and light, and for the descriptions of constellations and planets to express love: the lover's name of Astrophil combines "lover of a star" with Sidney's first name, and "stella," the beloved, personifies a star.[8] Scenes on Juliet's balcony under the night sky appear to echo several of Sidney's motifs. Juliet does not turn Romeo away, as Stella does Astrophil: that difference may have allowed Shakespeare his freedom with Sidney's poetry. The difference is a decisive one, since part of the impact of Shakespeare's play is in the importance of Juliet's voice, vision, and character. Stella, by contrast, is a major character but almost a virtual one, who rarely is given direct speech. Unlike the virtuoso verbal performances of Astrophil, the famous lines of Stella's refusal are almost painfully simple: "No no no no, my dear, let be." It is possible to imagine that far from the articulation and sensibility of Juliet, this simplicity shapes Joyce's portrayal of Gretta Conroy, once an uneducated Galway girl who owes some facets of her identity to Nora Barnacle Joyce. It also shapes the limitations of gender within Joyce's world, where claims for feminism are put into question by a sense of paranoia and a display of doubt that the novella reflects in its protagonist.

We do not learn why Capulet's cousin Rosaline had spurned Romeo, but if she had rejected him simply as a Montague, then the almost supernatural power of the sudden new love between Romeo and Juliet would be underscored. Shakespeare uses the considerable range of poetic love conventions to create something that points beyond them. In that sense, Eros the bittersweet is a major figure of excess that characterizes love beyond conventional courtship. In all its pleasure and pain, it is magical and poisonous, life-giving and deadly, illuminated and nocturnal. Most of the major conceits in the play derive from it. Seas, planets, constellations and stars, flowers, plants, birds, ships, and light in darkness—but also tears, weather, darkness in light, spilled blood, daggers, prisons, and tombs—all of these lend their figures to the combinations of love. Between purity and sin, "idolatry" (as Juliet calls her love for Romeo [2.2]) charts the course of the lovers. The colors of the sky and the sunrise—black and white, dark and light, paleness and redness—are the colors of lovers, dead and alive, of the sea and the stars. At the end of the play, the lovers' tragedy will have achieved a civil reconciliation, as the "ghostly father" had hoped, but only after an implacable series of deaths. For the modern temperament anticipated by Shakespeare, the promise of gold statues to portray the lovers is tinged with bitter irony. Two sets of cousins, Juliet's suitor, and Romeo's mother have entered the whirlwind of destruction that took the lives of Romeo and Juliet. The others linger for a few moments in the realm of the dead.

As enemies, advised by the "ghostly friar," Shakespeare's lovers are subjected to the pain of separations, to rivalry, and to the use of potions for supernatural effects. The love-potion of the Tristan and Isolde poems is not necessary—the lovers fall immediately in love. The Friar is experienced with philtres that simulate death while preserving life, or poisons that produce death. As in the Tristan texts, a love-triangle occurs: Paris seeks Juliet's hand before the feast when Romeo first sees her. As the play unfolds, Capulet speeds up the action as Paris, not Romeo, is promised his daughter's hand. Paris, however, is a weak figure of conventional love in the play, and his death is a pale echo of the powerful scenes with the wounded Mercutio or the violent and beloved Tybalt. *Romeo and Juliet* provides a key to the secrets of love and melancholy that explode in the tragic end of the play, the "lightning before death" that entrances Romeo at the edge of suicide, and the only possible resolution to calm the warring families. As in German mourning plays or

Trauerspiel, prophecy and proverbs are everywhere. Most of Shakespeare's characters in the play are prophetic: all wishes and threats come together. The opposition and reconciliation of love and death are reflected through the powerful images of Eros the bittersweet.

Love and death unite in prophecies from the beginning of *Romeo and Juliet*: the wedding-bed will be a grave, the grave a wedding-bed. The passion of "first" love—legitimate in Juliet—is rendered new and given voice by Romeo. His transformation begins with the feast. It is like an awakening from the dreamlike painful state of his frustrated infatuation with Rosaline (also a Capulet).

In 1.1, Romeo is miraculously oblivious to the violent action and the presence of important people, including the Prince, the Capulets, and his own parents. He appears before his cousin Benvoglio, laments the slowness of time, and asks: "Was that my father that went hence so fast?" (1.1.160). Romeo is at his most extreme point of self-enclosed depression in the play. Named for his good will (and for love itself), Benvoglio attempts to rouse him and encourages him to seek out a new love object. Thus, Romeo is first presented within a conventional portrayal of love-melancholy. Heavy as lead, he says he will not dance. Shakespeare anchors the character's floating consciousness in a stream of paradoxical images typical of baroque poetry:

> O me! what fray was here?
> Yet tell me not, for I have heard it all.
> Here's much to do with hate, but more with love.
> Why then, O brawling love, O loving hate,
> O anything of nothing first create
> O heavy lightness, serious vanity,
> Misshapen chaos of well-seeming forms
> Feather of lead, bright smoke, cold fire, sick health,
> Still-waking sleep that is not what it is
> This love feel I that feel no love in this
> (William Shakespeare, *Romeo and Juliet*, 1.1.171–180).

After this dizzying set of images of opposites (oxymora) that evoke the four elements and the opposed emotions of joy and sadness, Romeo arrives at the breathtaking images of the "Love is" verses. The oxymoron of the bittersweet crowns them:

> Love is a smoke made with the fume of sighs;
> Being purg'd, a fire sparkling in lovers' eyes;
> Being vex'd, a sea nourish'd with lovers' tears;

> What is it else? A madness most discreet,
> A choking gall, and a preserving sweet.
> Farewell, my coz (I. i. 188-193).

Eros the bittersweet is invoked many times in the play, but it is important that Romeo shifts from his conventionally presented love of Rosaline to something more powerful, in these lines that foreshadow a new love's language. Shakespeare inserts the bittersweet again, as Romeo begins to speak to Juliet at the feast. Chided by Capulet for wanting to throw Romeo out, Tybalt obeys his uncle but not without a note of prophecy that distantly recalls Sappho's Eros, bitter and sweet:

> I will withdraw; but this intrusion shall
> Now seeming sweet, convert to bitt'rest gall (1.5.90-91).

Shakespeare's particular and unforgettable combination of love and death in *Romeo and Juliet* is shaped in a mix of styles that also influence Joyce's modernist prose version. "The Dead" is perhaps the most dramatic of his works, and it includes performances of music, song, dancing, dramatic speech, and poetry in the contexts of love. "The Dead" is especially intriguing because of its extensive exploration of love. Its conclusion to *Dubliners* anticipates the play, *Exiles*, and the later works of *Ulysses* and *Finnegans Wake*; in breadth and in scope, "The Dead" signals a new development within *Dubliners*.

In *Romeo and Juliet*, the body and the soul intertwine, thanks to the transgressions of the Nurse and the Friar. Their emblems of the natural and the grey and spectral zones of the supernatural orient the physical realm of the body and sexuality (including suggestions of harlots and bawds), on the one hand, and the Franciscan spirituality of saints and ghosts on the other—but in both cases, love is present. The Nurse loves Juliet as the Friar loves Romeo. The Nurse's voice in particular will resonate throughout Joyce's later writings, especially in *Finnegans Wake*. It is as if Joyce had found that voice to be more moving and more real than all the others in the play.

The first character of "The Dead" is "Lily the caretaker's daughter," the only young girl, except for Gretta's memory of herself. The first conversation includes Lily's inelegant confession of having been exploited:

> —O then, said Gabriel gaily, I suppose we'll be going to your wedding one of these fine days with your young man, eh?
> The girl [...] said with great bitterness:
> —The men that is now is only all palaver and what they can get out of you.[9]

Lily's "bitterness" and the "palaver" of seduction embarrass Gabriel as if the accusation had something to do with his own desires and ambitions. The tragedy of "The Lass of Aughrim" is in the wings, but Gabriel does not ask any more questions. The identity of Shakespeare's Nurse is hidden in Gabriel's memory of Lily as a child at the threshold, "nursing a rag-doll" (177):

> There's no trust,
> No faith, no honesty in men. All perjur'd,
> All forsworn, all naught, all dissemblers.
> Ah, where's my man? Give me some aqua vitae.
> These sorrows make me old (3.2.85–89).

The Nurse's speech is echoed later when Gabriel surrenders to the tearful vision of Michael Furey's ghost. He swoons: the term occurs in 3.2 when the Nurse describes to Juliet the murder of her cousin by her lover:

> A piteous corse, a bloody piteous corse,
> Pale, pale as ashes, all bedaub'd in blood,
> All in gore-blood. I sounded [swooned] at the sight (3.2.54–56).

The description of her swooning resonates as she lyrically laments the loss of Tybalt and the dishonesty of Romeo. She calls for her man, clamors for whiskey, and complains of the weight of sorrow. In this scene of crisis, she and Juliet repeat many times that "Romeo is banished" and "Romeo is exil'd" (3.2.112–124, 133). Juliet's lines also echo Romeo's view of banishment as a form of death.

Shakespeare's Nurse holds the key to my reading of "The Dead" wherein the transformation of Gabriel suddenly reveals the meaning of the story in the final spectral epiphany. Gabriel wished to play the lovers' balcony scene with Gretta, but the sudden return of her long-repressed memory of Michael Furey, her first love, prevents Gabriel from rekindling their own "ecstasy" of passion. He resents the interruption, and at first he does not realize that his rival has been dead for many years. Gabriel's jealousy leads him to cross-examine his wife, as if she had been unfaithful: three times, he asks whether she loved the young man, and three times she answers in simple colloquial expressions that shy away from the name of love. But when he asks of the cause of death, Gretta answers in the guise of Juliet: "I think he died for me" (221). Gabriel reacts with terror. When Gretta falls asleep, Gabriel succumbs to his erotic failure and the new presence of Gretta's ghostly first love.

Gabriel weeps tears of melancholy and defeat as he drifts into the swooning that frees the ghosts to fly. Tears bring him closer to Gretta—his genuinely Irish wife who longs to return to the Galway of her youth—and to Ireland and the Irish (with whom he has struggled for intellectual life itself), even as they bring him to the edge of a death-like trance, an ecstasy of mourning. In "The Dead," Gabriel is weighed in the balance of love and found to be wanting:

> Poor Aunt Julia! She, too, would soon be a shade [...] He had caught that haggard look upon her face for a moment when she was singing *Arrayed for the Bridal.* [...] He thought of how she who lay beside him had locked in her heart for so many years that image of her lover's eyes when he had told her that he did not wish to live. [...] Generous tears filled Gabriel's eyes. He had never felt that himself towards any woman but he knew that such a feeling must be love. (224)

He is indeed more like Paris (mentioned in his speech) than he is like Romeo. Gretta's first love has upstaged him: here again, Joyce hides the reference to Shakespeare, this time by alluding to the Greek Paris who chose Aphrodite, rather than to the Count who seeks Juliet's hand and her father's wealth, and whose conventional language makes him a foil for Romeo's eloquent passion.

At the end of the novella, Gabriel is overcome with an emotion that takes him beyond himself. His mystical experience of death and ghosts and Ireland itself takes the form of a poetic passage in which the word "swoon" is repeated several times in an onomatopoetic and almost ritualized way, at a moment of incantatory magic:

> The tears gathered more thickly in his eyes and in the partial darkness he imagined he saw the form of a young man standing under a dripping tree. Other forms were near. His soul had approached that region where dwell the vast hosts of the dead. [...] His own identity was fading out into a grey impalpable world: the solid world itself which these dead had one time reared and lived in was dissolving and dwindling. [...] The time had come for him to set out on his journey westward. [...] His soul swooned slowly as he heard the snow falling faintly through the universe and faintly falling, like the descent of their last end, upon all the living and the dead. (224–25)

In between the lines, filled with repetitions and an incantatory mood that contrasts with all of Gabriel's recorded thoughts earlier in the evening, a lover's passion and death lead Gabriel into another world, in a figure of exile. Banishment and love, together, recall the melancholy love of Astrophil and especially the lamentations of Romeo, Juliet, and the Nurse in the second half of the play.

The balcony scene of *Romeo and Juliet* signals the poetry of love: Joyce includes a reference to it that connects aunt Julia with Gabriel and his late mother, whose needlework encloses him and brings darkness into his thoughts:

> Gabriel's eyes [...] wandered to the wall above the piano. A picture of the balcony scene in *Romeo and Juliet* hung there and beside it was a picture of the two murdered princes in the tower which Aunt Julia had worked in red, blue and brown wools when she was a girl. [...] for one year his mother had worked for him as a birthday present a waistcoat of purple tabbinet [...] A shadow passed over his face as he remembered her sullen opposition to his marriage. (186–87)

The bitterness of Lily, Gabriel, and others, with the repeated hints of crossings and shades and stars, confirmed by the banishment of the Lass in the song, are figures of exile that resonate through the novella. Romeo's exile as portrayed by Shakespeare may echo Dante's Canto 6, a bitter denunciation of Florence as a prostitute among princesses, and thus a lament of Dante's own exile. Even while denouncing his fellow Dubliners, Joyce explicitly displays the uniquely (for him) Irish virtue of hospitality in "The Dead" with its bourgeois surfeit of drink, food, musical entertainment, and discordant conversation. Exile hovers between the lines in most of Joyce's writings, and the injury of exile shapes the disappointment, anger, rage, and erotic violence that are evoked in the person of Gabriel and the terms of Gabriel's spectral ending.

The love interest is presented through Joyce's figure of a young servant girl (Lily), the maiden aunt Julia, or the virtuous loving wife, Gretta (whose name resonates together with Julia's name, to echo the name of Shakespeare's heroine). Gabriel is jealous and doubts his wife's chastity. He looks at the boots and clothes she has left in disorder, dispersed around the hotel room: "Perhaps she had not told him all the story" (223). "The Dead" presents "The Lass of Aughrim" as an Irish anti-*Romeo and Juliet*, with some precautions taken against it being recognized as such: the cipher of the servant Lily as a child at the door, the back staircase, the poor singing performance, Bartell D'Arcy's rudeness—and its impact on Gretta, whose immense grief could be read as a silent and perhaps unconscious reflection on Gabriel's (and Joyce's?) regard for her as a subject in her own right. The terrors of paranoia hover among the final shades.

The challenges of reading "The Dead" include Joyce's "disappointing representations of women"[10] and the narrative sympathies deployed in defense of the protagonist, Gabriel Conroy. Norris brings out the contradictions implicit in confronting Joyce's claim to take up Ibsen's dramatic feminism and Joyce's use of masculine weakness to cover for the misogyny that lurks beneath the surface. In addition, Norris's critical exploration of the characters, their speeches and their silences, claims the textual existence of a narrator less neutral than the ones appearing in Flaubert's fiction, a widely appropriated modernist model of free indirect discourse. The blurring of character and narrator at several moments in "The Dead" is the result, including the final paragraph with its intense repetitions and the flourish of the swoon. It is not without impact that Gretta has here disappeared, again, as she did several times earlier in the evening. Finally, she is no longer even present in her husband's thoughts.

I will suggest an alternative view to the spectral epiphany of Gabriel's final spiritual swoon: the contrast between Gretta's narrative and the eroticism that Gabriel feels and thinks seem to tear the couple apart. The figure of dismemberment occurs with a possible reference to Romeo's threat in the churchyard when Gabriel succumbs to jealousy and paranoia: he cannot admire his wife's beauty, she has lost it in his eyes. The frequently thematized staleness of women no longer young is evident throughout *Dubliners.*

In Gretta's verbal act of remembering, so poorly received by her husband, she sees the eyes of Michael Furey, not those of her husband. The poetic repetitions that move through the story culminate in her words, following the song that he used to sing and the failed balcony scene of the boy in the rain. The repetitions become increasingly incantatory as Gretta's story is accompanied by a tacit undressing that Gabriel apparently does not even notice. The figure of Romeo's threat of dismemberment may be recalled in Gretta's dispersed and disorderly clothes and boots. The rhyme words and repetitions include Gretta/great with him; as well the cold (outside and even inside, with Bartell D'Arcy's cold), and the snow, from beginning to end, covers everything up, even the lack of sound that Gabriel strangely seems to hear as falling snow, after he doesn't notice Gretta undressing. He doesn't notice a lot of things outside himself. He drowns his sorrows in the repetitions and the swoon that is not a swoon of love.

But the final swoon paragraph with its gloss over the events of the evening is perhaps yet another of Gabriel's dissimulations, repressions, or coverups. The snow and the cold, repeated throughout, are figured in Gabriel's response ("coldly") to his wife who wishes to see Galway. The cold includes Bartell D'Arcy's hoarseness—the white voice—of the fragmented rendition of "Lass of Aughrim," a song imperfectly membered by its singer, whose fit of temper is nearly abusive of his hostesses. Norris's readings of these passages include the hidden seduction upstairs and the contrast between the much-admired D'Arcy who can't sing and the deeply accomplished vocal art of Julia Morkan whom no one can look at. The old woman exiled from her church, the black singer discussed at table and defended by Freddy Malins, and even the young Mary Jane whose performance interests none of the men—no one wants to look at them, or to see them. And then Gretta isn't as pretty as she once was! The expectations seem rather demanding.

Norris correctly indicates John Huston's misinterpretation—in the scene that threatens to derail the film with a dismaying and gratuitous example of misogyny—in the great Irish-American director's final film, "The Dead," apparently a vehicle for nostalgia for Ireland but also a showcase for the director's daughter, Angelica Huston, playing a romanticized Gretta.[11] But it is in the stifled back answers that Norris finds a way to reconcile a claim for feminism with the evidence of misogyny, and thus to maintain her suspicious readings that lead throughout *Dubliners* to end in the novella of balconies, star-crossed lovers, dismemberment and dissolution—and the onlooker, outside love.

Shakespeare's idealized love is unimaginable outside of the worked image above the piano. The feminine as portrayed in "The Dead" falls back on the clichés of youth, age, virginity, and the role of women as nurses and nursemaids. Only music offers a way out in the Morkan household. The brutality of betrayal, poverty, and the powerlessness of the girl, unrecognized, homeless, and perhaps banished with her rape-child in the lyrics of "The Lass of Aughrim" are suggestive of Lily's new bitterness, of Molly Ivors's self-exile from hospitality, and of Gretta's sense of loss in the return of her repressed memories and Gabriel's jealousy. Lily and Molly have disappeared, and in the dark hotel Gretta's innocent confession is absorbed into Gabriel's overstated swooning. All the crossing of rooms and thresholds, the flights of movement, the stars, and the shades and shadows, lead to a final imagined scene about going West. It has been customary to follow the author's cues to read the debasement of the feminine as one more portrait of colonial Ireland, and to view the abjection of Leopold Bloom as an ostracized Dublin Jew and a womanly man in the same light, but those didactic touches have not aged well, and all the swooning at the end of "The Dead" may sound indigestibly Victorian.

But Shakespeare's elaboration of the lovers' final scenes in the Capulets' crypt—and Joyce's allusion to it in the Gresham Hotel—is not lost on Samuel Beckett, Joyce's fellow exile in Paris, who turns it into a moment of extremely dark comedy. In *Malone meurt*, the title character fondly pens a line about himself and his ancient lover: "C'est l'amour qui nous conduit/ La main dans la main vers Glasnevin (1) 1.Nom d'un cimetière local très estimé" *[It's love that leads us/ Hand in hand toward Glasnevin (1)1.Name of a very respected local cemetery.*[12] In Beckett's general sweep toward minimalism, these comically and grotesquely rendered overtones of Shakespearean love and death (but in a famous Irish cemetery!) do not reappear in his English translation. For Beckett, love is exile and banishment; the dance of shadows crossing leads only to a cemetery. In Joyce's later work, by contrast, the Shakespearean combination of eroticism, love, and war among political powers is everywhere. Beginning with the sensations of the damp earth and the winter, with its anticipated cold and Aunt Julia's death, Shakespeare's losses of love, the naked ground that swallows Romeo, and ghosts seen through tears falling like rain mark the bittersweet Irish ending of "The Dead."

Notes

1 Ed. René Weis, *Romeo and Juliet* (London: Bloomsbury, 2012).
2 James Strachey, Gen. Editor, *The Complete Psychological Works of Sigmund Freud* (London: The Hogarth Press and the Institute for Psycho-Analysis, 1966), vol. 1, pp. 222–28. The topic is central to Freud's life-work on psychology and on culture from at the latest 1895 until his last writings (vol. 23). Lacan's "return to Freud" includes the major concepts of repression and its return.
3 Margot Norris, *Suspicious Readings of Joyce's Dubliners* (Philadelphia: University of Pennsylvania Press, 2003), 216–38.
4 Ed. Daniel R. Schwartz, James Joyce, *The Dead* (Boston: Bedford/St. Martin's, 1994), 190–205.
5 *The Complete Poems of Sappho*, trans. Willis Barnstone (Boston: Shambhala Publications, 2006), 43 and *Sappho*, trans. Mary Barnard (Berkeley and Los Angeles: University of California Press, 1958), 39. Guy Davenport, *Seven Greeks* (New York: New Directions, 1966. See Beryl Schlossman, *Objects of Desire: The Madonnas of Modernism* (Ithaca: Cornell University Press, 1999).
6 Edgar Wind, *Pagan Mysteries of the Renaissance* (New York: Norton, 1969), Chapter X, and especially 73.
7 Dante Alighieri, *Purgatorio*, ed. and trans. Charles Singleton (Princeton: Princeton University Press, 1973), 60 (VI: 106).
8 Sir Philip Sidney, *The Major Works*, ed. Katherine Duncan-Jones (Oxford: Oxford University Press, 2002).
9 James Joyce, "The Dead," *Dubliners*. Penguin Classics (New York: Penguin, 1992), 177–78.
10 Margot Norris, "Not the Girl She Was," in Schwarz, James Joyce. The Dead. 192.
11 Margot Norris, *Suspicious Readings of Joyce's Dubliners*, 232.
12 Samuel Beckett, *Malone meurt*. Paris: Minuit, 1951, 148. My translation.

Chapter 9

EPHEMERAL SPECTACLES: ART, POLITICAL THEATER, *ULYSSES*

Ellen Carol Jones

The "Messianic scene" of the "Circe" episode of *Ulysses* both critiques and parodies religious and political spectacles in Ireland deriving from the urban festivals and processions that flourished throughout monarchical and imperial Europe. The torchlight procession and Bloom's investiture as "undoubted emperor-president and king-chairman, the most serene and potent and very puissant ruler of this realm," Leopold the First (*U* 15.1471–73), are in apostolic succession to these urban spectacles of pomp and circumstance staged to legitimize the power of political rule. This Circean burlesque re-inscribes the streets of subaltern Dublin and thereby also recalls the resistance to imperial politics and the reclamation of public space enacted by nationalist counter-spectacles, questioning their own claim to historical truth and exploring the power relations that undergird the dialectic of history and memory. Such a re-inscription critiques both utopian and dystopian sociopolitical visions of colonial Ireland. In staging a performative resistance to structures of power, this re-inscription posits and yet also critiques the subversive, even revolutionary, function of an avant-garde or modernist experimental art in a colonial state; and it questions the possibility for such an art to launch a system-immanent critique of itself under subaltern conditions. Margot Norris notes that historically Joyce is situated "at the precise moment when the avant-garde's self-critique was made possible by its confrontation with aestheticism's disavowal of art's social origin." As such, Joyce's own avant-gardism is located in "a dramatic and dynamic textual performativity whose end is not autotelic [...] but political." The Joycean text is "the *staging* of a cultural phenomenon," she argues: "as an artist of (and, as Irishman, prostituted to) the dominant culture," his art is "literally inscribed in the textualization of Ireland's political and economic life." In demonstrating "art's resistance to, and suppression by, civic and commercial systems responsive to a hegemonic order," Joyce thereby recovers its "implied violence."[1]

Throughout Europe, how religious, funereal and, especially, political processions moved circuitously through the streets of a city, and how a city served as stage set for these theatrical ceremonies, demonstrated how urban space could serve as vehicle for messages of power. In royal entries into a subject city or in military triumphs, modeled on Roman triumphs, the ruler or the victor as representative of imperial might, usually seated on a horse and accompanied by a military entourage, was met at the city's gate by the highest-ranking government and religious officials and, in an elaborate ceremony, presented the keys to the city. The ruler and entourage then processed through the city in a parade that included all governmental and religious officials, noblemen, militias and trade guilds. Marking the routes of early modern European processions were elaborate ephemeral structures designed by such eminent artists as Peter Paul Rubens in 1635: arches, porticos and stages where *tableaux vivants* were posed or plays were performed. Texts, art and symbolic figurations on these ephemeral structures not only praised the ruler, glorifying his or her royal ancestry as well as military victories and deeds of state, but also expressed the desires of the ruled, supplicating their ruler to act in accord with their welfare.

Triumphs and entries, the elaborate ceremonials of theaters of power enacted in both metropolitan and subject cities, enabled a ruler to confirm his or her inherent right to rule, to celebrate military victories, to demonstrate the ruler's largess and judiciary power, to appeal directly to various classes of the ruler's subjects, to receive the allegiance and subservience of those subjects to this rule, and, especially in the Low Countries where entries had a quasi-democratic charge, to pledge protection of the rights and safety of the citizens. In the Low Countries, the *joyeuse entrée* charter—the *blijde inkomst* sworn by Joanna, Duchess of Brabant, and her husband, Wenceslas of Luxembourg, on their entry into Louvain/Leuven in 1356—constituted a fundamental constitution for all the provinces of the Netherlands, confirming the rights and privileges of the ruled; a ceremonial ratification of this charter marked all subsequent entries of rulers to the cities of the Low Countries. The conflicting political messages of these spectacles of power yet also of reciprocity—particularly those staged in lands where the *blijde inkomst* guaranteed subjects' rights—clarify why the royal visits to Ireland of George IV, Victoria, and Edward VII became increasingly contested as Irish nationalism evolved in power and scope. Irish nationalist resistance to imperial power entailed both acts of individual dissent and the public political theater of counter-monarchical, anti-imperial spectacles.

Art as ephemeral as the temporary but ornate and extraordinarily complex iconographic arches, stages and porticos constructed for actual processions—or the even more ephemeral massive woodcut compilations of the early sixteenth-century paper triumphs Albrecht Dürer and other artists created for Maximilian I to disseminate throughout his empire to consolidate his imperial authority, the prestige of the emperor and the artists, the visual splendor of the paper triumphs, and, paradoxically, their very ephemerality increasing their aura—served not only as advertisements of power, but also, in some cases, as petitions to that power in the political theater of Renaissance and Baroque Europe. Nineteenth-century royal visits of the British monarchs to Ireland reinstated, albeit in attenuated form, the elaborate celebrations of Baroque Europe; the revival of royal ritualism and the invention of novel "traditions" by the British monarchy were judged necessary counterweights both to the danger of popular democracy and to the danger of political unrest in the metropolitan colony of Ireland. Royal visits to Ireland demonstrated the might of the British ruler and the monarchy's power to destabilize opposition, as in the 1821 post-coronation visit of George IV, "the Messiah of royalty," the first visit by a monarch to Ireland in nearly one hundred and thirty years and one of the most visually recorded public events in early nineteenth-century Ireland. Sir Richard Morrison was the architect for the wood and canvas triumphal arch, constructed in thirty hours at the top of Sackville Street. The king was greeted with idolatrous enthusiasm in Ireland, perhaps due to the misconception he supported Catholic Emancipation, which he reluctantly granted only in 1829:

> No monarch on the earth ever received a more enthusiastic tribute of devotional attachment to the royal person than the king received from his faithful Irish people on the ever-memorable 17th August. The splendid ovation, the pompous triumph of "olden time," were but the shadow of a shade to the stupendous spectacle—the magnificent entry of the British Monarch into the capital of his Kingdom of Ireland. Dublin yesterday exhibited a display of pomp and pageantry, and pride, unsurpassed by anything in modern London.[2]

For Lord Byron, this reception was the cause of "My contempt for a nation so servile, though sore, / Which though trod like the worm will not turn upon power."[3] Even Lord Castlereagh, Irish chief secretary during the crucial years of the United Irish Rising and the vote and institution of the union, 1798–1801, was cheered during this royal visit, a sign, the London *Times* suggested, that the Irish were "at once the most credulous and most forgiving of mankind."[4]

The performances Daniel O'Connell, leader of the Irish members of Parliament, staged to repeal the Acts of Union—processions, mass meetings, even a mock coronation—contested the very authority of the merged

Parliament of the United Kingdom established by the 1800 Acts of Union between the Kingdoms of Great Britain and Ireland. With the launch of his Repeal Association in 1840, O'Connell intensified his prior advocacy for "repeal but not separation," arguing for the reinstatement of Ireland's own parliament, with "the Commons representing the people possessed of universal suffrage."[5] Hailed by his compatriots as "Liberator" for his roles in securing Catholic Emancipation and agitating for repeal, and, in an honorific once given to Gerald FitzGerald, as the uncrowned king of Ireland—the latter term also accorded to Charles Stewart Parnell, "Erin's uncrowned king" (*U* 16.1495)—O'Connell initially was careful to style himself a servant of the monarchs but ultimately during Victoria's reign assumed a theatrical counter-monarchical role. Agitation for repeal intensified in 1842–43 when O'Connell held almost fifty "monster" meetings in Ireland to pressure the British government for legislative independence, meetings that raised the specter of mass uprisings and violence through ostensibly pacific mass gatherings. The monster meetings conflated loyalty to the Crown with allegiance to O'Connell, deploying the pageantry, processions of the trades and fraternal orders with their banners, temperance bands in military array, carts and floats, horsemen ranked around the outskirts of the meetings, and even the symbolic ephemeral architecture usually reserved for triumphs and royal entries: a triumphal arch at the monster meeting at Dundalk was inscribed, "The Queen, O'Connell agus Erin go bragh." Another arch depicted Queen Victoria and Prince Albert but addressed O'Connell: "Ireland's Moses, who crushed our foes, welcome to Dundalk."[6] These processions and monster meetings fused royal and religious ceremonials to market O'Connell as savior for a people in bondage; a banner spanning the Ennis parade route, hung over chains cut by a swordsman as O'Connell's carriage passed underneath, proclaimed: "The Liberator of Ireland Will Cut Asunder The Chains of Slavery We Labour Under."[7] In a burlesque coronation at the Mullaghmast monster meeting on October 1, a deputation presented O'Connell with "The Irish National Cap" in the form of the old Milesian crown. For the "august and triumphant meeting" at Tara, County Meath, O'Connell's progress from Dublin to Tara, John Mitchel wrote, was "a procession and a triumph. Under triumphal arches, and amidst a storm of music and acclamations, his carriage passed through the several little towns that lay in his way." Exhibits and stages for street theater lined the parade route. A harper, styled as bardic, played before him in his triumphal chariot. The crowd came "with naked hands; but the Agitator knew well that if he had invited them they would have come still more gladly with extemporaneous pikes and spears. [...] He knew that every soul in that host demanded its enfranchisement at *his* hand."[8] But in "Aeolus," Stephen Dedalus questions the suasions of

O'Connell's propaganda, equating his words with the "leperous distilment" King Hamlet claims his usurper "in the porches of my ears did pour": "Gone with the wind. Hosts at Mullaghmast and Tara of the kings. Miles of ears of porches. The tribune's words, howled and scattered to the four winds. A people sheltered within his voice. Dead noise. Akasic records of all that ever anywhere wherever was. Love and laud him: me no more" (*Hamlet* I.v.64, 63; *U* 7.880–83).

The British government forced O'Connell to cancel the monster meeting at Clontarf or risk arrest and military reprisals, yet nine days later O'Connell and other leaders of the repeal movement were arrested for conspiracy and other measures. O'Connell was found guilty on February 10, 1844, fined and sentenced to prison for a year commencing May 30; but the House of Lords overturned his conviction on September 6, a quashing Prime Minister Sir Robert Peel termed "Mr. O'Connell's Liberation."[9] The day following that reversal, "there was a triumphal procession thro' the streets of Dublin. Mr. O'Connell was elevated in a car drawn by eight horses, the concourse of People was immense."[10] O'Connell staged his own "royal visit" to Dublin on the first "anniversary of the 'Martyrdom'" of his imprisonment, processing through the streets and hosting a national levee at the Rotundo, playing the role of "monarch of the Irish heart." As Wellington wrote to Graham, ten thousand people paraded before a crowd of a hundred thousand "idlers" lining the streets: "It was in short as impudent a demonstration of the popular force as ever was witnessed in Ireland."[11] And the *Evening Mail* described the "outrage on royalty" of O'Connell "sitting in aristocratic state in the throne room" at the Dublin levee: "A man, professing in words to be a subject—assuming in reality the prerogatives of a Sovereign, surrounded by a *regalia*, an etiquette resembling in all points that of a constitutional monarch."[12] The *Cork Examiner* detailed the styling of O'Connell as he reprised his role as "monarch of the Irish heart" in a procession through the streets of Cork: "He sat on an elevated chair beneath a large canopy that towered twenty feet above the ground. Holding the canopy aloft were four female figures representing Justice, Truth, Fortitude, and Prudence. [...] An enormous repeal cap and a huge shamrock crowned the top of the vehicle."[13] At his death, O'Connell was honored in the largest funeral procession the country, suffering in the midst of the Famine, had yet seen.

Shared suffering, oppression, injustice, trauma: all unite more firmly than shared joy, Ernest Renan has argued: "En fait de souvenirs nationaux, les deuils valent mieux que les triomphes; car ils imposent des devoirs; ils commandent l'effort en commun."[14] Mass gatherings in Ireland for public funerals, the funeral processions' symbolic insurrectionary routes, the funerals' emblematic ceremonies replete with nationalist oratory and motifs—for

O'Connell in 1847, Terence Bellew MacManus in 1861, Charles Stewart Parnell in 1891, and Jeremiah O'Donovan Rossa in 1915—"established the rhetorical and ritual framework for the messianic style of nationalist remembrance."[15] These funeral spectacles, a type of *theatrum mortis*, reinscribed the city's streets as nationalist territory, creating stations for real or imagined pilgrimages. Invoking the "protean power of martyrdom, where the stark and depressing facts of abject failure and death can be mysteriously transfigured into triumph,"[16] the centennial commemorations of the 1798 and 1803 United Irishmen Risings were exercises in such redemptive remembrance. So, too, were the mass processions and elaborate ceremonies to lay foundation stones and unveil monuments to both constitutional politicians and nationalist separatists, symbolic routes and rituals that reenacted the funereal spectacles for the nationalists and created sacred nationalist spaces in the metropolitan colony. The parades, street decorations and illuminations of the city to mark the consecration of space in these nationalist dedicatory ceremonies themselves rivaled and at times surpassed the official celebrations for royal visits. The public political theater of counter-monarchical and counter-unionist commemorative spectacles staged in Ireland in the late nineteenth and early twentieth centuries attempted both to invoke and to control public memory and acts founded on that memory, countering royal visits and both the state-sponsored and parallel populist celebrations of British anniversaries and Protestant deliverances and triumphalism that had marked—and continued to mark—the civic life and public spaces of Ireland. As such, these theatrical spectacles transformed spaces that could not yet be controlled permanently into "a temporary stage on which they dramatise the power they still lack." This symbolic capturing of a city or capital thus expresses "political ambitions before the political means necessary to realise them have been created."[17]

Joyce's texts register the demotic, sub-elite community remembrance of royal visits and celebratory spectacles as well as nationalist funerals and commemorative processions, revealing Irish resistance to, even burlesque of, imperial spectacles, but also critiquing the claims to historical truth staged in these counter-spectacles. To bear witness to the past is to invoke its spectral repetition in the present. In ceremonies of messianic remembrance, in these symbolic reworkings of the past, the past is sublated: preserved by being transmuted by the rituals of memory, revivified by an act of imaginative "remembrance," then elevated through sacralization. Ultimately that past is canceled, Joyce recognizes, as memory creates a past never actually experienced or known by the "rememberer"; Joyce's texts examine how public "memory" is created by projecting a future not yet realized—a projection that is, paradoxically, also a retrospective arrangement of a past that never occurred: the historical past comprehended as idea, fabled by the daughters of memory.

Not until 1849 did the "Famine Queen" sail to Ireland for her first visit to Cork, Dublin and Belfast, "bringing her and this excitable nation into contact for the first time." A hazardous experiment to be sure, Queen Victoria's visit was nevertheless intended to pacify dissent and stabilize the political system, to further integrate Ireland into the governmental structures of the United Kingdom and thus abolish the office of Lord Lieutenant, to promote investment in the island, and to "celebrate" the official end of the Great Famine, *an Gorta Mór*, of 1845–49. Anger at the devastation caused by the Famine—starvation, disease and approximately a million deaths; evictions of poor tenants; the destruction of the countryside of Ireland; and the emigration of over a million Irish—drove nationalist criticism of Queen Victoria's visit.

Petitions and supplications during royal visits to Ireland occurred not in the official ephemeral art greeting the monarch but in loyal addresses, if made at all. Cork city's address of loyalty mentioned the country's distress and hope for future good government, a mild petition given the trauma resulting from the Famine; Dublin Corporation's loyal address of welcome failed to mention the Famine or the call to repeal the Union or clemency for imprisoned or exiled Irish political leaders. The royal couple's formal procession through the Cork city streets decorated with flowers and triumphal arches was greeted by "very noisy and excitable but very good humored crowds." The harbor at Kingstown, when the royal yacht and accompanying steamers landed, was "covered with thousands and thousands of spectators, cheering most enthusiastically." For the delighted queen, "the enthusiasm and excitement shown by the Irish people was extreme."[18] To account for the crowds, John Mitchel surmised a "great army of persons" in Ireland were "paid to be loyal" through their economic, social and political privileges and therefore "were expected to get up the appearance of rejoicing."[19] The Dublin procession of the queen inscribed an Ascendancy-dominated route through the city. At the Royal Triumphal Archway erected on Baggot Street bridge over the Grand Canal, the ceremony of royal entry to the city took place: an "equerry demanded entry for the queen and the gates were duly opened by the city marshal. The lord mayor presented the queen with the keys of the city 'with some appropriate words, spoken in an amazing brogue'," as the queen noted his speech in her journal. The final triumphal arch of the parade route made an overt plea for peace: a dove, olive branch tied around its neck, was "let down into my lap," Queen Victoria wrote in her journal; delighted, she had the bird caged. The procession, the queen pronounced, was "a never to be forgotten scene, particularly when one reflects on what state the country was in quite lately, in open revolt and under martial law."[20] The Dublin celebrations—their extravagance belying the Famine's devastation of the country and its impoverished populace—included illuminations and light beams, military reviews, receptions, concerts, dinners and a ball at the vice regal lodge. "Dublin has been during the week like a city risen from the dead."[21]

In their "calculated pageantry," royal processions—and, to a lesser extent, their vice regal re-stagings—like their Baroque forebears, merged Church and State on a higher plane and were "designed to overawe and enthrall the eye."[22] The parallel entry ceremony for incoming lords lieutenant emphasizes how the viceroy functioned as monarchial substitute: the annually elected lord mayor of Dublin Corporation laid the mace and civic sword at the viceroy's feet and offered him the city keys; the viceroy then processed through the city. The vice regal cavalcade that concludes "Wandering Rocks," as with actual vice regal cavalcades accompanied by outriders instituted in 1882 by Lord Spencer after the Phoenix Park murders, replays in part the theatrical processions of British monarchs.

"Wandering Rocks" foregrounds the control of Church and State over the lives of citizens and the very physical fabric of the city, the hostile environment, as well as Dubliners' acquiescence or resistance to that control. The process of historical fabrication is made explicit in the street theater of this episode as the material and the human interact. Tellingly, Joyce opposes a different kind of ephemeral art and a different kind of marketing—advertisements of populist entertainers—to the marketing of power and control that State or Church pageantry deploys. As Carla Marengo Vaglio points out, in the total spectacle of simultaneous movement through the city "disjointed and apparently self-contained vignettes reach out for each other, potentiated by the mutual recognition and interaction of cardboard characters and flesh and blood ones" as the poster for Marie Kendall's variety show, plastered throughout the city, sets into motion the vice regal cavalcade and the advertisement for Eugene Stratton's blackface song and dance act appears both to inaugurate Father Conmee's pastoral walk across Dublin and to welcome the vice regal cavalcade to Ascendancy territory.[23] The 1798 United Irishmen Rising is restaged as late nineteenth-century nationalist resistance: the 1898 counter-procession to lay the foundation stone for a monument to Wolfe Tone, the leader of the Rising—an act of consecration Stephen Dedalus in *A Portrait of the Artist as a Young Man* had judged a "scene of tawdry tribute" (*P* 184)—inscribed a symbolic route through the streets of Dublin, reclaiming the space of the subaltern city from imperial control. This route echoed the insurrectionary detour to Glasnevin cemetery the Fenians had plotted for the funeral procession of Terence Bellew McManus in 1861, reinscribed by the funeral cortege for Parnell in 1891 and unconsciously retraced by Tom Kernan in "Wandering Rocks" on June 16, 1904: Wolfe Tone's house in Stafford Street; St. Michan's Church, where the remains of the Brothers Sheares lie unburied; Moira House, where many United Irishmen sheltered; Thomas Street, where Lord Edward FitzGerald was arrested in 1798 and where Robert Emmet was executed in 1803. In "Wandering Rocks" the statue's absence is sandwiched by a parade of walking advertisement: "Five tallwhitehatted sandwichmen between Monypeny's corner and the slab where Wolfe Tone's statue was not, eeled themselves turning H. E. L. Y'S and plodded back as they had come" (*U* 10.377–79). But what is presented as absence in *Ulysses* became the site, in the heart of Ascendancy Dublin, of annual commemorative pilgrimage, a marker for nationalist funerals to file past, and the starting point for most of Dublin's nationalist marches, centenary celebrations and dedicatory parades, forging a symbolic link between these spectacles and the separatist ideas the Tone memorial symbolized, creating a metaphor for revolutionary action and thus challenging imperial Britain's control of Ireland. Offering a subaltern history, these contrived celebratory stagings were designed to effect a radical transformation of Irish society.

On February 29, 1900, to commemorate the gallantry—and deep losses—of her Irish soldiers in the British Empire's war against two Boer states in South Africa, Queen Victoria had created a new regiment of Irish Guards in the British army and had ordered that the hitherto prohibited shamrock be worn on St. Patrick's Day by all ranks in her Majesty's Irish regiments. In April 1900, Victoria, shamrock-bedecked, came to Ireland on what was billed as an unofficial, non-political visit, but called the "Boer War Tour" by Irish nationalists who saw her tour as a tool to recruit soldiers for the war. Joyce in 1907 echoed the nationalist claims: "the Queen came over for the purpose of capturing the easy-going sympathies of the country, and adding to the lists of the recruiting sergeants" (*CW* 165). As George Moore remarked, she had driven through the city "a shilling between her finger and thumb, a bag of shillings under the seat."[24]

Rituals repeated at every royal entry were intended to invoke the past, real or invented, and legitimize the present: the Queen approached the city boundaries and her heraldic officer requested entry by the Lord Mayor and Aldermen; she was presented the civic sword and the keys to the city and ceremoniously returned them. The gateway, designed by Sir Thomas Drew, erected for this 1900 ceremony at the entrance of the municipal boundary at Leeson Street Bridge, represented the old city gate.[25] Maud Gonne describes the Lord Mayor and Aldermen, escorted by foot and horse police, riding in a gilded Mayoral coach through streets lined with military to present the keys of the city to the queen. Or, as Bloom images the queen's procession through the poorer parts of the city: "From Ailesbury road, Clyde road, artisans' dwellings, north Dublin union, lord mayor in his gingerbread coach, old queen in a bathchair" (*U* 8.708–10).

Voicing the anti-imperialist and pro-Boer stance of radical nationalists, Yeats declared, "Whoever stands by the roadway cheering for Queen Victoria cheers for that Empire, dishonours Ireland, and condones a crime … her crime in South Africa."[26] Joyce in his 1907 Trieste lecture, "Ireland, Island of Saints and Sages," argued that one would realize a "moral separation already exists" between Great Britain and Ireland if one "had been in the streets when Queen Victoria entered the Irish capital the year before her death" (*CW* 163). Echoing John Mitchel's portrayal of the divided Irish response to the queen's 1849 visit, Joyce contrasts the cheers of the "officials," "unionist employees" and "tourists" to the citizens' silent, almost pitying, reception:

> The Queen's carriage passed, carefully protected on all sides by an impressive body of guards with bared sabres, and within was seen a tiny lady, almost a dwarf, tossed and jolted by the movements of the carriage, dressed in mourning, and wearing horn-rimmed glasses on a livid and empty face. Now and then she bowed fitfully, in reply to some isolated shout of greeting, like one who has learned her lesson badly. She bowed to left and right, with a vague and mechanical movement. The English soldiers stood respectfully at attention while their patroness passed, and behind them, the crowd of citizens looked at the ostentatious procession and the pathetic central figure with curious eyes and almost with pity; and when the carriage passed, they followed it with ambiguous glances. This time there were no bombs or cabbage stalks, but the old Queen of England entered the Irish capital in the midst of a silent people. (*CW* 165)

Yet contemporary accounts differed: as one witness noted in disgust, "all the snobs in the country" were "like mad people now with loyalty."[27] The queen's procession passed under inscriptions hung over the road: "In her a thousand virtues closed as Mother, Wife and Queen"; "Blest for ever is she who relied on Erin's honour and Erin's pride."[28] The constitutionalist Dublin Corporation presented the customary loyal address of welcome to the queen—to the anger of radical nationalists. Particularly offensive to nationalists were the Union Jacks draped over the statue of Henry Grattan: Victoria's royal tour coincided almost exactly with the April 2 centenary of the introduction in the British parliament of the Acts of Union and thus the end of "Grattan's Parliament," Ireland's effective legislative independence granted by the Constitution of 1782.[29] On its return from the royal procession, the Mayoral coach "was sorely battered and its glass broken by the infuriated crowd on the quays and, white and trembling, the Lord Mayor and his revolutionary secretary were barely saved by the police from a dip in the Liffey."[30]

In 1903, Edward Martyn urged nationalist Ireland to tell the British government "with one voice that if they bring the King here under any other guise than as a restorer of our stolen constitution, they will regret their rashness."[31] Opposition to Edward VII's royal visit was organized, so that of the over eighty addresses of welcome, ultimately not one came from a publicly elected body in Dublin. As Joyce noted in 1907, the usual protocol was for the Lord Mayor to receive the monarch "at the gates of the city. But, in fact, the last monarch who entered had to be content with an informal reception by the sheriff, since the mayor had refused the honour" at the Royal Triumphal Arch designed by Frederick Batchelor constructed on Leeson Street (*CW* 163).[32] And when the royal party traveled in state from the Vice Regal Lodge in Phoenix Park past Kilmainham and Thomas Street to a formal reception in Dublin Castle, the affront to the memory of Robert Emmet—whose 1803 rebellion in the area of Thomas Street, imprisonment in Kilmainham Gaol, and execution outside Saint Catherine's Church on Thomas Street the nationalists were commemorating that centennial year—was unmistakable. Nonetheless, Dubliners, some loyal, some mistakenly believing the king supported Home Rule, enthusiastically "raised the cheer of the gratefully oppressed," compelling an observer to remark wryly: "And these are the people whom some call disloyal."[33]

The carnivalesque phantasmagoria of the "Messianic scene" of "Circe"—Joyce's "paper triumph"—traffics in public spectacle, mass delusion, utopian political fantasies but dystopian execution, transformations and transfigurations, and martyrdom. The center of the inauguration of "socialist" utopianism in *Ulysses*,[34] this scene reveals how the utopian desires of colonial subjects are molded and controlled by imperial power—indeed, how subjectivity itself is exteriorized. "Circe," as a "portrait of cultural psychosis," is "as much the world of an imperialized experience as it is of the unconscious," a world of economic oppression concomitant with political oppression, the goal being sustained social control.[35] The private and internalized dream becomes public spectacle; yet reciprocally, public spectacle becomes private and internalized.[36] The political theater of this scene reveals the performativity of politics and the protean nature of identity, identifications, affiliations. In the torchlight procession of this scene, in the neo-baroque excess of its spectacle—amid the Venetian masts, maypoles, festal arches, street banners with legends in Irish and Hebrew; the papal standard and the civic flag and the cloth of estate; windows, balconies and streets thronged with sightseers; military regiments and fife and drum band; imperial eagles; political, civic, religious, royal and colonial officials; guilds and trades and trainbands; buglers and beefeaters; parliamentary officials and members of the royal court, including the high constable carrying the sword of state, Saint Stephen's iron crown, chalice, bible—Bloom appears, as did rulers throughout Europe, under an arch of triumph. Echoing the apocalyptic coming of the Messiah, Bloom is seated on a milkwhite horse with long flowing crimson tail, and garbed in a crimson velvet mantle trimmed in ermine. He is bearing "*Saint Edward's staff, the orb and scepter with the dove, the curtana,*" religious and royal insignia that symbolize his power extending over the world. All spectators uncover their heads for the "world's greatest reformer" (*U* 15.1398–1460).

For the pageantry, catalogues, oath, and declarations of this self-consciously theatrical scene, Joyce echoes and parodies newspaper reports of funereal, religious and political spectacles such as the 1903 funeral of Pope Leo XIII and election and coronation of Pius X; the 1902 coronation of British king Edward VII; the 1903 visit to Ireland of Edward VII and attendant triumphalist spectacles of Ascendancy Dublin; the 1899 Wolfe Tone Demonstration; the centenary demonstrations of Emmet's 1803 rising and execution. And he echoes Arthur Griffith's mockery, in his 1904 *The Resurrection of Hungary*, of "the magnificent procession" staged in Pesth in 1857 to honor the Emperor of Austria.[37] As in royal entries, the "*freedom of the city is presented to him embodied in a charter. The keys of Dublin, crossed on a crimson cushion, are given to him*" (*U* 15.1519–20). The oath administered to Bloom by William, Archbishop of Armagh—"Will you to your power cause law and mercy to be executed in all your judgments in Ireland and territories thereunto belonging?"—is predicated on an empire of Ireland and parallels that administered to Edward VII by the Archbishop of Canterbury in 1902 (*U* 15.1480–82). The strength of the crown by the time of Edward VII's coronation resided in its symbolic representation of the idea of imperial unity. The performative ceremonies "Circe" mocks—ceremonies that actuate the very transformation they enact, as in a coronation the acts of anointing and crowning create the king, and thus his embodiment of the body politic—constitute theatrical spectacles. Michael, Archbishop of Armagh, anoints Bloom's head with oil in an echo of papal and royal coronations. By declaring in the formula announcing a new pope and incorporating the national saints of the United Kingdoms of Great Britain and Ireland—"*Habemus carneficem.* Leopold, Patrick, Andrew, David, George, be thou anointed!" (*U* 15.1487–89)—"We have an executioner," the coronation alludes to the coercive power undergirding that union: the constellation of religious, economic, legal, military, and political structures that enforce that coercion.

Joyce was not the first to theatricalize the coronation of Edward VII; in a film Joyce may have seen, Georges Méliès—his producer Charles

Urban having been denied permission to film the actual coronation—staged "an absolutely perfect reproduction of the ceremony in Westminster Abbey" according to the boast of an American newspaper advertisement for the 1902 silent short: "The Most Magnificent Spectacle of the 20th Century Produced by Méliès, of Paris, at a Cost of $10,000."[38] Initially, illusionist and filmmaker Méliès toyed with the idea of filming in the artificial style or "spectacular expression" of his *féeries*, or fantasy films, even suggesting to Urban that the recently deceased Queen Victoria would appear in a vision. Joyce may have adopted Méliès' "baroque *mise-en scenes*," mechanized stage effects, and methods of trick cinema of his *féeries* to fashion "the deliquescent dreamscape of 'Circe'," a dreamscape in which dreaming becomes a form of stylized self-watching, a viewing of protean performances, and dreams are framed within dreams.[39] However, for this film, Urban opted for a realistic "pre-enactment" of the ceremony, and Méliès filmed in ordinary sequence, casting his actors based on physical resemblance to their counterparts in the actual ceremony. Edward was played by a washhouse attendant who later reprised his kingly role in Méliès's fantasy *Le Tunnel sous la Manche/Tunneling the English Channel* (1907). Queen Alexandra was played by a dancer/actress from the Théâtre Municipal du Châtelet, a Parisian theater that specialized in fantasy spectacles.

Filmed prior to the actual coronation for release on Coronation Day, *Le Sacre d'Édouard VII/The Coronation of Edward VII* experienced a delayed opening when the actual coronation, scheduled for June 26, 1902, was postponed due to the future king's sudden illness from perityphlitis, necessitating an emergency operation. Because of Edward's weakness, the ceremonies, when performed on August 9, 1902, were attenuated, yet still denounced by James Connelly as "a piece of Royalist and Capitalist propaganda."[40] Even in their reduced forms, the ceremonies were performative, transforming Edward's civil status to that of king: in staging such ceremonies that are themselves elaborately staged, with highly choreographed ceremonial gestures instituting that transformation, Méliès deployed many of the pantomimed gestures of his *féeries* or magic acts.[41] In early cinema, Carla Marengo Vaglio points out, even the documentary film recuperates its "dynamic and provocative potential," represented in "the 'translation of actualities' into 'visual hyperboles' or 'spectacular scenes' that, enlarging and penetrating the visual field, would tend to a 'total mastering of the possibilities of space,' a space in which natural and artificial aspects blend and exchange their qualities,"[42] a space that fluctuates between the secular and the sacred. The film as anticipatory *actualité reconstituée*—preconstructed "reconstructed news"—was a popular success, including with Edward VII himself, who delighted in the imitation ceremony, its interplay between reality and fantasy: "If I didn't know that the king and queen in the film were impersonators, I'd be convinced that we were looking at ourselves, so perfect is the resemblance! [...] Many congratulations! This is splendid! What a marvelous apparatus cinema is. It's found a way of recording even the parts of the ceremony that didn't take place. Now that's really fantastic!"[43]

Composed during the summer of 1921 as an addendum to "Circe" and completed at least by August 11, just a month after the July 9 truce ending the fighting of the War of Independence, the "Messianic scene" of Bloom's political ascendance and ultimate immolation, as well as the later Circean scene of Dublin burning, obliquely address not only the United Irishmen Risings of 1798 and 1803 or the destruction by the British of the center of Dublin during the Easter 1916 Rising and the subsequent mass internments and the executions of sixteen leaders of the Rising, but also the chaos throughout Ireland during the 1919–21 War of Independence: the assassinations and military reprisals; boycotts and intimidations; sacking of towns, cities and townships; burning of part of the city of Cork; martial law, imprisonments and hunger strikes of a war that Joyce claimed had turned his country into a "slaughterhouse."[44] But in Bloom's proclamation that "a new era is about to dawn" and in the opening of the Court of Conscience (*U* 15.1542, 1629), the "Messianic scene" also obliquely addresses the establishment of a de facto republic on January 21, 1919, when Members of Parliament from Sinn Féin elected in 1918 to serve in the British House of Commons abstained from Westminster and instead established Dáil Éireann, creating an alternative administrative and judicial system that operated independently of British-administered rule. The British government initially failed to proscribe Dáil Éireann, enabling it to operate at least underground, and not officially declaring it illegal until September 1919. The *Declaration of Independence*, read at that January 21 meeting, confirmed the Easter 1916 *Proclamation of the Irish Republic* and its democratic principles, pledged to secure the republic and affirmed the rights of Irish citizens to equality and freedom. The Democratic Programme, *Clár Oibre Poblacánaighe*, a paper presented to and confirmed by the Dáil that day, stressed labor and socialist principles that Bloom echoes in his socialist stump speech: "We declare in the words of the Irish Republican Proclamation the right of the people of Ireland to the ownership of Ireland, and to the unfettered control of Irish destinies to be indefeasible, and [...] we declare that the Nation's sovereignty extends not only to all men and women of the Nation, but to all its material possessions, the Nation's soil and all its resources, all the wealth and all the wealth-producing processes within the Nation, and [...] we reaffirm that all right to private property must be subordinated to the public right and welfare."[45] This last clause, inserted by the Labour Party, was, as Oonagh Walsh points out, "a radical statement by any standards, and one which implied that all citizens should have a fair share in the country's resources in return for their work," thus ensuring that labor, even socialist, principles were declared at the first Dáil.[46] But as Joyce suggests in "Circe," hope in the revolutionary initiative of the working class may be misplaced, as the people veer from moral and political adulation of Bloom—"He's a man like Ireland wants"—to denunciation of him: "He's as bad as Parnell was" (*U* 15.1540, 1761).

Or the people may realize that Bloom's seemingly progressive political message is predicated on imperial structures of power. In this "Messianic scene" Bloom's proclamations and manifestoes, his advocacy of social and economic progressivism and even his government's ceremonies modeled on British templates, echo the proclamations, manifestos and ceremonies of Dáil Éireann of 1919–1921. Progressive social and economic proposals advocated by socialism, syndicalism and labor, Joyce recognized, could be subsumed and even undermined by utopian idealism, for that idealism could be used to legitimize the very structures of power that would subvert a progressive politics. As Norris notes, Joyce dramatizes "texts as a *mise en scène* of ideological formations, as a stage" on which various discourses execute ideological projects.[47] Bloom's three stump speeches in "Circe" shift from socialist demagoguery to the religious propaganda and promises of utopian messianism (and "the legitimization of dictatorship through utopian idealism") and, finally, to a more practical messianic politics that fails to address the needs of an impoverished, distressed populace, their dire plight foregrounded by setting this episode in Nighttown.[48] By 1904, living conditions in Dublin, a city in great economic and social distress, were grim. The construction of the new Bloomusalem in the Nova Hibernia of the future, trumpeted as utopian but executed as dystopian, entails the demolition of buildings, monuments and houses; the displaced inhabitants "*are lodged in barrels and boxes, all marked in red with the letters: L. B. Several paupers fall from a ladder. A part of the walls of Dublin, crowded with loyal sightseers, collapses,*" and as they die, they hail Bloom with the salute vanquished gladiators gave to the emperor (*U* 15.1550–57). The power of Bloom, "acclimatized Britisher" (*U* 15.909), as Messianic ruler is predicated on models to which the Irish were subject, as Wolfgang Wicht has also argued: "Bloom's Irish socialist authority suggests identification with specifically British and religious protocols, categories and discourses of hierarchy. Thus, the text tells us that Bloom's inauguration of utopian desires is still deeply immersed in Ireland's colonial status."[49] In "Ithaca" Bloom—recognizing that every human problem must be considered from the standpoint of time yet confronted with the "irreparability of the past" and the "imprevidibility of the future"—is despondent because "at the critical turning point of human existence he desired to amend many social conditions, the product of inequality and avarice and international animosity," yet he cannot do so, unable to surmount his own, and Ireland's, political and economic subordination (*U* 17.975, 980, 990–92). Yet the "enduring historical power" of Joyce, Norris claims, is his ability, through art, to expose that subordination: to imbricate and interweave "the life of the art in ways that ravel modernism's myth of aesthetic and artistic autonomy," and, in doing so, to reveal art's "revolutionary" political and social potential.[50] *Ulysses*, raveling that subordination it so expertly anatomizes, establishes itself as a counter-site: "outside all places, oppositional both to messianic utopias and contingent social practice, resisting totalization and constructing a place of heterotopia,"[51] the productive and revisionary space of the construction of culture as incommensurable difference, the space in which the conflictual heterogeneity of the public sphere, in all its contestations of national identity and openness to the other, is enacted.

Notes

1 Margot Norris, *Joyce's Web: The Social Unraveling of Modernism* (Austin: University of Texas Press, 1992), 5, 24, 22, 9, 31, 19, 14.

2 *Freeman's Journal* August 18, 1821; quoted in Ryle Dwyer, "A Royal Welcome?" *The Irish Examiner* March 5, 2011.

3 Lord Byron, "The Irish Avatar," *The Poetical Works of Lord Byron* (London: John Murray, 1876), 575; quoted in James Murphy, *Abject Loyalty: Nationalism and Monarchy in Ireland During the Reign of Queen Victoria* (Washington, D.C.: Catholic University of America Press, 2001), xxv.

4 *Times* August 22, 1821; quoted in Murphy, *Abject Loyalty* 9.

5 *Freeman's Journal* July 14, 1840; quoted in Murphy, *Abject Loyalty* 32.

6 *Freeman's Journal* July 1, 1843; quoted in Murphy, *Abject Loyalty* 35.

7 Gary Owens, "Hedge Schools of Politics: O'Connell's Monster Meetings," *History Ireland* 2.1 (Spring 1994) https://www.historyireland.com/18th-19th-century-history/hedge-schools-of-politics-oconnells-monster-meetings/.

8 John Mitchel, *The Last Conquest of Ireland (Perhaps)* (First published serially: Tennessee: *Southern Citizen* 1858) (Glasgow: Cameron, Ferguson, 1876), 34, 35. Emphasis in original.

9 Royal Archives, Windsor Castle, A 16/121, Sir Robert Peel to Queen Victoria, September 22, 1844; quoted in Murphy, *Abject Loyalty* 47.

10 Royal Archives, Windsor Castle, B 8/154, Sir James Graham to Queen Victoria, September 8, 1844; quoted in Murphy, *Abject Loyalty* 46.

11 *Times* June 2, 1845; Royal Archives, Windsor Castle D 14/147, The Duke of Wellington to Sir James Graham, May 30, 1845; quoted in Murphy, *Abject Loyalty* 55, 56.

12 *Evening Mail* quoted in *Freeman's Journal* June 2 and 3, 1845; cited in Murphy, *Abject Loyalty* 56.

13 *Cork Examiner* June 9, 1845; quoted in Gary Owens, "Nationalism without Words: Symbolism and Ritual Behaviour in the Repeal 'Monster Meetings' of 1843–45," in James S. Donnelly, Jr. and Kerby A. Miller, eds. *Irish Popular Culture, 1650–1850* (Dublin: Irish Academic Press, 1998), 242–70 (250).

14 Ernest Renan, *Qu'est-ce qu'une Nation*, ed. Joep Leersen (1882; Leiden, 1994), 28.
15 Ian McBride, "Memory and National Identity in Modern Ireland," *History and Memory in Modern Ireland*, ed. Ian McBride (Cambridge: Cambridge University Press, 2001), 1–42 (31).
16 Alan Ford, "Martyrdom, History and Memory in Early Modern Ireland," *History and Memory in Modern Ireland*, ed. Ian McBride, 43–66 (43).
17 John Berger, "The Nature of Mass Demonstrations," *New Society* (May 23, 1968): 755.
18 Royal Archives, Windsor Castle, Queen Victoria Journals, August 3, 5, 1849; quoted in Murphy, *Abject Loyalty* 88, 89.
19 Mitchel, *The Last Conquest of Ireland (Perhaps)* 215.
20 Murphy, *Abject Loyalty* 91, quoting Royal Archives, Windsor Castle, Queen Victoria Journals, August 6, 1849. Royal Triumphal Archway, Baggot Street, Dublin, Engraving, 1849: https://www.archiseek.com/2012/1849-royal-triumphal-archway-baggot-street-dublin/.
21 *Freeman's Journal* August 10, 1849; quoted in Murphy, *Abject Loyalty* 95.
22 Luke McKernan, "The Other Diamond Jubilee," *The Bioscope*, https://thebioscope.net/2012/06/16/the-other-diamond-jubilee/.
23 Carla Marengo Vaglio, "Futurist Music Hall and Cinema," *Roll Away the Reel World: James Joyce and Cinema*, ed. John McCourt (Cork: Cork University Press, 2010), 86–102 (95, 96).
24 George Moore, quoted in W. B. Yeats, *Autobiographies*, ed. William H. O'Donnell and Douglas N. Archibald. Vol. III of *The Collected Works of W. B. Yeats*, Richard J. Finneran and George Mills Harper, gen. eds. (New York: Scribner, 1999), 329.
25 Sir Thomas Drew, architect, Royal Triumphal Archway, Leeson Street, Dublin 1900: https://www.archiseek.com/2012/1900-royal-triumphal-archway-leeson-street-dublin/. Film of this procession can be accessed at https://www.britishpathe.com/video/queen-victoria-in-dublin.
26 *Freeman's Journal* April 4, 1900; quoted in Senia Pašeta, "Nationalist Responses to Two Royal Visits to Ireland, 1900 and 1903," *Irish Historical Studies* 31.124 (November 1999): 488–504 (491).
27 Letter to John MacBride, April 10, 1900 (N.L.I., F. J. Allan papers, MS 26755); quoted in Pašeta, "Nationalist Responses" 491.
28 Royal Archive, Windsor Castle, Queen Victoria Journals, April 4, 1900; quoted in Murphy, *Abject Loyalty* 284. See Thomas Moore's "Rich and Rare Were the Gems She Wore."
29 Pašeta, "Nationalist Responses" 491.
30 Maud Gonne, *The Autobiography of Maud Gonne: A Servant of the Queen*, ed. A. Norman Jeffares and Anna MacBride White (1938; Chicago: University of Chicago Press, 1994), 269.
31 *Freeman's Journal* April 4, 1903; quoted in Pašeta, "Nationalist Responses" 497.
32 Frederick Batchelor, architect, Royal Triumphal Arch, Leeson Street, Dublin, 1903: http://www.archiseek.com/2012/1903-royal-triumphal-arch-leeson-street-dublin/.
33 *D* 42. Comment quoted in Sidney Lee, *King Edward VII: A Biography*, 2 vols. (London: Macmillan, 1927), 63; cited in Murphy, *Abject Loyalty* xxv.
34 Wolfgang Wicht, *Utopianism in James Joyce's "Ulysses"* (Heidelberg: Universitätsverlag C. Winter, 2000), 39.
35 Cheryl Herr, *Joyce's Anatomy of Culture* (Urbana and Chicago: University of Illinois Press, 1986), 167, 170.

36 Wicht, *Utopianism in James Joyce's "Ulysses"* 43.n.21.

37 F. L. Radford, "King, Pope, and Hero-Martyr: *Ulysses* and the Nightmare of Irish History," *James Joyce Quarterly* 15.4 (Summer 1978): 275–323.

38 Georges Méliès, *Le Sacre d'Édouard VII/The Coronation of Edward VII*: https://www.youtube.com/watch?v=AoGYll8gX14.

39 Philip Sicker, "Mirages in the Lampglow: Joyce's 'Circe' and Méliès' Dream Cinema," *Roll Away the Reel World: James Joyce and Cinema*, 69–85 (70, 72, 82, 84).

40 Austen Morgan, *James Connolly: A Political Biography* (Manchester: Manchester University Press, 1988), 35; quoted in Murphy, *Abject Loyalty* 295.

41 Elizabeth Ezra, *Georges Méliès* (Manchester: Manchester University Press, 2000), 67, 68.

42 Marengo Vaglio, "Futurist Music Hall and Cinema" 89, 91.

43 Edward VII quoted in Ezra, *Georges Méliès* 67.

44 Letter to Valery Larbaud, c. August 11, 1921, *Letters* I, 168, 169. Letter to Mrs. William Murray, October 14, 1921, *SL* 286.

45 https://en.wikisource.org/wiki/Democratic_Programme_of_the_First_Dáil.

46 Oonagh Walsh, *Ireland's Independence, 1880–1923* (London and New York: Routledge, 2002), 59.

47 Norris, *Joyce's Web* 21.

48 Wicht, *Utopianism in James Joyce's "Ulysses"* 73–104; quotation from 92.

49 Wicht, *Utopianism in James Joyce's "Ulysses"* 89.

50 Norris, *Joyce's Web* 3, 8, 14.

51 *U* 17.975, 980, 990–992; Wicht, *Utopianism in James Joyce's "Ulysses"* 107.

Part V

The Value of James Joyce: Ethico-Political Readings

Chapter 10

"FOREIGN WORDS ARE THE JEWS OF LANGUAGE": JOYCE'S PHILOLOGICAL ANATOMY OF ANTI-SEMITISM AND THE DIASPORA OF JOYCEANS[1]

Valérie Bénéjam

In her article on "Fact, Fiction, and Anti-Semitism in the 'Cyclops' Episode of Joyce's *Ulysses*," Margot Norris offers a scrupulous study of how "anti-Semitic stereotypes are consolidated and disseminated into a community as true."[2] This essay will take its inspiration from what Norris identifies as the "narratological anatomy of anti-Semitism" (171) unfolding in "Cyclops," and from her preoccupation with the circulation of gossip and the authentication of information. It will contend that this "narratological anatomy" is complemented in *Ulysses* with a *philological* anatomy of anti-Semitism, which Joyce further pursues in the diasporic linguistic program of *Finnegans Wake*, and which must be met by a diasporic response from his readers.

The episode that displays the most explicit level of anti-Semitism in *Ulysses* is also that which explores the limits of unreliable narration, with a narrator who has variously been called by critics a "barfly," "the Nameless One," or a "dun" (Norris's choice, 164), and who in our day and age would probably be termed a troll. Joyce himself explained that he was influenced by the character of Thersites, from Shakespeare's *Troilus and Cressida*, a malevolent, envious Greek warrior who insults and systematically attributes the most cynical motivations to the legendary heroes appearing on stage.[3] The "Cyclops" narrator reacts similarly to the characters appearing in the pub, and his voice is further foregrounded, since his narrative and interpretation are the only ones provided. In Shakespeare as in Joyce, this riling speaker is allowed to have the last word, and in "Cyclops," apart from the parodic interpolations—which are but interpolations and never narrate new events in the pub—he is never interrupted or contradicted.

The "Cyclops" narrator is an expert at circulating unreliable narratives, and therefore his connection with anti-Semitism—defined by Theodor Adorno as "the rumour about the Jews"[4]—should not come as a surprise. The anti-Semitic narratives circulated in "Cyclops" are founded on stereotypes about Jews. Into these stereotypes, what is known—or what is believed to be known—is reorganized to fit in: reality is bent to correspond to set phrases and hackneyed formulas, whose only pretension to the truth is that they have been heard before and are part of a general store of clichés. Only a philological approach may deconstruct these linguistic forms. Victor Klemperer, in his remarkable study of the language of the Third Reich (*Lingua Tertii Imperii*),[5] has examined in thorough, frightening detail the invasion of a language by such clichés, "endorsed without so much as a second thought," which at first seem harmless and gradually take hold of a language (24). He has studied "as a phenomenon in itself" the "hysteria of language" (28) and the process through which it eventually morphs into a full-blown cancer—the linguistic environment of a vitiated social and political regime. One's maternal tongue becomes, instead of a tool for thinking and writing, its exact opposite: "a language which writes and thinks for you" (24).

Klemperer's philologist's despair at not finding "in the language of this regime a single, truly honest word" (32), his belief that "language reveals all" (11), would certainly have resonated with Joyce's constant preoccupation with the sincerity of language and his pragmatic denunciation of all the clichés that "think for [us]." Joyce's language is always a multi-layered affair, which presents the lie while exposing its dishonesty, and probes the lack of authenticity of the words in spite of the very speaker who has mouthed them. Such linguistic denunciations have always been at the core of Joyce's writing. In the "Epiphanies," each set phrase awkwardly placed makes us aware of painfully coarse interactions, such as Skeffington's "Still [...] it hurts [...]" in response to the death of Joyce's younger brother.[6] In "The Dead," Gabriel's aesthete's phrases—the impersonal title "Distant Music,"[7] or the pedantic color scheme he deploys when referring to his wife's skirt as he admires her on the staircase ("terracotta and salmon pink," *D* 209)—only betray his incomprehension of the actual situation, of his wife's true feelings, together with, ironically, his own *distance* from the emotions aroused in her by the *music*. Set phrases, be they *recherché* or vulgar, always threaten to distort the truth. Gabriel's poetic construction is the intellectual, learned side of a phenomenon that takes place every time we pigeonhole reality into formulas inherited and not re-examined, thus losing the authenticity of language and its exact correspondence to reality. Nor is the phenomenon all black and white, or anyone immune, for language acquisition—as *A Portrait of the Artist as a Young Man* illustrates—is all about finding, within a language we have culturally inherited, the words that will fit the new reality with which we progressively become acquainted. As the cyclical phases of confidence and of imbalance in each chapter demonstrate, linguistic authenticity is not a radical decision one can make once and for all: it is a life-long training process, a series of fine re-adjustments that require our constant vigilance and alertness. Hence the need for a perpetually renewed, perpetually watchful, philological approach.

Anti-Semitism appears early in the discourse of some of the characters in *Ulysses*, and the dialogic and linguistic strategies Joyce deploys in relation to this cancer are both subtle and extremely efficient. In "Nestor" lies the scene, and the first developed occurrence of the illness. For Joyce's exposure of anti-Semitism is that the prejudice appears before the Jew: it pre-exists Bloom's arrival in *Ulysses*, making it clear that there is no need for the presence of a Jew, or for any Jewish action, to spur anti-Semitism. In fact, the presence of a Jew, such a central presence in the novel, becomes the joke Joyce plays on the anti-Semite: we leave Deasy at the end of the second chapter with his repeated quip about never letting the Jews enter Ireland ("Ireland, they say, has the honour of being the only country which never persecuted the jews. Do you know that? No. And do you know why? [...] Because she never let them in. [...] She never let them in," *U* 2.437–46), only to discover the distinctly Jewish name of "Mr. Leopold Bloom" as the very first words of the fourth chapter, together with his gentle, "softly" moving presence, eating "with relish," quite comfortable in his kitchen, not at all hindered from entering Ireland (*U* 4.1–6).

Deasy, on the other hand, appears rather out of sorts as he utters his poor joke: he needs to halt as he runs after Stephen, "breathing hard and swallowing his breath" (*U* 2.436), and his state of health worsens between the two utterances of the punch line: "A coughball of laughter leaped from his throat dragging after it a rattling chain of phlegm. He turned back quickly, coughing, laughing, his lifted arms waving to the air" (*U* 2.443–45). Here also, the joke is played at Deasy's expense, revealing that anti-Semitism is no matter for pleasantry, but a medical condition, whereby what comes out of the anti-Semite's mouth—coughing and phlegm—is the medical equivalent of anti-Semitism within the body politic. Deasy's laughter is a "leaping coughball" over which he manifestly has no control, "dragging after it a rattling chain of phlegm" that comes with the reiterated tagline, as if anti-Semitic language had a life of its own and controlled the anti-Semite's body, infecting it and producing mucus and puppet-like gesticulation together with the words.

Another revealing stylistic feature of the extract is the apparently awkward repetition of the verb "to say" in the beginning of Deasy's joke: "—I just wanted to say, he said. Ireland, they say [...]" (*U* 2.437). This inelegant repeat, underlined by the narrator ("he said" interjected between Deasy's two occurrences) confirms that anti-Semitism is first and foremost a question of discourse, and more specifically of unverified rumor ("they say") which one willingly repeats ("wanted to say"). Anti-Semitism functions because of such dialogical cowardice, which leads one to absorb and transmit a joke, which is not a joke but an infection. Listening and repeating ensures the pandemic's progress, one which would be better curbed by the wearing of earplugs than that of facial masks.

In this respect, Stephen's "beginning" of a "smile" (*U* 2.441) is not entirely reassuring, as we wonder whether he is donning a polite mask or enjoying the quip. In the first draft of "Cyclops," Stephen was included among the drinkers and even participated actively in the anti-Semitic taunting of Bloom in Barney Kiernan's pub. In fact, he originally was the one answering the question "Why can't a Jew love his country like the next fellow?" with "when he's quite sure which country it is" (*U* 12.1628–30).[8] The notion that the figure of the "artist as a young man" was first conceived as anti-Semitic in *Ulysses* is one worth pondering over in the light of some of the young Joyce's questionable statements, for instance in his early essay on Munkacsy's *Ecce Homo* painting (1899). There, he described the Jewish characters in the picture by remarking on "that horrible cast of countenance, so common among the sweaters of modern Israël," and notes that "in their small beady eyes twinkles the fire of rejection, the bitter unwisdom of their race."[9] *Pace* Ira Nadel's interpretation that these early missteps "are not to suggest that Joyce was anti-Semitic"[10]—an interpretation that would go radically against his otherwise well-argued study of Joyce's affinities with Jewish culture—I would contend that the young Joyce may very well have shared the prevalent anti-Semitism of his native city, and that perhaps his own early falling to the contagious linguistic infection later made him particularly aware of the disease's powerful infectious routes and of its severe symptoms.

Once the unsavory joke has been told and its teller exposed as a sick man, the very last lines of "Nestor" present another, radically different transformation of Deasy's appearance: "On his wise shoulders through the checkerwork of leaves the sun flung spangles, dancing coins" (*U* 2.448-49). These coins function like the "small gold coin [shining] in the palm" that Corley displays "to the gaze of his disciple" in the epiphanic ending of "Two Gallants" (*D* 60), which exposes the mean trick he has played on the skivvy with whom he spent the evening. Similarly, the "dancing coins" on Deasy's "wise shoulders" work as a final epiphanic revelation at the end of the episode. Its extent can only be fully grasped when going back to the very beginning of Deasy's unsavory anti-Semitic rant. Deasy has given Stephen his letter about the foot-and-mouth disease, and asked for his help in publishing it, since it could not get printed in England because of "difficulties," "intrigues," "backstairs influence"—a revealing crescendo typical of conspiracy theories, the source of which he presently explains:

> He raised his forefinger and beat the air oldly before his voice spoke.
> —Mark my words, Mr Dedalus, he said. England is in the hands of the jews. In all the highest places: her finance, her press. And they are the signs of a nation's decay. Wherever they gather they eat up the nation's vital strength. I have seen it coming these years. As sure as we are standing here the jew merchants are already at their work of destruction. Old England is dying. [...]
> —Dying, he said, if not dead by now. (*U* 2.345–54)

This is the passage that triggers Stephen's rather problematic memory of Jews and their "full slow eyes" forming a "[g]abble of geese" on the steps of the Paris stock exchange (*U* 2.364–72): Deasy's stereotypical discourse suggests stereotypical images in Stephen's mind, demonstrating how such discourse is performative (or contagious) in producing anti-Semitic perceptions.

This first developed occurrence of anti-Semitism in *Ulysses* concentrates Joyce's techniques for processing this type of discourse. Deasy's speech has all the typical features of nineteenth-century anti-Semitism, or indeed of any racism: born from frustration and a feeling of persecution, it soon turns into conspiracy theories, presenting itself as a lesson that would give a thorough explanation for everything that is wrong and could not be explained otherwise—here the supposed decadence of England. The sentences are simple, with few nuances or modality, and a consequent predominance of the verb "to be": "England *is* in the hands of the jews," "they *are* the signs of a nation's decay," "the jew merchants *are* already at their work of destruction" and "Old England *is* dying [...] if not dead by now." It is an apocalyptic revelation, a discourse that presents itself as both the identification of a most serious state of affairs, and of its unilateral cause. Ironically, given its own contagious nature, it takes the form of a medical diagnosis ("Old England," "she," is mortally ill). Here the Jews are agents of destruction because of their de-territorialized nature: they are dispersed in various nations, but if you let them organize their diasporic communities in each nation ("wherever they gather") they will eat up the "vital strength." Thus the illness is of the parasitic form.[11]

The nation, here England or Old England, does not require to be defined or delimited, but manifestly being part of it is not simply about being "born here," as Bloom puts it in "Cyclops." A similar dialectics will resurface when the "Citizen" puts to Bloom the old question, "What is your nation if I may ask?" (*U* 12.1430), and the other drinkers later note that a Jew may only "love his country like the next fellow" if "he's quite sure which country it is" (*U* 12.1628–30). Nor can nationality be acquired with economic success which, if anything, would make Jews even more suspect. This was indeed the core of the Zionist argument: whatever efforts Jews may make toward integration, the anti-Semites will always consider them exterior to the national group—a form of exclusion rendered easier by the lack of precision in defining the group. In fact, the exclusion of the Jew tends to replace any other criteria as the chief common ground for the group: in "Telemachus," in what is the very first occurrence of anti-Semitism in *Ulysses*, Haines claimed "—Of course I'm a Britisher [...], and I feel as one. I don't want to see my country fall into the hands of German jews either. That's our national problem, I'm afraid, just now." Haines has no other definition of "a Britisher" than anti-Semitism.

In "Circe," which is the land of stereotypical and stage characters, Bloom's father Rudolph comes dressed "*in the long caftan of an elder in Zion*" (*U* 15.249), an allusion to the forgery of the *Protocols of the Elders of Zion*, which supposedly exposed the true nature and the extent of the Jewish conspiracy to take control of the world.[12] The Jewish control over nations as purportedly divulged in the *Protocols* would be based on typically international (or "cosmopolite") activities—namely finance, trade and the press. The infamous triad can be recognized in Deasy's speech as he complains that England's "finance" and "press" are in the hands of the Jewish "merchants." These three stereotypical de-territorialized activities will also recur throughout *Ulysses* in relation to Bloom, a travelling salesman and ad canvasser for the press, whose capacity at making heaps of money from "throwaways" raises no doubts for the drinkers in "Cyclops."

In Joyce's final version of *Ulysses*, Stephen resists contagion a little better, and answers Deasy as a philosophically minded philologist, by defining the word merchant with precision and independently from religious or racial distinction: "A merchant, Stephen said, is one who buys cheap and sells dear, jew or gentile, is he not?" (*U* 2.359–60). Deasy then feels the need to fall back onto the original—Christian rather than the later racialist—vein of anti-Semitism: the Jews have "sinned against the light," this has left some "darkness in their eyes." And then he utters the old diasporic curse: "that is why they are wanderers on the earth to this day" (*U* 2.361–63). When Stephen asks "who has not?," Deasy is in no condition of mind to understand that this query relates to his own comment about "sinn[ing] against the light" and alludes to the universality of original sin. Stephen's answer further emphasizes the motif of light in the text. For the sunbeam that Deasy has walked into underlines his typically Aryan blue gaze ("his eyes coming to blue life as they passed a broad sunbeam, *U* 2.352–53), and recurs at a short interval ("His eyes open wide in vision stared sternly across the sunbeam in which he halted," *U* 2.357–58). Joyce's technique of characterization often employs such repetitions, where the stylistic choice to reuse exactly the same words or turns of phrase alerts readers to a symptomatic quirk or mannerism in the character, which is often the symptom of some underlying, hidden problem. This is observable in *Dubliners* for instance, when Maria's "tip of her nose" twice nearly meeting "the tip of her chin" in a witch-like grin nourishes our suspicions that all is not as "nice" in her world as her laughter would suggest (*D* 101). Through a comparable effect of characterization, in "An Encounter," the pervert's mind is twice mentioned as "circling round and round" as if "magnetised" by his own "speech" (*D* 26, 27), and we realize the symptom is the same whether he expounds upon his liberal views on sweethearts or extols the virtues of a good whipping: our suspicions are thus confirmed that his turnabout has only shown us the two sides of the same mad coin. In both cases, as with Deasy in *Ulysses*, readers are encouraged to observe the characters like psycho-analysts consider their patients, on the watch for symptoms of a wider, subconscious dysfunction. When the sunbeam returns in the very last lines of the "Nestor" chapter, it creates a play of spangling light and shadows on Deasy's shoulders that turns into coins and makes him a gentile merchant, to be therefore treated like any merchant, be he "jew or gentile." Stephen may not explicitly condemn the anti-Semitic ranting because he needs the coins that appear so effortlessly off Deasy's "wise shoulders."

In "Cyclops," anti-Semitic discourse mostly bears the same features, with the added ironic dimension that it comes as easily to the Irish nationalists as it came to the defenders of "Old England." They are blind to the parallels between the persecutions suffered by the Jews in Eastern-European pogroms and those suffered by the Irish at the hands of the British. The Citizen also fails to see the irony of denouncing the international conspiracy of covertly organized Jews, whilst calling for the support of the Irish diaspora ("our greater Ireland beyond the sea") in Old Testament rhetorics: "those that came to the land of the free remember the land of bondage" (*U* 12.1364–75) refers to the Biblical exodus of the Jews—"I *am* the LORD thy God, which brought thee out of the land of Egypt, from the house of bondage" (*Deuteronomy* 5:6). As with Deasy's discourse, Joyce presents us in "Cyclops" with a collection of hackneyed phrases and stereotypes, all borrowed elsewhere—therefore recognizable as well as traceable if we acquire a historical knowledge of these words and phrases and of their usages. Reading Joyce will encourage us to pursue this typically philological knowledge, for this is his habitual ironical, satirical treatment—piling up in the characters' discourse such a profusion of clichés that readers come to realize there is no independently formed thought behind their words: as Klemperer noted, the language "thinks for you."

Speech becomes a form of mechanical repetition of set phrases, and the comic effect produced corresponds to the very definition of humor by Henri Bergson, "*du mécanique plaqué sur du vivant*" ("something mechanical encrusted on the living").[13] Anti-Semitic discourse is thus laughable, as Joyce's anti-Semitic characters damn themselves by their own words.

Deasy's speech in fact was not delivered directly by him but, in keeping with the mechanical generation of such language, he "raised his forefinger and beat the air oldly before his voice spoke." "Oldly," referring to his age and echoing "Old England," draws the readers' attention by the very process of coining a neologism. "[H]is voice spoke" is another hint of "something mechanical" in his character. Similarly, when in "Telemachus" Haines constructed his "Britisher" identity on a hatred of German Jews, his anti-Semitic speech was introduced by "Haines' voice said" (*U* 1.666). The dissociation between the speaker and his voice, accompanied in Deasy's case with the senile beating of the forefinger, is a symptom revealing that this mechanical, parrot-like repetition of stereotypes has no connection to reality. Whilst the anti-Semite views the Jews as degenerate, uprooted, and their de-territorialization as a parasitic disease of the nations where they have settled, it is on the contrary anti-Semitism that Joyce comically exposes as spreading across nations a physiological and linguistic disease that produces mechanical, thoughtless speech.

A philological detour is required to contextualize and grasp all the implications of Joyce's anti-Semitic critique. "Anti-Semitism" itself is a word that appeared in the vernacular European languages toward the end of the nineteenth century, together with two connected words, Zionism and diaspora. The word "anti-Semitism" is actually Joyce's contemporary: the *OED* gives the literary magazine *The Athenæum* issue of September 3, 1881, as the first occurrence for "anti-Semite" and "anti-Semitic" in English. In direct connection with "anti-Semitism," "Zionism" (or *Zionismus*) is also precisely traceable, to May 16, 1890, in an article by the Austrian publicist Nathan Birnbaum, in his Viennese periodical *Selbstemanzipation.* Theodor Herzl's *The Jewish State* was itself published in Vienna, in February 1896, a book spurred by Herzl's witnessing of the degradation of Captain Dreyfus in Paris eleven months earlier. Zionism is constructed as the only possible response to the rise of anti-Semitism and the impossibility of integration, and Herzl actively construes the Zionist project as the negation of diaspora. *The Jewish State* contains the word "diaspora" in its traditional negatively connoted application to the Hebrews, but not in the original Biblical meaning of a divine curse to scatter; now its reversal, the return to the homeland, depends on the determination of humans.

Diaspora had long been related to Jewish identity, and in the nineteenth century became a core notion of anti-Semitism. Διασπορά (*diaspora*) derives from a verb (διασπείρω, *diaspeírō -ein*, to scatter, disperse), itself formed from the prefix διά (*diá*, across or beyond) and the verb σπείρω (*speírō -ein*, to sow, to scatter). Its first meaning is thus not so much that of a dispersed community, nor of the territory where this community may be found, but refers rather to the *act* of dispersion itself.[14] In the Bible, *Diaspora* was the consequence of the Exile of the Hebrews, and appeared for instance in *Deuteronomy*, when Moses explains how would be cursed those that disobeyed the ten commandments: "The Lord shall cause thee to be smitten before thine enemies: thou shalt go out one way against them, and flee seven ways before them: and shalt be *removed into* all the kingdoms of the earth" (28:25).[15] Later the curse is emphasized: "the Lord shall scatter thee among all people, from the one end of the earth even unto the other" (28:64); "among these nations shalt thou find no ease, neither shall the sole of thy foot have rest: but the Lord shall give thee there a trembling heart, and failing of eyes, and sorrow of mind" (28:65); and "thy life shall hang in doubt before thee; and thou shalt fear day and night and shalt have none assurance of thy life" (28:66). This ancient word happens to be Joyce's sense of "diaspora," as we find it in *Finnegans Wake*, just before the sixth peal of thunder, in the phrase "in deesperation of deispiration at the diasporation of his diesparation" (*FW* 257.25–26), where diaspora is combined with despair, desperation, God in Latin (*dei*), death (to die), and additional echoes of the medieval hymn *Dies irae*—thus a particularly negatively connoted view of diaspora, bordering on the apocalyptic.

The emergence of the word has strangely Joycean echoes. Its origin can be traced very precisely to its *hapax*—or first, referential usage, from which all subsequent usages derive. *Diaspora* first emerged in the third century B.C., in Alexandria where, according to legend, seventy Jewish scholars translated the Hebraic Bible into Greek.[16] This Greek translation, the work of the seventy scholars or *septuaginta interpretes*, is therefore known as the *Septuagint*. In "Oxen of the Sun," we find a reference to "the wit of the septuagint" (*U* 14.381). Besides being witty, they were also linguistically creative, for the word *diaspora* had never appeared as such in Greek literature before and was a neologism. The verb διασπείρω (*diaspeírō -ein*) was common, although not in the meaning of scattering a whole people, but the noun itself has no previous occurrence. There was nothing very bold about adding a final -ά to form a noun from a Greek verb, but it proves a creative approach to the language. In fact, as Dufoix explains, the language of the *Septuagint* translation as a whole shows a great sensitivity to the question of language and to that of the confrontation between languages. The community in which this translation occurred was one where the understanding of the original Hebrew language had been lost, and so the seventy scholars were required to translate the sacred text into Greek, but also to shape the Greek language so that it could give a flavor of the old Hebrew version to those who no longer had access to it. It is to this confrontation between languages that can be traced the creation of the neologism, *diaspora*, a neologism which was probably even more significant since this was the word referring to the very process of dispersion that had rendered the translation necessary. The aim of the *Septuagint* translation was to ensure the community could again meet and share the sacred text.[17]

Historically, *diaspora* then entered a phase of Christian usage, as the text of the *Septuagint* was progressively abandoned by the Jews, and the word *diaspora* disappeared in subsequent translations of the Hebraic Bible. But it was reinvested among Christians, first in the Eastern Roman (or Byzantine) Empire, where the Greek language was widely spoken and used for theological writings, and then in its Latin translation as *dispersio*. "Diaspora" came to relate to the Jews and to the Jewish refusal of the Christian faith, as if that was the cause of the original divine punishment of dispersion: this would be the early "anti-Semitic" phase of the notion. From the eighteenth century, the Protestant tradition gave a positive meaning to the word *diaspora*,[18] in its Greek form, and this is how it progressively entered European vernacular languages, where it took about a century to be fully accepted.[19] As a Greek word, no longer translated but transplanted in its Greek form into European vernacular languages, "diaspora" is also Joyce's contemporary.

This, however, was not the word the anti-Semites employed, but instead that which derived from its Latin translation—dispersion. In nineteenth-century anti-Semitic discourse, the notion tended to lose its character of divine punishment, to become a racial feature of "the Jew," the proof of the Jewish supposed incapacity to have a homeland, therefore the mark of a parasitic race, all the more dangerous because they seemed to be able to thrive without a homeland. This is related to the idea of being uprooted, degenerate, prone to living in hiding, therefore a possible source of instability for national communities. The "paradigm of de-territorialization," as the French historian of anti-Semitism Marc Angenot has termed it, became one of the bases of anti-Semitic discourse, in parallel with the development of nationalisms, as racial hostility progressively supplanted religious hostility.[20]

In *Finnegans Wake*, *diaspora* becomes a linguistic program. In Theodor Adorno's collection of aphorisms and short texts, *Minima Moralia*, just after the aphorism about anti-Semitism being the rumor about the Jews, may be found another aphorism: "*Fremdwörter sind die Juden der Sprache*" ("Foreign words are the Jews of language," *Minima Moralia*, 110).[21] *Fremdwort* (or foreign word) is a specific German notion, referring to the terms, many of them of Latin origin, which entered the language at a rather late stage—mostly starting with the Renaissance. *Diaspora*, of course, is a *Fremdwort* in German.

This aphorism may only be fully understood in relation to the specific lexical structure of German, and more particularly within the wider question of the supposed authenticity of pure, organic language, which itself requires resituating within the historical—both philological and philosophical—debates surrounding these questions in German.[22] In "Les mots étrangers sont les juifs de la langue" (a French translation of Adorno's aphorism), Jean-Jacques Lecercle develops the concept of "foreign words," which for him is not restricted to German. What foreign words bring to the language, Lecercle explains, is de-familiarization, and this further entails a political function, as foreign words achieve a form of resistance against nationalism (which always has linguistic aspects, since nations very often define themselves and their territories linguistically). Foreign words are charged with subversion, and this also touches the erotic, as they "represent a form of exogamy of language" (21). While ordinary language is the vehicle for historically sedimented clichés, foreign words on the contrary de-doxise the language we speak and write. Further, foreign words teach us that a language is not an organic, natural totality, but a cultural construct, the result of struggles and compromises—a human history. Foreign words de-naturalize language, and thus contribute to dissolving the naturalistic illusion that it is the mirror of thought: they introduce dissonance in this fictional harmony and expose how language may imprison its speakers. Foreign words resist nationalism and irrationalism in language; they are a lesson in demystification, by forcing a language to be conscious of its real past, in opposition to its mythical origins: instead of withdrawing back into a supposed mythical past, they open up a language to its future. All this, foreign words do because they remain—like the construct of the Jew—a foreign entity within a language, never fully assimilated, but always mobilized against linguistic conventions, harassing the language from within, producing—not hybridization, but a form of linguistic *agôn*, or conflict, that never disappears.

The connection is obvious with what Joyce does in *Finnegans Wake*. The dissemination of languages in the *Wake* has already been much discussed. Perhaps most precisely informed is the work of Laurent Milesi, who is enough of a polyglot to give justice to Joyce's multi-linguistic project. Milesi first examined Joyce's work on foreign languages in the *Finnegans Wake* Notebooks, studying the thematic lists of foreign words, and confronting the crossed-out occurrences with the final text.[23] He makes the crucial distinction between the "langues de compétence" (competence languages: English, Italian, French, Latin, Dano-Norwegian, German and modern Greek), in which Joyce was fluent; the "langues d'apprentissage" (learning languages: Spanish, Dutch, Russian, Irish), in which Joyce took lessons or taught himself with some regularity; and the "langues de recherche" (research languages), some sixty other languages, over which Joyce worked methodically, revealing his aim to compose a form of universal language, "a language to transcend all languages, all linguistic and historic nationalisms and ideologies."[24] Milesi's conclusions harken back to the *septuaginta* and its seventy translators, connecting the magic number to the Babel motif and the Babelization of language in the *Wake*, as seventy, according to subsequent exegeses, would be the legendary number of languages resulting from the destruction of the tower of Babel. Milesi even supposes that the reason why some of the research languages present in Joyce's notebooks have not been used could be that Joyce wanted, in keeping with the Babel myth, to limit the number of languages in *Finnegans Wake* to the symbolic number of seventy.

Further relevant information relates to Anglo-Irish—a term Milesi uses to be faithful to what Joyce would have called the language which we now call Hiberno-English—as it constitutes what he terms the "middle-voice" of *Finnegans Wake*, i.e. the basis, the stable, underlying music of the book, which gets spared foreignization.[25] Milesi notes that Hiberno-English elements very rarely enter into the composition of portemanteau words, and that they remain "uncontaminated by foreign linguistic intrusion."[26] Thus, Joyce has taken "Anglo-Irish," and particularly its Dublin variety—a non-normative, both lexically and syntactically fluid language, which is itself a form of *contact* language—as the acoustic and affective basis of *Finnegans Wake*. Around this stable, musical "middle voice" (61), he has deployed his dissemination of seventy languages—not the actual but the symbolic totality of foreign languages, creating in the process a veritable diasporic linguistic program.

This program also corresponds to what happens to languages in diasporic situations—a parodoxical and complementary phenomenon that involves the bringing into contact of foreign tongues—in the form of bilingualism or trilingualism or more, or of possible hybridization, creolization, in other words creation of contact languages, where the superstratum tends to be the language of the new land and the substratum the original language.[27] Diasporic communities distinguish themselves by efforts to preserve either their original language or that which has become the language of the community, by a form of linguistic voluntarism, or activism, whereby the language becomes the vehicle of an identity which is symbolically and affectively invested. With Wakese, Joyce did in fact implement a diasporic linguistic program, which both preserves and affectively invests the original Hiberno-English, and through the dissemination into English of the symbolic totality of foreign languages, achieves not only the deconstruction of the superstratum of English, but also the creation of a universal tongue for all the sub-species and "sibspeeches of all mankind [that] have foliated (earth seizing them!) from the root of some funner's stotter all the soundest sense to be found immense" (*FW* 96.30–32).

Finally, a typical feature of languages in diaspora is that, not only are they the objects of much linguistic activism, but by the same token they also tend to be much invested by collective discourse, and to produce a form of meta-language and interpretations of themselves. In "Two Words for Joyce," Derrida had already developed the idea that Joyceans, as an institutionalized academic community, are the "*joyciciel*" (or "Joyceware," a pun on *logiciel*, meaning software in French), because whatever discourse is produced about Joyce was already programmed in his work. Perhaps Joyce readers' own diasporic, philological dynamics works in response to the diasporic linguistic program of Joyce's work, which already contains it. And this is why Joyceans may have a form of responsibility to be faithful to Joyce's diasporic linguistic program of defamiliarization and demystification, of resistance against sedimented clichés and any form of uncritical usage of language—which seems much needed these days. Eventually, a "Diaspora of Joyceans"—like a flock of (preferably wild) geese, or a bevy of blushing maidens—is the phrase I would like to offer for the community of Joyceans, not in contradiction to Jacques Derrida's famous 1982 phrase for the institutionalization of Joyce studies, "*James Joyce Inc.*"[28]—but rather in re-actualization of his phrase, and in homage to Norris's reading of anti-Semitism in Joyce. Our "Diaspora of Joyceans" should be understood in the sense in which Joyce speaks, in *Finnegans Wake*, of a "diasporation of [all] pirates" (*FW* 463.21).

Notes

1 Some of the thoughts presented here were first articulated in a plenary talk at the *Diasporic Joyce* conference in Toronto in June 2017. I would like to thank Michael Groden and Tim Conley for their invitation.

2 Margot Norris, "Fact, Fiction, and Anti-Semitism in the 'Cyclops' Episode of Joyce's *Ulysses*," *Journal of Narrative Theory* 36:2 (Summer 2006: 163–89), 186. Further references to this article will appear parenthetically. Norris further elaborates her ideas in "Stephen Dedalus's Anti-Semitic Ballad: A Sabotaged Climax in Joyce's *Ulysses*" (*De-Familiarizing Readings: Essays from the Austin Joyce Conference*, *European Joyce Studies* 18, eds. Alan W. Friedman and Charles Rossman, Amsterdam & New York: Rodopi, 2009, 65–86).

3 See Joyce's own letter to Budgen from September 10, 1933 (*LI* 337); Frank Budgen, *James Joyce and the Making of Ulysses* (Oxford: Oxford University Press, 1972), 158, 171; Ellmann's biography (*JJII* 459).

4 Theodor Adorno, *Minima Moralia: Reflections on a Damaged Life*, translated from the German by E. F. N. Jephcott (London: Verso, 1974), 110.

5 Victor Klemperer, *The Language of the Third Reich: LTI—Lingua Tertii Imperii: A Philologist's Notebook*, translated by Martin Brady (London: The Athlone Press, 2000). Further references will appear parenthetically within the text. The original, *Lingua Tertii Imperii: Notizbuch eines Philologen*, was published by AufbauVerlag in 1947.

6 James Joyce, *Poems and Shorter Writings*, eds. Richard Ellmann, A. Walton Litz and John Whittier-Ferguson (London: Faber, 1991), 182.

7 James Joyce, *Dubliners*, eds. Robert Scholes and A. Walton Litz (New York: Viking, 1967), 210. Further references will appear parenthetically in the text as *D* followed with page number.

8 See V.A.6, fols 2r, 2v, quoted in Michael Groden, *Ulysses in Progress* (Princeton: Princeton University Press, 1977), 136.

9 "Royal Hibernian Academy 'Ecce Homo'," in James Joyce, *Occasional, Critical, and Political Writing*, ed. Kevin Barry (Oxford: Oxford University Press, 2000), 19, 20.

10 Ira B. Nadel, *James Joyce and the Jews* (Gainesville: University Press of Florida, 1996), 57. On the same subject, see also Neil R. Davison's *James Joyce, Ulysses, and the Construction of Jewish Identity: Culture, Biography, and "the Jew" in Modernist Europe* (Cambridge: Cambridge University Press, 1998); Marilyn Reizbaum's *James Joyce's Judaic Other* (Stanford, CA: Stanford University Press, 1999).

11 For a study of the anti-Semitic sources that inspired Joyce's critique here, see Ira Nadel's section on "Anti-Semitism" (*James Joyce and the Jews*, 57–69). Of particular interest for Deasy's quip is Arthur Griffith's article in the *United Irishman* from 23 January 1904: "Mr Davitt is proud — so are we — that Ireland is the only country in Europe where 'the Jews were never persecuted.' But that is all the more reason why Jews should not persecute Ireland" (60).

12 The *Protocols*, probably forged by the Russian secret police, appeared in 1903. It was exposed as a hoax by the London *Times* in 1921, but this did not hinder its circulation.

13 Henri Bergson, *Le rire: Essai sur la signification du comique* (Paris: Presses Universitaires de France, [1940] 1983), 29; and *Laughter: An Essay on the Meaning of the Comic* (trans. Cloudesley Brereton and Fred Rothwell, Mineola, New York: Dover, 2013), 18.

14 I am much indebted here to Stéphane Dufoix's *La Dispersion, Une Histoire des usages du mot diaspora* (Paris: Éditions Amsterdam, 2011), which has been published in English by Brill as *The Dispersion: A History of the Word Diaspora* (Amsterdam: Brill, 2017).

15 "*[R]emoved into*" is the fragment that corresponds to the word *diaspora.*

16 seventy or seventy-two: the number had magical or ritual value so should not be taken too literally.

17 There is a dialectic relation between dispersion and gathering, around the sharing of the text, which has interesting echoes for Joyceans.

18 To lament the dispersion of Christian communities, "diaspora" became associated with several myths of importance to Joyce: the Fall, Babel, the Wandering Jew.

19 First in German (first dictionary entry in 1880), then English (1895 or 96 for first *OED* entry; although dictionaries of Protestantism have it from 1860).

20 Marc Angenot, *Ce que l'on dit des Juifs en 1889. Antisémitisme et discours social* (Saint-Denis: Presses Universitaires de Vincennes, 1989), 159–77.

21 This is the literal translation of the sentence, but to clarify what is meant in regards to the history of the German language, translators usually give *Fremdwörter* as "German words of foreign derivation."

22 Thorough references would include essays by Theodor Adorno, but also Walter Benjamin, and Martin Heidegger. I will be content here with citing my chief inspiration for this reflection: Jean Jacques Lecercle's thought-provoking article, "Les mots étrangers sont les juifs de la langue" (in *L'Étranger dans la langue*, eds. Emily Eells, Christine Berthin, Jean-Michel Déprats, Nanterre: Presses Universitaires de Paris-Ouest, 2013, 17–36); further references, translated by me, will appear parenthetically.

23 Laurent Milesi, "L'idiome babélien de *Finnegans Wake*: Recherches thématiques dans une perspective génétique," in *Genèse de Babel: Joyce et la création*, ed. Claude Jacquet (Paris: Editions du Centre national de la recherche scientifique, 1985), 155–215.

24 Milesi, "Introduction: Language(s) with a Difference," *Joyce and the Difference of Language*, ed. Laurent Milesi (Cambridge: Cambridge University Press, 2003), 4.

25 Milesi, "The Perversions of 'Aerse' and the Anglo-Irish Middle Voice in *Finnegans Wake*," *Joyce Studies Annual* 4 (Summer 1993), 98–110.

26 Milesi, "In-Law and Out-Lex: Some Linguistic Aspects of "Barbarity" and Nationalism in *Ulysses* and *Finnegans Wake*," in *Papers on Joyce* 3 (1997), 57–71.

27 See for instance: Bettina Migge, "Creole formation as Language Contact: The Case of the Suriname Creoles," John Benjamins, 2003 (ffhal-01494340f); or John P. Hughes, "The Irish Language and the 'Brogue': A Study in Substratum, " *Word* 22:1–3 (1966), 259–75.

28 Jacques Derrida, "Deux mots pour Joyce," 23. Geoff Bennington's translation ("Two Words for Joyce," published in Attridge and Ferrer's *Post-Structuralist Joyce: Essays from the French* [Cambridge: Cambridge University Press, 1984, 145–59], as well as in Mary T. Reynolds ed. *James Joyce: A Collection of Critical Essays* [Prentice Hall, 1993, 206–20]), is taken from an earlier transcription of Derrida's conference rather than from the Galilée Paris edition of 1987, and does not contain the phrase "James Joyce Inc." The phrase may have been either not transcribed from or not spoken in the 1982 conference (which Derrida himself describes as "*bref et improvisé à partir de quelques notes*" ["brief and improvised from a few notes"], 11), but it appeared in the 1987 French publication of this conference.

Chapter 11

ALWAYS A GOOD TURN: VETERANS OF THE JEWISH SUBJECT IN JOYCE

Marilyn Reizbaum

One of my first memories of Margot Norris is of her plenary address at the Copenhagen Joyce Symposium, in 1986, in which, as in the article it became, she tracks "the riddle of desire" through the overdetermined helio-trope. That the upward movement of the figure is not always uplifting corresponds to her critical sensibility—a light narratological touch with an exquisitely sharp edge. Another essay I invariably return to in teaching "The Dead" is Norris's essay on "back-answers," where she mobilizes (Althusserian) ideas of relative autonomy and Lacanian theories governing desire to make a claim for the narrative's canny and uncanny use of suspect ideological propositions: as she describes it, "Joyce's dramatization of the politics of art's determination to conceal its own politically oppressive functions."[1] Her topic there is gender, in particular, but she continues to demonstrate the sometimes tricky balance between complicity and exposure in the subjects Joyce treats. In her Introduction to *Suspicious Readings of Joyce's Dubliners* (2003) (the volume in which that essay on "The Dead" has finally been collected), Margot refers to herself as a "bricoleur, taking this or that tool as it comes to hand and as it fits the purpose of reading whatever story is before" her. She elaborates: "my theoretical inspirations [...] have in common an oppositional, or dialectical, or dialogical logic that I find necessary for reading the stories *otherwise* rather than simply as reinforcements or paraphrases of the narrations themselves."[2] In approaching Joycean texts in these ways, *Dubliners* in particular, she posits the "problem" of multiple interpretations as both generous and intolerably ambiguous. Margot Norris talks about how she herself may be intolerant of such ambiguity, coming down on one side or another in her readings, but acknowledges the ethical stance in such toleration (e.g., Derek Attridge's refusal to fill in the gaps in reading for Clay, for example, in order to respect the other as other), and, at the same time, the ethical challenge to being a detective, enthralled still by the search for answers.[3] As Margot Norris's readers, we thrill in her search.

In this tribute to Norris's work, I want to consider the gorgeous didacticism of her discussion of Jewishness and anti-Semitism in Joyce's work through her engagement with possible worlds theory in *Virgin and Veteran Readings of Ulysses* (2011); I read this theory in conjunction with her concept of suspicious reading, a critical disposition about which there has been considerable contest recently. In fact, we might see these critical propositions of possible worlds theory and the hermeneutics of suspicion as antithetical, the former reparative of the latter; but in the hands of the expert bricoleur, they cooperate to enrich the understanding of this subject especially, even when they clash. While it has been my contention that Jewishness is a heuristic for the narrative form in Joyce's work—that is, that the flashpoint figure of marginality, the premier other (certainly in Joyce's milieu), complements and helps to explain Joyce's formal choices—Norris's narratological approach to the Jewish subject tweaks the proposition, suggesting that one understands the subject through the novel's formal strategies, thereby elucidating the novel's deployment of Jewishness. I will confess that I was somewhat surprised initially to discover her interest in and address to this topic. Though there has been a variety of approaches to the "Jewish angle" in Joyce's work, some less parochial than others, most have been culturally based. In my own work on the topic in Joyce, I have sometimes had to check the instinct to rehabilitate the subjects of Jews and Jewishness and, resisting, have sought instead to show the formal function and significance of the subjects. For Margot Norris, the cultural aspect of the Jewish subject is integral to what she argues is Joyce's didacticism, which is revealed through the narratological stakes of *Ulysses*. And these stakes match her own. Her skin in the game, as it were, is one I emulate in my own work, to make Jewishness a critical, heuristic subject for Joyce and modernism. Margot Norris does not presuppose what Jewishness we bring to Joyce's work; she asks us as readers to think about Bloom, Jewish Dublin, anti-Semitism, and to *examine*—what we know, how we know, and when we knew it?

Before turning to several examples of Norris's analysis, here is a brief overview of the theoretical approaches she brings to this topic:

The general principle governing "virgin" and "veteran" readers is presented in response to an idea about the untenability of a virgin reading of *Ulysses*—where they would know nothing about the novel in advance of picking it up. Such untenability is defined in one way by Karen Lawrence's "spatial approach" and theory of re-reading, which posits that "the text's narrative discontinuities make the work unintelligible unless the reader has 'the entire book in mind; he must see the beginning in terms of the end'."[4] Norris counters that the virgin reader is not untenable since many first-time readers are obliged to follow "a consecutive or sequential reading in which the text is confronted with attention to the narrative development of events produced by the temporal disbursement of information [...] even if their knowledge of the implications of what they read remains flawed and incomplete."

> From a critical and heuristic perspective, however, a simultaneous procedure for reading the work from a virgin and veteran perspective concurrently is not precluded. In that case, the virgin reading simulates a first-time encounter with the narrative *innocent* of later information that will eventually modify or clarify earlier events and character appraisals. At the same time, a veteran reading shadowing it makes the significance of what is withheld from the virgin available to us.[5]

Norris makes a similar case about reading *Dubliners*, but from a different standpoint. In discussing the narratorial heurism of the stories that "make[s] the operations of texts explicit and visible," she notes the history of her own re-reading, aided by the different theories and reading that the critical trends have brought to bear on interpretations of the stories; "a re-reading that has gradually turned into a *re-writing*," which sometimes seems a "speculative counter-narrative." Her interpretive suspicion, she tells us, configures the narrator or narrative voices as unreliable. What is withheld is here delimited as gnomonic. Her approach to the gaps is to press for "specific rationales" rather than to let them stand for themselves: "What the narrators fail or refuse to tell, as well as how they tell things, is always significant because it opens a silent counter-discourse that presses the possibility of an interpretation in opposition to that prompted by the narrative voice."[6] Addressing the narrative disjunctions one encounters in the text, Margot Norris establishes that—

> Reader "suspicion" or "distrust" of the narration is produced precisely by unease or dissatisfaction with what I would call *narrational prompts*. [...] By resisting these prompts or cues, "we" readers are transformed from narratees into critics, in the sense that, instead of passively following the narrational lead toward certain judgements of the characters and events in the story, we begin to objectify and evaluate the narrational practice itself. One could take the implications of this shift or split in the reader even further by locating it in the transformation of a consumptive reading into an ethical reading.[7]

In this "transformation," the naïve reader turns into a questioning or resistant and self-conscious reader about their interpretive stances. The suspicious reader in this way would seem to conjoin virgin and veteran practices. The Jewish subject is the perfect proving ground for the conjunction of these theories, in that there are disjunctive prompts that attend it, gaps that press for solutions (and may be unresolvable despite the reader's best efforts or due to their worst indifference); the subject itself is inevitably suspect, regardless of what critical frame one brings.

Margot Norris confirms the view that the Jewish, or in the case of Bloom, the Jew-ish subject, is suspect by arguing, contradictorily, that Joyce has a heuristic strategy for the revelation of Bloom's Jewishness so as not to diminish him or make him threatening in the eyes of his readers as it does his fellow citizens. Even Stephen, who deals better with the hypothetical idea of Jews than most others in the novel, is unsettled by Bloom's gestures toward familiarity or familiality. The reason for his unease is debated by Norris and others, and I will make the case below, in the discussion of the Ithaca chapter. Her conclusion that the way Leopold Bloom is introduced in *Ulysses is* "carefully orchestrated over many pages" to build sympathy for him seems persuasive and yet it is hard to imagine many readers of this text who are "innocents" on the particular subject of Jews.[8]

When Bloom's Jewishness remains unspoken, inferred, displaced, etc., the gap is significant both as a referent and as an omission. The history of the novel, which until the latter part of the twentieth century had rendered Bloom and the Jewish subject overall as minor, has demonstrated a passive resistance (or not so passive) to the writerly engagement that Norris suggests: "Joyce's acute anatomy of anti-Semitism entails not only the reader's passive register of its representation: it further requires the reader's active engagement in sorting out its operation and thereby playing an ethical role in its interventions."[9] At the very least, the success of Joyce's strategy, according to Norris, to build sympathy for Bloom and by association Jewishness, is not borne out by the critical history of the novel. And this is its own heuristic. Bloom had either been too Jewish—often paradoxically rendering Bloom invisible or insignificant—or not Jewish enough for the likes of many of his readers. In fact, Bloom became sympathetic when Jews became "possible" subjects.

Norris contends Joyce put the strategy into action because he knew "his reader was unpredictable" on the matter of sympathy toward Jews; but I wonder if this narratological unfolding has as much to do with predictability?[10] Though Bloom's Jewishness is obliquely presented in the first few chapters, beginning with Calypso, there is knowingness on display, as is the *pretense* of innocence (e.g., Hades, Cyclops, etc.), which is one operation of prejudice. Looking at it this way does not change her contention that the reader may become an agent in the register and ethics of anti-Semitism. But does not the history of the novel demonstrate the unpredictability of the reader's capacity to glean Joyce's strategy and respond accordingly? This reminds me of Margot Norris's argument about "The Dead," and Joyce's strategy there to expose art's concealment of its oppressive functions, in that case to do so with the representation of gender. To the degree that Joyce's anti-Semitism has been debated, I will weigh in to suggest that the same liability is at work—as that which she identifies in "The Dead"—except in that case it is Joyce's sexism at issue. *Ulysses*' exposure of anti-Semitism in such a strategic manner is *necessarily* at once a reproduction of it.

> By being largely female, the back answers in "The Dead" suggest that Joyce uses the politics of gender to conduct his self-critique of art in the story. But he does this by having the story's art replicate the problems of sexual politics in society by twisting its plot in such a way that the ubiquitous oppression of woman is both blatant and discounted, unmistakable and invisible at the same time. [...] Art's self-critique requires Joyce to dramatize that art's representation of woman is inherently oppressive and thereby obliges him to specularize his own role as male artist for the purposes of critique.[11]

The staging of Bloom's Jewishness in *Ulysses* might not seem as specularizing of the role of the artist as that which Norris describes for The Dead, except perhaps in Ithaca, as we shall see. Her argument here resists the charge of anti-Semitism for Joyce and for the novel, but Joyce's sleight-of-hand makes the work susceptible of such an accusation; "the anatomy of anti-Semitism" is both performative and becomes a speech act. The strategy to make Bloom sympathetic does nothing for Jews in general, unless he becomes a stand-in, which I believe the novel goes to pains to deflect by making Bloom Jew-ish. Norris's narratological approach does similar work, rendering both the author and the work sympathetic.

In what follows, I will read along with Margot Norris, examining with her several of the instances that she presents as constituent of Joyce's narrative strategy, serving "as a heuristic tool for the reader's education in the operation and effects of prejudice":[12] in particular, the slow reveal of Bloom's Jewishness in Calypso and Lotus Eaters; and the enigmatic scene in Ithaca, in which Stephen insinuates an anthem of blood libel into the exchange with Bloom. The perspectives Norris brings from Possible Worlds theory that "revisit the conventional problems of narration, plot, character, and interpretation" correspond to her other critical stance regarding "virgin readings of self-disputing texts, where the outcome of such reading can be to demonstrate that the production of conflicting interpretations is the integral aim of the textual project, one that is already staged in the writing itself."[13] The uncertainty about Bloom's Jewishness is heuristic in these terms.

Calypso and Lotus-Eaters

Margot Norris discusses Bloom's fastidiousness, his contempt for the shabbiness of several of the people he encounters, "a disgust [...] grounded in matters of hygiene." She moves through these encounters with McCoy, Sweny, Bantam Lyons, etc., in a sequential manner within the novel so as to "simultaneously simulate the hypothetical virgin reader's encounters with them." Her argument that through these meetings Bloom's "position in the social hierarchy of the text's agential constellations is registered as socially upper middle class and having social confidence is belied by what we have seen in his interactions with his wife, his status at home, and by his thoughts, some metonymously self-reflexive."[14] Wondering why mice never squeal when cats handle them cruelly, he concludes—"Seem to like it" (4.28).[15] The meeting with M'Coy unsettles him—"wished he had not met that M'Coy fellow" (5.210–11). M'Coy might be "picking at his mustache stubble" (5.163), but he is mostly picking at Bloom's sore about Molly; and in wondering if he is "pimping after me," Bloom follows him with his eyes to the sign advertising *Leah*, which then leads to a series of associations about betrayal, apostasy and his father's suicide. Instead of exuding confidence, Bloom appears on each of these occasions as someone who has been wronged in a social sense, and whose private contempt is a kind of psychological revenge or tit for tat.

The Sweny reference is of particular note—the chemist who sells Bloom the lemon soap and orange flower water for Molly. While Bloom thinks of Sweny's "sandy shrivelled smell" (5.473), he also thinks of a smell that "can almost cure you" when thinking of all the drugs and potions that saturate the air. Bloom seems to be reminded of many things as he stands there—the poisons that kill the body, such as his father's aconite; the scents that bathe and nourish the body, like Molly's. Perhaps for a virgin reader, the focus on smell is as yet unconnected to the stereotype of the Jewish odor (which will come up later, in Cyclops, and Circe). In her terrific essay on Lotus Eaters and the organ of the skin, Maud Ellmann contends that "Bloom's task in 'Lotus-Eaters' is to save his skin, threatened by wounding from without, by leakage from within, as well as by the skin diseases that befuddle this distinction." She refers here to the "contemporary fears about degeneration," as what accounts, in part, for the copious images of skin disease in the chapter;[16] such "contemporary fears" are a stand in for the threat of Jew-ish disease.[17] It is true that the Jew's "smell" has not yet been directly invoked by the text in Calypso or Lotus Eaters, but it hovers there as a fixed stereotype about Jews, certainly in the period in which the novel was written and in concert with Bloom's obsessiveness about this feature.[18] Norris claims that this idea of social consciousness about cultural stereotypes, etc. kicks in only after it is revealed that Bloom is Jewish. But I wonder if the clues activate the prejudice as much as the knowledge. One cannot help but see the irony in Bloom's contempt, unless one is clueless, which is, of course, Norris's argument. I am not arguing that Bloom is being ironic here, but that his lashing out, importantly in private thoughts only, may be read as ironic, in context.

Norris does concede that along the way, there have been "signs and clues to the features of Jewishness in Bloom's knowledge world," which the reader recognizes in retrospect.[19] She raises Bloom's mention of friendship with other Jews, such as Citron and Mastiansky, "foreign" names which would read as Jewish, especially in the context of Bloom's reverie about Palestine.[20] More significantly, who other than someone Jewish would muse about the kosherness of mice (4.275–76), or imagine the contradiction in Arthur Griffith's vision of Irish liberatory home rule by exposing his anti-Semitism ("Ikey"—4.102); for an ostensible "virgin" reader, might these be observations that refuse to register? One clue Norris does not mention is Bloom's reference to "mazzoth" when in the church in Lotus Eaters and while thinking about the wafer, body of Christ. He makes the connection to Passover, the scene of the last supper—is it unwittingly?—and holds up the Jewish ceremonial traditions in another sort of tit for tat: the "unleavened shewbread […] all like one family party […] all in the same swim […] In our confraternity" (5.358–64); all sounds a bit cynical, especially given the other implicit references to matza/the wafer/the body of Christ, and the reference to ritual murder in Ithaca. The question about Bloom's knowingness arises again there.

Ithaca

Now to move to Norris's discussion of the enigma of the Ballad of Harry Hughes; most readers find inexplicable the appearance of this notorious ballad in Ithaca. In general terms, Norris's narratological analysis achieves at least two things: it uses the Jewish subject to give us a sharper focus on the ethical and social stakes of the ballad's cultural specificity and it reinforces the necessity, the embeddedness of suspicious reading, which the Jewish subject in turn makes necessary.[21]

There are two questions about this scene that continue to niggle in ways that interpretation does not relieve or satisfy: Why is Bloom's hospitality met with Stephen's churlishness (a polite term for anti-Semitism)? Followed by, why include the text and the music of the ballad, with notes in Joyce's own hand, no less? Joyce's text seems particularly resistant to explanation.[22]

The First Question

One way this has been answered has to do with the economy of exchange in this scene, suitable to the catechistic paradigm: the sliding signifier of the "victim predestined," which on the one hand trades positions between Harry Hughes and the Jew and in the second, between the Irish and the Jews (17.833–40; 725–60).[23] In the first instance, Harry Hughes is the Christian victim of ritual murder, predestined by the crucifixion and therefore allegorically a stand in for Christ, whose shed blood displaces the blood of the lamb that marks the doorposts of the Jews, thereby sparing their firstborn sons from God's wrath against the Egyptians.[24] The Passover story becomes the Easter story (ergo the bloody matza) and thereafter all Christian boys fill the position, including Stephen. Second, Bloom becomes the victim predestined of an anti-Semitic offense, which has been proven throughout the day. But as Norris points out, it is unclear who makes the designation of "victim predestined" here—Stephen or the narrator. She wonders in the exchange between the two positions, "What does this mean—that Bloom can be identified with little Harry as a victim of excessive retaliation."[25] In part, she answers "If the reader is prompted to regard Bloom as both the spurious threat and the victim of Stephen's anti-Semitic attack, then we are not only made to serve witness to this tortuous and pernicious logic but to participate in an analysis of its construction."[26] But this does not entirely explain what it means for the Jewish perpetrator to be identified with his own victim. The reading of the mirror between the Irish and the Jews as historical victims, what Michael Rothberg calls "multidirectional remembering," yields an understanding of different histories of suffering through the lens of each other.[27] But this, too, seems unsatisfying given the assault on Bloom, one reminiscent of that in Cyclops by the Citizen, where, in my reading, there is a mirroring of oppressed parties and a performance of nationalist bravado that is mocked by the narrative (and narrator, in different ways); in Ithaca, the note is more deadly serious.[28]

In all cases, as Norris argues, the appearance of the ballad performs an act of narratological sabotage, both by disallowing a satisfactory denouement for the father–son motif and in the gap the text produces in refusing to explain Stephen's presentation of the ballad at a moment of ostensible bonding. It sabotages the expectation of a "virtually transcendent possibility of communion, not only between Stephen and Bloom as individuals, but between the Irish and the Jewish people as races with analogous genealogical, cultural, and political histories."[29] The ethics of such equivalencies has been questioned by critics so as to suggest that the text itself poses the question of their legitimacy. Abby Bender explains the explanatory gap by assessing, "Stephen ultimately forces us to confront our uncritical celebration of the solidarity of the oppressed—it brings a tolerated anti-Semitism into the present."[30]

Norris is trained on the omission of the motive for Stephen's intervention, which, as she argues, puts the reader in the role of detective around a subject that might be typically evaded, narratively and otherwise. The narrative's avoidance is therefore heuristic. This way of thinking about it then shapes the act of detection. To determine that it is inexplicable is productive in these terms. In fact, Norris goes so far as to say that even if one might impute motive, as have certain critics—(e.g., Stephen feels threatened, strange, etc.)[31]—"yet a brutal attack on an innocent man is so out of character with everything we have seen of Stephen's thoughts, encounters, and behavior throughout the day that it is simply unthinkable."[32] As to why Joyce would wish to obscure the possibility that Stephen's rudeness in singing the ballad might have been inadvertent, she responds that perhaps because any explicit *excuse* for Stephen's behavior would simultaneously *absolve* the reader from concern about the ballad's anti-Semitism and its possible harm. The upshot for Norris is narratological and ethical. She capaciously concludes:

> By shocking the reader with Stephen's anti-Semitic ballad at the climax of the novel, Joyce forces us to explore why such outbursts are produced, to reexamine their historical origins, and to worry about their pernicious future effects not only on Leopold Bloom, but on a larger European population.[33]

But this does not preclude the assessment of Stephen as harboring anti-Semitism. And why would it be "unthinkable" for him to use the best weapon to hand to stave off his perceived threat? After all, he has been primed by Haines in Telemachus and Deasy in Nestor, warned about Bloom by Mulligan in Scylla and Oxen; and finally he registered the "strange kind of flesh of a different man approach him, sinewy and wobbly and all that" in Eumaeus, when he comes face to face with Bloom, and Bloom takes his arm to escort him to his house, saying "then you'll feel a different man" (16.719–22). He does. Primed by history to see the Jewish other differently and the invitation of hospitality as a threat. At the chapter's end, Stephen is not a changed man, in the other meaning of that platitude.[34]

Norris questions the use of the word "strange" in Bloom's request for a "strange legend on an allied theme" (17.795–96) after singing Hatikvah to Stephen, "partially in anticipation of that multiple, ethnically irreducible consummation" (17.761–62).[35] An allied theme would be nationalist, which makes Stephen's choice both perverse and apt—anti-Semitism, after all, has a nationalist underpinning. It is difficult to parse "ethnically irreducible" here, but in one reading of this multiple consummation, a national anthem, however much allied or parallel, would seem to counter such a wish—is it ethnically or multiply irreducible? The word "legend" is interesting in this context, not only because it is allied to the ballad, a genre which is handed down, but because it is the word associated with Theodor Herzl's famous statement regarding the establishment of a Jewish state—"If you will it, it is no legend."—another meaning of ethnically irreducible (cannot be watered down), one might say. All of this is strange for Stephen, who, at the very least, does not know Hebrew. The request by Bloom to be allied and the fear of the strange seem to be prompts for Stephen's anti-Semitic act.

In the way that the narrative technique of Ithaca simulates questions and answers in a catechistic form, with a foregone or predestined answer, Stephen may be a sort of ventriloquist of what Norris describes in Cyclops as "the consolidated and disseminated anti-Semitic stereotypes." We might even consider the preclusion of explanation of Stephen's motive for presenting the ballad in terms of biblical injunctions, as with laws in Judaism that are considered inexplicable: "chukim" are divine statutes that are beyond human reasoning or are given without explanation, such as the kosher laws and laws like it, where the deity tests discipline, adherence and faith, and authority. Such testing of authority mimics the author's position, which Ithaca does so well. Maimonides and Talmudic thought textually frame this exchange between Bloom and Stephen, reinforcing the paradox in the centrality of exegesis to Jewish law (Maimonides' "Guide to the Perplexed") combined at once with the law that evades interpretation by design—a reflection of the narrative strategy that Norris ascribes to Joyce (17.710–25).

The Second Question

Margot Norris suggests that Stephen enjoys "delivering creative or cultural set-pieces to Bloom: the Jeep song, the mountain hotel scenario, his parable, and finally "The Ballad of Harry Hughes";[36] but the latter is of such a different nature from the others, that the question about why the text and music are included seems to go unanswered. She also suggests that their inclusion cures the reader of any virgin status with respect to such anti-Semitic set pieces.[37] While Norris ascribes to Joyce an ethical motive through his narrative strategies, Joyce would appear to collude with a kind of anti-Semitism by including personally inscribed musical notesheets of the ballad. I am reminded again of her discussion of "The Dead" as exemplary of Joyce's illustration of the relationship between politics and art; here, in Ithaca, he stages an anti-Semitic scene, one that is as historically entrenched as the sexist "Distant

Music" scene in "The Dead"—arguably more. In doing so, Joyce exposes a symbolic order and the racial subject within it; the exposure inevitably implicates the author who has marked the scene by insinuating and inscribing his own copy of the set text, and it provides him with some specularizing distance. No one in the milieu is exonerated: the social does not allow a Stephen to bond with a Jew and neither *may* Joyce.[38]

Some argue that a "virgin status" regarding these recycled set texts is hard to come by. They are embedded in a kind of cultural memory or collective non-consciousness. Astrid Erlls discusses the inclusion of the ballad in Ithaca in terms of pre-, re-, and hyper-remediation. She writes from a perspective of media memory studies:

> James Joyce's *Ulysses* represents *premediation*—a process that connects both minds and texts with collective memory as it is produced in media cultures. Premediation is the (usually non-conscious) process by which images and narratives recalled from representations circulating in media culture turn into powerful schemata and preform imagination, experience, memory, storytelling, and action. It is a forward-facing, generative dynamic of memory. [...] It is through histories of remediation that stories such as those of Jewish blood libel solidify into cultural memory.[39]

The recirculation, especially of variants of such stories and images, constitutes a hypermediated presentation, which might account for Joyce's choice to include the text and the music, just as Child includes numerous versions, while disavowing the veracity of ritual murder and condemning the "horrible consequences" perpetrated by the false accusation.[40] Textual evidence is a feature of these remediations, despite the oral transmission that seems to attend them. One thinks also of "The Protocols of the Elders of Zion," whose origin story begins with a forged document found on a dead Jewish Russian soldier—or so the myth goes. The pernicious hyper-mediation of that text is legendary. The variants of the Hugh of Lincoln ballad might also account for Bloom's seeming ignorance when he hears the first part of Stephen's recitation.

> How did the son of Rudolph receive the first part?
>
> With unmixed feeling. Smiling, a jew, he heard with pleasure and saw the unbroken kitchen windows. (17.809–11).

But it is just as likely that the variant rehearsed by Stephen does not seem to Bloom at this moment to apply to himself. Stephen will spare him.[41]

Erll continues:

> The "Ballad of Little Harry" in the "Ithaca" episode shows that pre-mediation is not a blind fate to be accepted in increasingly hyper-mediated memory cultures. It is the effect of a process of remediation in which everyone is implicated, in which different variants can almost always be imagined or retrieved, and in which we all have the choice what to transport, what to elide, what to ignore—only, however, on the condition that non-conscious narrative schemata are made conscious, and then (self-)critically scrutinized, thus breaking the hidden power of implicit cultural memory.[42]

Joyce's staging of the scene can be characterized as (self-) critical scrutiny, but I am also struck by Erll's reference to the breaking of the hidden power of cultural memory, and the breaking of the windows that necessarily occurs in this scene, which Bloom at first does not detect; its readers, too, have sought to understand the break, perhaps reflecting on our lack of self-scrutiny.[43]

Conclusion

The narrative form of Ithaca invites many generic associations, most commonly parodies of both scientific method and catechistic devotions. Norris at one point characterizes Bloom's and Stephen's exchange as an "ethnic game, whose irony is, of course, the ambiguous relationship each man has with his own ethnic heritage."[44] If theirs is a game "of producing analogous Irish and Jewish cultural signs," then Stephen wins by stunningly fracturing it, in Norris's term, through which he sabotages a climax in accordance with Joyce's formal aims.[45] Of course, games or puzzles are the generic associations by which Joyce's enterprise is often questioned or disparaged—what is his motive? Are his readers the victims of "a gigantic hoax, of one of the most enormous leg-pulls in history," to quote Oliver St. John Gogarty.[46]

Take the riddle, which Joyce favors, itself a paradigm of predestination; it is a figure that is often used to represent and also disparage Joyce's method. It makes him suspect. The impetus to solve it is met with the impossibility of such resolution borne of the nature of riddles, which are proleptic in the sense that they embed an answer which belies the proposition of guessing. One must almost already know the answer to solve the riddle—the answer then precedes the question, as in a catechism. It pertains to the way in which Jewishness functions in the novel—as a property always already known, even when, as Norris argues, "nothing in Calypso *tells* us that Bloom is Jewish" [my italics].[47] This paradigm embodies both the virgin and the veteran, an exchange, which

Norris has set up as a sort of inter-play. She says the game is fractured, but maybe this is the game, where one ups the ante to win. She beautifully works through the interpretive logic of this exchange to help the reader, as she says, work out an explanation for Stephen's behavior that is a "matter of ethical judgement."[48] The act of interpretation to understand why Stephen might wish to injure or offend Bloom with his ballad requires the reader to work through the logic of understanding how civilized peoples might persecute a minority by perceiving it, wrongly, as a threat. And yet, so well-rehearsed is this scenario, that part of its pleasure is in the repetition.

Another form that both appears in Ithaca and might be applied to its narrative is the pantomime. After all, the voiceover narrator reports, acting as a conduit, a duenna perhaps, while our actors perform parts that are "predestined." Pantomimes and games return us to Norris's discussion of the heliotrope, which she qualifies as an "answer to the riddle of desire in Joyce's work." She discusses various forms of desire for which the heliotrope functions as a trope, but it is as an "intellectual paradigm suggesting a model of reading Joyce's work that is unconventional both in its procedures and its goals," that turns me again and again to Margot Norris's essay and to her work overall as she charts for us a heliotropic reading of Joyce, keeping our eye on "the movement, longing, reaching, turning, communicating and dancing that signifies" the desire of our search for pleasure in Joyce's work.[49]

Notes

1 Margot Norris, "The Politics of Gender and Art in 'The Dead'," *Suspicious Readings of Joyce's Dubliners* (Philadelphia: University of Pennsylvania Press, 2003), 227.
2 Norris, Introduction, *Suspicious Readings of Joyce's Dubliners,* 13.
3 Ibid., 11, 12.
4 Margot Norris, *Virgin and Veteran Readings of Ulysses* (New York: Palgrave Macmillan, 2011), 2.
5 Ibid., 3.
6 Ibid., 9. Norris references others on the subjects of gaps: "In somewhat different registers both Sonia Bašić and Derek Attridge argue against the interpretation of gaps and mysteries, Bašić to preserve their power to subvert and Attridge in the interest of ethics." In *Suspicious Readings of Joyce's Dubliners,* 11, 12.
7 Ibid., 10.
8 Norris, *Virgin and Veteran Readings of Ulysses,* 262.
9 Ibid., 213.
10 Ibid., 102.
11 Norris, "The Politics of Gender and Art in 'The Dead," 218.
12 Norris, *Virgin and Veteran Readings of Ulysses,* 102.
13 Introduction, *Suspicious Readings of Joyce's Dubliners,* 15.
14 *Virgin and Veteran Readings of Ulysses,* 102–3.

15 All citations to quotations in James Joyce's *Ulysses* refer to the Random House Edition (New York, 1986).
16 Ellmann, Maud, "Skinscapes in 'Lotus Eaters,'" in *Ulysses—En-gendered Perspectives: Eighteen New Essays on the Episodes*, eds. Kimberly J. Devlin and Marilyn Reizbaum (Columbia: University of South Carolina, 1999), 65.
17 See Reizbaum, *Unfit: Jewish Degeneration and Modernism* (London and New York: Bloomsbury Academic, 2020) for an explanation of my use of the hyphenated "Jewish" (9). It might signal partiality or a constellation of ideas associated with Jews, Jewishness and Jewish subjects.
18 In *Virgin and Veteran Readers of Ulysses*, Norris draws on Lubomir Doležel's ideas about "social representations" when discussing Bloom's social status and interaction with others.
19 Ibid., 101.
20 My thanks to the editors for pointing out the context for Bloom's reference to Mastiansky and Citron.
21 *Virgin and Veteran Readings of Ulysses*, 212.
22 See my previous address to this subject in "Urban Legends," *Eire Ireland* 45: 1& 2 Spr/Sum 2010: 247–49.
23 Astrid Erll, "Homer, Turko, Little Harry: Cultural Memory and the Ethics of Premediation in James Joyce's Ulysses," *Partial Answers: Journal of Literature and the History of Ideas*, 17, no. 2, June 2019: 242.
24 A secessionist version of the Passover story appears in Matthew, in the form of Herod's Slaughter of the Innocents, in which Herod, responding to the prophecies of the coming of Christ, orders the execution of all male children under the age of 2. They figure as the first Christian martyrs. A reference to the "Slaughter of Innocents appears in Lestrygonians and Oxen of the Sun. In the first instance, Bloom thinks of it in Davy Byrnes while riffing on hunger, the prohibitions, religious and otherwise, associated with eating, and the casualties thereof. This oblique reference underscores the irony in having a feast day associated with the slaughter of children.The body of Christ and cannibalism hover over these deliberations. My thanks to the editors for this suggestion.
25 *Virgin and Veteran Readings of Ulysses*, 208–9.
26 Ibid., 211.
27 Erll recalls Joyce's remark of the "epic of two races Israelite-Irish" (236).
28 See my "When the Saints Come Marching In: Re-deeming Cyclops," in *Ulysses—En-gendered Perspectives*, 167–84.
29 *Virgin and Veteran Readings of Ulysses*, 206.
30 See Erll and Abby Bender, "A Bloomsday Seder: Joyce and Jewish Memory," *Memory Ireland: James Joyce and Cultural Memory*, eds., Oona Frawley and Katherine O'Callaghan (Syracuse: Syracuse University Press, 76.
31 See, for example, Vicki Mahaffey's discussion of the perceived threat Bloom presents to Stephen, in "Sidereal Writing: Male Refractions and Malefactions in 'Ithaca'," in *Ulysses—En-gendered Perspectives*, 254–66.
32 *Virgin and Veteran Readings of Ulysses*, 208.
33 Ibid., 213.
34 In fact, there is a parallel scene in Eumaeus, where ethnicity and nationalism are part of the exchange between Bloom and Stephen. Bloom's revelation to Stephen about the anti-Semitism he experienced at the pub is delivered with both a proud

identification with Jews and demurral about being Jewish which might later account for the equivocal expression of Stephen's apprehension of Bloom's Jewishness: "He thought that he thought that he was a jew whereas he knew that he knew that he knew that he was not" (17.530–31). Stephen's response to lay claim to Ireland rather than Irishness and Bloom perceives Stephen's response to what he has confided as a kind of rebuke.

35 *Virgin and Veteran Readings of Ulysses*, 207.
36 Ibid., 205.
37 Ibid., 208.
38 Thanks to the editors for their suggestions here.
39 Erll, 229, 242.
40 See Mahaffey, 262; *Virgin and Veteran Readings of Ulysses*, 211.
41 Erll recounts the American variant that elides the anti-Semitism, 243, 44.
42 Erll, 245.
43 I can't help thinking of Virginia's Woolf's plaint about Joyce's need to "break the windows," which doubles as admiration. In "*Mr. Bennett and Mrs. Brown*," (London, Hogarth Press, 1924), 21.
44 *Virgin and Veteran Readings of Ulysses*, 206.
45 Ibid.
46 Oliver St. John Gogarty, "They Think They know Joyce," *Saturday Review of Literature* xxxii (March 18, 1950), 8.
47 *Virgin and Veteran Readings of Ulysses*, 88.
48 Ibid., 208.
49 Norris ("Joyce's Heliotrope," *Coping with Joyce: Essays from the Copenhagen Symposium* (Columbus: Ohio State University Press 1989), 3, 4.

Chapter 12

JAMES JOYCE'S HUMANE COMEDY[1]

Michael Patrick Gillespie

While living in Trieste, during his first ten years of self-imposed exile from Ireland, James Joyce not only threw himself into his career as an author—publishing *Chamber Music*, completing *Dubliners*, and transforming *Stephen Hero* into *A Portrait of the Artist as a Young Man*—but, when he was not giving language lessons, he also reaffirmed his ongoing commitment to understanding the process of creativity through an intense study of the works of other authors. His reconstituted library from that period indicates, unsurprisingly, that he was drawn predominantly to fiction. In terms of quantity, nineteenth century French and Russian authors attracted more of Joyce's attention than did any others, and of those writers he showed a particularly strong interest in the gritty, realistic approach of Honoré de Balzac. During this time in Trieste, Joyce acquired a dozen and half works by that author, including fifteen books from Balzac's *La Comédie humaine* series.[2]

While one might ascribe any number of reasons for this predilection, an obvious explanation is that their shared interest in the mores of the bourgeoisie led Joyce to give Balzac's work pride of place in his library. However, a striking distinction obtains between the attitudes that shaped the two authors' observations. Balzac's narratives stand aloof from the characters that he created, sustaining a dispassionate, analytic view of them throughout his works. Joyce's discourses, on the other hand, show an interest in doing more than pillorying the Irish through acerbic accounts that simply highlight critiques of their actions and attitudes.

Certainly, Joyce was fascinated by the mundane details of ordinary existence, and he never hesitated to draw attention to the peculiarities and weaknesses of any of his characters. At the same time, he was never aloof, punitive, or contemptuous in his representations of human failings. Indeed, he understood and sympathized with the imperfections of his characters, and he would not suppress acknowledgments of their humanity in order to turn them into vehicles for excoriating the culture that shaped them. Instead, in an understated but insistent way, Joyce's prose reminded readers that a range of feelings and attitudes shape any nature. Even in individuals with outsized traits that seem to dominate their beings, Joyce was careful to introduce other impulses that enabled readers to expand their understanding of the characters' motivations and actions.

It strikes me that Joyce's writing seems to take particular care to endow any of the figures who receive extended examination in his works with the ability to see aspects of the world in an amusing fashion that meliorates harsher features of their environment. Because Molly, time and again, refuses to take seriously the portentousness in the world around her, she can label the singer Ben Dollard a "base barreltone" without giving it a second thought. Granted, her sense of humor does not often rise above an inclination towards malapropisms, but those observations neatly inject a measure of playfulness and even tolerance into the otherwise self-absorbed personality that emerges in her monologue in Penelope.

An appreciation for wit, if not necessarily the ability to carry it off, also gives an added feature to Bloom's nature. One sees this in Hades when he attempts to tell the anecdote about Reuben J. Dodd's hapless son. Although he so muddles his delivery that the generally mild-mannered Martin Cunningham intervenes to finish the story, there is never any doubt that Bloom has a clear sense of the silliness of the situation. Equally so, Joyce knows that, in keeping within the limits of Bloom's personality, he can give Bloom some appreciation of humorous incidents that he encounters time and again in Dublin without being able to endow him with the ability to use them to entertain others.

Although Stephen Dedalus also displays the mellowing traits of a comic appreciation of the world, he presents a greater test of any intention by Joyce to insinuate a sense of humor into his personality. Because of Stephen's love of language, his quick wit (quite similar to his father Simon's), and his sardonic view of the world around him, a satirical tone time and again inflects his discourse. However, the keen powers of observation and the pithy forms of expression that make Stephen's character so unique do not lead immediately to a clear or consistent comic sense emerging from his personality. When he is being funny, his aims shift quickly and often from self-aggrandizement, to self-criticism, to self-defense, at the same time his observations are both more acute and more spontaneously than the studied performativity of Buck Mulligan, the "Mercurial Malachi." It can be a challenge to follow his machinations and an even great challenge to understand how they relate to his character.

Critics from Robert Boyle to Edmund Epstein to Margot Norris to Karen Lawrence and Joseph Valente—to name a few of his most astute examiners—have offered insightful readings of Stephen's nature, each emphasizing important traits that inform the reader's understanding. It is most certainly not my aim here to present yet another version of interpreting Stephen. Rather, with a more modest purpose, I seek to show how Joyce's representation facilitates the range of understandings proposed by a variety of sophisticated critics by focusing on the way a single aspect of Stephen's nature—his sense of humor—gives readers a greater awareness of his humanity and from there a broader sense of how he can be interpreted.

For me, this approach is nowhere more evident than in the representation of Stephen Dedalus' character in *A Portrait of the Artist as a Young Man* and *Ulysses*. Although an unswerving aesthetic ambition and a relentless artistic egoism seem to dominate his nature, Joyce skillfully insinuates demonstrations of a range of other feelings that enhance and humanize a reader's sense of Stephen. One can point to a number of traits that contribute to this perception, but I would like to undertake my own suspicious readings of Stephen's sense of humor, though with no pretentions to deploying the skill and grace that Margot Norris brought to her examination of *Dubliners* in the Norton Critical Edition.

Like the terms patriotism, piety, and pornography, humor is easier for an individual to recognize than to define. Attempting to resolve the mutability of its meaning would leave little space to apply the term to Joyce's work. Here I look at its manifestations in attitudes ranging from whimsical mimicry to biting ridicule, and I leave it to each reader to apply the concept in a way that best suits her or his personal understanding.

Joyce introduces us to Stephen's early flashes of humor in the gentle and charming opening of *A Portrait of the Artist as a Young Man*:

> Once upon a time and a very good time it was there was a moocow coming down along the road and this moocow that was coming down along the road met a nicens little boy named baby tuckoo [...]
>
> His father told him that story: his father looked at him through a glass: he had a hairy face.
>
> He was baby tuckoo. The moocow came down the road where Betty Byrne lived: she sold lemon platt.[3]

Of course, the imbedded ambiguity of these opening lines make it impossible to identify the speaker definitively as Stephen, the narrator, or, at least for the first few sentences, Simon Dedalus. Nonetheless, the final portion singles out Stephen as a willing, unselfconscious participant in a whimsical farce. The next line goes on to capture the spontaneous charm of a small child's "seriocomic" sententiousness while offering innocent amusement to the adults and readers who hear him: "When you wet the bed first it is warm then it gets cold" (5).

In short order, however, as Stephen moves from a toddler to a young boy, capriciousness turns to caution. First, he learns that both admitting to and denying kissing one's mother leads to ridicule. Then, the trauma of the Christmas dinner scene and the horror of Father Dolan's pandying make Stephen even more aware of the violent consequences and maddening perfidy of linguistic imprecision. These experiences blunt childish impulses to indulge spontaneous exuberance, and they metamorphose into a more concentrated, more disciplined, and less open application of wit.

By the time he had become a student at Belvedere College, Stephen learned to use an incisive wit to turn language against his tormentors. An example of his ability to apply it occurs outside the school just before a theatrical production. There Stephen encounters his class rival, Vincent Heron, another figure with a Balzacian taste for exploiting vulnerability, who, demanding information about a supposed girlfriend, mixes banter and threat to embarrass and intimidate Stephen:

> Stephen's moment of anger had already passed. [...] He scarcely resented what had seemed to him at first a silly indelicateness [...] and his face mirrored his rival's false smile.
>
> —Admit! Repeated Heron, striking him again with his cane across the calf of the leg.
>
> The stroke was playful but not so lightly given as the first one had been. Stephen [...] bowing submissively, as if to meet his companion's jesting mood, began to recite the *Confiteor* [author's italics]. The episode ended well for both Heron and Wallis laughed indulgently at the irreverence. (68)

The moment turns on the skillful manipulation of language and meaning. Heron cannot pursue his intention to humiliate a rival because he cannot run the risk that brushing aside Stephen's mild blasphemy—the invocation of a prayer from the Latin Mass as a comic answer to a demand for information. To do so would make him seem the religious prig and admit an inability to form a clever response to Stephen's sally. Wit has come to serve as the young Stephen's defense against the world, and language has become his weapon to deflect and disarm its hostility.

Nonetheless, in this and other instances of Stephen's cleverness in *A Portrait of the Artist as a Young Man*, his wit is circumscribed by its defensiveness. Most significantly, Stephen's banter is never self-directed. He employs rhetorical skills to hold others at arm's length and to blunt the force of too intense scrutiny. Whatever humor emerges from his remarks comes closer to *schadenfreude* than to anything else.

In fact, as Stephen grows older he takes himself increasingly seriously and has apparently little time for wit and none for other aspects of humor. At the opening of Chapter III, sitting in an algebra class, waiting for the appearance of the teacher, Stephen tries to dispel his boredom by mimicking the solicitations he has heard from whores in Nighttown:

—Hello, Bertie, any good in your mind?
—Is that you, pigeon?
—Number ten. Fresh Nelly is waiting on you.
—Good night, husband! Coming in to have a short time! (89)

The staleness of the dialogue matches the torpor that envelops the adolescent Stephen, but it reveals a bit more. This is not Stephen performing for his friends; rather it is an unvoiced sardonic, rather than erotic, recollection. The public exercise of humor has become a danger, carrying a threat of self-exposure that Stephen forestalls by keeping his performance sequestered.

In Chapter 4, religious devotion and aesthetic ecstasy underscore Stephen's conception of the world as a serious place. While the self-absorption of this section of the novel may seem to circumscribe rather than elaborate Stephen's humanity, the absence of humor rather than its presence enhances our sense of his nature. As any parent will testify, Joyce here has perfectly captured the characteristic sullenness that overwhelms most of us as teenagers.

In Chapter 5, Stephen pompously expounds his aesthetic theory to Lynch and humorlessly debates religious belief and filial duty with Cranly. The observations that he makes are often quite canny, but Stephen never achieves a sense of self-awareness that would allow him to deflect and deflate the inclination towards defensive pretentiousness that accompanies these disquisitions. Cranly does succeed in bringing Stephen, if only momentarily, to remembering the power of a pithy reply. When cataloguing the achievements of his father Simon, Stephen concludes dismissively: "and at present a praiser of his own past" (213). Later, after making clear his intention to break from the Catholic Church, Cranly asks Stephen if he then intended to become a Protestant, Stephen responds with biting dismissiveness. "I said I lost my faith, not my self respect" (215).

By the end of the novel Stephen's sense of humor has constricted in a way that reflects the self-importance which has come to characterize his nature. In the final lines of the novel, he mythologizes himself in his penultimate journal entry, reiterating his determination for independence while linking it to a commitment to his artistic vocation: "I go to encounter for the millionth time the reality of experience and to forge in the smithy of my soul the uncreated conscience of my race" (224). The novel closes with Stephen feeling not the least self-consciousness about his bravado or showing a glimmer of recognition of the irony inherent in his choice of the word "forge."

It would be easy to see all this as a narrowing rather than an expanding view of Stephen's humanity. Certainly, from the time he is the exuberant Baby Tuckoo to when he becomes the guarded and aloof artistic rebel, Stephen's inclinations for expressing his amusement, frustration, and even bewilderment with the world around him become increasingly circumscribed. At the same time, because of the way they echo the stages of his emotional development, our cumulative sense of his nature increases rather than diminishes.

The reserve and introspection readers see at the end of *A Portrait of the Artist as a Young Man* have changed little by the time we see Stephen in *Ulysses*. The failed academic sojourn on the Continent and his bittersweet return to Dublin to witness his mother's death that have taken place in the interval between the two novels have done little to blunt his egoism or to diminish his sense of isolation. However, he also now shows both a greater self-awareness as someone on the brink of artistic achievement and a larger sense of insecurity as a character now more vulnerable to the incestuous environment of Dublin literary life. As a response to it all, his humor reflects a newfound ability to laugh at himself as well as an even greater wariness of the world around him.

The narrative presents a compelling example of the challenges to his identity that Stephen now faces when the opening lines introduce the Balzacian presence of his nemesis: "Stately, plump Buck Mulligan [coming] from the stairhead" to summon the sleepy and somewhat surly Stephen Dedalus into the narrative with the peremptory command—"Come up, Kinch! Come up, you fearful Jesuit!"[4] With this flourish the mercurial Malachi conflates a comic rendition of the opening prayers and the moment of consecration at Mass to assert his claim to the role of wry, self-aggrandizing comic commentator on Dublin mores whose censorious wit will punctuate various episodes in the narrative until his farewell performance in Circe.

The humor of Buck Mulligan always delights us because of its underlying nastiness and disrespect. His flippant blasphemy—seen in "The Ballad of Joking Jesus" later in the chapter—and his bawdy cleverness—exemplified in a passage in the Scylla and Charybdis chapter when he proposes to write a play entitled "A Honeymoon in the Hand, or Every Man His Own Wife"—insure that what he says will engage out attention whenever he appears.

With derisive disregard for all consequences, Mulligan demonstrates that he, not Stephen, is the rightful heir to the tradition of vituperative mockery exemplified by Simon Dedalus—"such a criticizer" as Molly reminds us. Both men are entertainers seeking to please their audience through merciless catalogues of the foibles of any target of their humor. To amplify the impact of their ridicule, they willingly oversimplify their representations, and never show themselves as more than superficial commentators on human fallibility.

Stephen rejects the implicit invitation to take up their malicious clowning and become another barroom wit. However, his commitment to a higher form commentary on the human condition does not signal the loss of his sense of humor. Rather, we see emerging a self-effacing comedy, merciless in its interrogation of his own nature and wryly aware of the foibles of those around him.

The narrative almost immediately offers telling examples of this wit in the face of Mulligan's bombastic performance, though Stephen's early morning grogginess makes it more understated than representations later in the day. Buck Mulligan, waving his shaving mirror and posturing, invokes the spirit of Oscar Wilde: "The rage of Caliban at not seeing his face in the mirror. [...] If Wilde were only alive to see you." Stephen responds by saying: "It is a symbol of Irish art. The cracked looking glass of a servant" (1.143–146). Mulligan is delighted by the phrase: "Tell that to the oxy chap downstairs and touch him for a guinea" (1.154–155). Stephen lets the remark pass, not bothering to inform Mulligan that the line he finds so amusing was cribbed from "The Decay of Lying," an extended essay by the writer Mulligan has just invoked.

In the Nestor episode, Stephen is now wide awake, but faces an audience for his wit that proves even less receptive to cleverness than were the occupants of the Martello tower. His initial attempt, an observation that the Kingstown Pier is "a disappointed bridge," (2.39) produces only confusion among the Dalkey schoolboys whom he teaches and must be filed away for "Haines's chapbook [...] amid wild drink and talk, to pierce the polished mail of his mind" (2.42). When the sententious Garrett Deasy gives Stephen his biweekly salary, he urges his young employee to acquire a "little savingsbox" to hold his coins. Aware of his own spendthrift ways, Stephen replies with grim humor: "Mine would be often empty" (2.232) to which Deasy can only respond by quoting Iago "*Put but money in thy purse*" (2.239, author's italics) in a context that shows a complete misunderstanding of both Stephen's and Shakespeare's sentiments.

Whether or not a reader finds Stephen's witticisms particularly amusing, the way Joyce uses Stephen's self-deprecation gives us a clearer picture of the struggle with ego and insecurity that is an essential part of his nature. Little things enforce this idea. In a preemptive gesture, Stephen imagines Mulligan's mockery over conveying Deasy's foot and mouth disease letter to newspaper editors: "Mulligan will dub me a new name: the bullock befriending bard" (2.430–431). In this easy, dismissive fashion Stephen announces that he is no longer intimidated by the thought of seeing his weaknesses exposed, and he uses a keen wit to anticipate and thereby blunt such criticism from others.

As he walks along Sandymount Strand in Proteus, Stephen is clearly in a more reflective frame of mind, yet he nevertheless shows an even greater willingness to lampoon his own pretentions. In a relentless, self-parodic dialectic with himself, he offers a witty interrogation of his artistic pretensions, as critical and as humorous as anything that Mulligan could devise:

> Reading two pages apiece of seven books every night, eh? I was young. You bowed to yourself in the mirror, stepping forward to applause earnestly, striking face. Hurray for the Goddamned idiot! Hray! No-one saw: tell no-one. Books you were going to write with letters for titles. Have you read his F?O yes, but I prefer Q. Yes, but W is wonderful. O yes, W. Remember your epiphanies written on green oval leaves, deeply deep, copies to be sent if you died to all the great libraries of the world, including Alexandria? Someone was to read them there after a few thousand years, a mahamanvantara. Pico della Mirandola like. Ay, very like a whale. When one reads these strange pages of one long gone one feels that one is at one with one who once [...] (3.136–146).

In this brief paragraph, Stephen lampoons his youthful ambitions, makes his erudition seem ridiculous, sneaks in a *Hamlet* reference, and parodies the stylistic techniques of pretentious critics even as he tacitly admits to seeking just the sort of praise that serves as the object of his derision.

At the same time, he does not limit his humor to self-flagellation. Earlier in the same episode Stephen also suggests that he has inherited his father's gift of mimicry—including the ability to imitate Simon's derisive language "O, weeping God, the things I married into" (3.67). In an extended account of a visit to his aunt and uncle's house in Strasbourg Terrane, he catches all of the idiosyncrasies that punctuate the discourses of his Uncle Richie and Cousin Walter. Stephen's mimicry is both critical and sympathetic, and it captures the humanity of both Richie and Walter—interspersed with evocations of Simon Dedalus' caustic perspective "Papa's little bedpal. Lump of love" (3.88)—with such dexterity that it can come as a minor shock to find that the entire comic episode took place in Stephen's imagination. "I have passed the way to aunt Sara's. Am I not going there? Seems not" (3.158–159).[5]

With all these changes, Stephen's humor remains understated, personal, and localized. On a visit to the offices of the *Freeman's Journal*, the editor, Myles Crawford, seeks to compliment Stephen by suggesting a career as a journalist. "I want you to write something for me, he said. Something with a bite in it. You can do it. I see it in your face" (7.616–617). For Stephen, who just spent an hour on Sandymount Strand obsessing about his future as a creative writer, the suggestion that he might become a newspaperman is at the very least unpleasant. In response he again invokes his gift for mimicry, but with a twist that will be repeated in the next chapter: "See it in your face. See it in your eye. Lazy idle little schemer" (7.616) recalls the language of Father Dolan in Chapter I of *A Portrait of the Artist as a Young Man* immediately before pandying the terrified Stephen. Crawford's affront is verbal and unintended, and Stephen's unvoiced response shows both the sting he feels and his skill at using irony to diffuse his lacerated feelings. Wit has become an internalized way of deflecting pain rather than an external demonstration of cleverness.

Later, in the Nationals Library of Ireland, Stephen now faces an openly hostile audience. A. E., John Eglinton, and—midway through the chapter—Buck Mulligan. They challenge Stephen's intellectual assumptions and the dexterity of his polemics not with the aim of finding greater insight in the topic under discussion but with the purpose of humiliation. His comebacks vary according to the person confronting him, and at times slip into unvoiced retorts that allow him to salvage self-esteem without giving offense to those who retain the power to impede his ambitions. In a range of examples over the course of the chapter, Stephen shows that along with his newly found capacity for self-criticism he retains a willing inclination for responding with ridicule when challenged.

The exchanges begin when Thomas Lyster, the "quaker librarian" makes an innocuous comment about Goethe. Stephen, in a gesture that suggests he is already feeling defensive, responds with insulting sarcasm that seems to tip well into rudeness: "Monsieur de la Palice [...] was alive fifteen minutes before his death" (7.16–17). The next example indicates that Stephen has cause to keep up his guard as AE tries to patronize him by deriding, before the talk has actually begun, the premise of Stephen's Shakespeare theory as akin to "the speculation of schoolboys for schoolboys" (7.53). Stephen tartly turns the words back on his critic: "The schoolmen were schoolboys first [...] Aristotle was once Plato's schoolboy" (7.56–57). Clearly, when Stephen now feels the criticism of others, he uses his wit to respond far more directly than he did as a young boy confronted by Vincent Heron.

Nonetheless, aware of the power they have over him, Stephen does not always choose to share all his cleverness with the other men gathered in the National Library. While talking to Eglinton, A. E., Best, and Lyster about Shakespeare's creative process in writing *Hamlet*, Stephen conducts a private conversation with himself, full of the same archness and talent for mimicry that he previewed in Proteus. Alternating between exaggerated Elizabethan language and the discourse of scholarly disputation, Stephen mixes references to *Hamlet* and recollections of his childhood experiences with echoes of Deasy's pedantic self-congratulation.

In one of the first of the chapter's inner dialogues, he uses a dialectic that recalls a debt to A. E., attempts to rationalize not repaying it, and then finally humorously accepts his obligation:

> How now, sirrah, that pound he lent you when you were hungry?
>
> * * *
>
> You spent most of it in Georgina Johnson's bed, clergyman's daughter.
> Agenbite of inwit.
> Do you intend to pay it back?
>
> * * *
>
> Wait. Five months. Molecules all change. I am other now. Other I got pound.
> Buzz. Buzz.
> But I, entelechy, form of forms, am I by memory because under everchanging forms.
> I that sinned and prayed and fasted.
> A child Conmee saved from pandies.
> I, I and I. I.
> A.E.I.O.U. (9.192–213)

For me this is a wonderful example of Joyce showing the complexity of Stephen's feelings while letting readers make of them what we will. The argument for avoiding repayment of a loan is clearly just rationalizing. The punning conclusion may seem to be feeble humor, but its tone, far more self-deprecating and less confrontational than in other instances, offers a nice contrast: Stephen defends his ideas publicly and wrestles with his faults in his musings.

Of course, he remains attentive to the usefulness of any of his private thoughts and shortly after the passage quoted above he deftly integrates the image of molecular change into his lecture as a response to the carping commentary of Eglinton: "As we, or mother Dana, weave and unweave our bodies, Stephen said, from day to day, their molecules shuttled to and fro, so does the artist weave and unweave his image" (9.376–378). In playing with the loosely applied imagery from the Celtic Revival and punning on the title of a journal that Eglinton edited, *Dana*, Stephen can toy with the twin concepts of flattery and mockery without seeming to compromise himself in either case.

When Mulligan abruptly appears in the librarian's office door Stephen's tone changes. His wit becomes introspective. Emphasizing self-consciousness over bravado, he silently and ponderously quotes King Ahab's response to the chastisement of the prophet Elijah: "Hast thou found me, O mine enemy?" (9.483).

Paradoxically, however, Mulligan begins with public praise for Stephen's wit by quoting his telegram—"*The sentimentalist is he who would enjoy without incurring the immense debtorship for the thing done*" (9.550–551, author's italics)—and then critiquing it. "O, you peerless mummer! O, your priestified, Kinchite" (9.554–555). However, despite this passing nod, Mulligan's bawdy humor, featuring speculation on the masturbatory habits of the Dublin literati, expels subtlety and dominates the remainder of the chapter's comic effusions.

The disquisition in the National Library proves to be the high point of Stephen's display of wit. After this episode, with the exception of a desultory exchange with his sister Dilly in Wandering Rocks (10.800–880), Stephen disappears from the narrative until the Oxen of the Sun episode. There, he has become young Boasthard oblivious to efforts by Bloom to calm him "for he had in his bosom a spike named Bitterness which could not by words be done away" (14.429–431). Drink has made Stephen sullen and has dulled every aspect of his humor. Language no longer serves as a shield from the criticism of others because alcohol has distorted his judgment and suppressed the discipline that wit always requires.

Stephen seems less defensive and a good bit more demonstrative in the Circe episode, but again his drunkenness, combined with the hallucinations which he experiences, make a great deal of his discourse only associatively intelligible. Whether chanting "the introit for paschal time" (15.74), performing a wild solo dance in the parlor of Bella Cohen's whorehouse (15.4121–4128), imaging an apparition of his dead mother (15.4147–4220) or blithely ignoring the menaces of Private Carr (15.4370–4750), Stephen has slipped into a world of self-amusement.

In Eumaeus, while Stephen seems to have a clearer sense of the world than he displayed in the previous chapter, an alcoholic fog still obscures his thoughts, and a sullenness creeps into his observations that corrodes whatever wit he attempts to express. When Stephen and Bloom encounter John Corley, reduced from the relative affluence of the *Dubliners* story "Two Gallants" to little more than an itinerant, Stephen tells him: "There'll be a job tomorrow or next day [...] in a boys' school at Dalkey for a gentleman usher. Mr Garret Deasy. Try it. You may mention my name" (16.157–159). Even Corley sees it as a ridiculous proposition, and we are left to wonder whether Stephen has temporarily lost his powers of concentration or if an incipient hangover has fanned a nasty impulse towards ridicule in his nature.

Later, in the cabman's shelter, with even less subtlety, Stephen abruptly cuts off conversation with Bloom: "We can't change the country. Let us change the subject" (16.1171). At this point in the narrative drink and exhaustion have blunted his wit and turned his humor to cruelty and rudeness. While these final examples offer little insight into the dexterity of Stephen's mind, they do give readers a sense of the meanness that can overtake him given the proper conditions.

In Stephen's last appearance, late at night in Bloom's kitchen, the question-and-answer format of Ithaca makes his sentiments nearly as difficult to follow as they were in Oxen of the Sun. Though slowly sobering up, his clumsy attempt at entertainment goes badly when he sings an anti-Semitic song about the murder of the young Harry Hughes. The appalling choice stands in contrast to his resistance to Deasy anti-Semitism in the Nestor episode. However, it is not that one gesture cancels the other but rather that, even making allowances for the dilatory effects his debauchery, Stephen's nature remains malleable and suggestable over the course of the narrative.

Admittedly, none of the examples that I have cited establish Stephen as one of the great fictional humorists or even as a popular amateur entertainer on the level of his father, Simon Dedalus, or his frenemy, Buck Mulligan. However, whether or not one judges Stephen as genuinely funny, his efforts reveal distinguishing features in his nature from the opening whimsicality of *A Portrait of the Artist as a Young Man* to the emotional exhaustion at the close of *Ulysses*. That is not to say that the two novels trace a metamorphosis in Stephen's character. Clearly, he has not ceased to be aloof, self-absorbed or thin-skinned, but the way he employs humor now also admits to a measure of vulnerability that makes his character much more accessible.

I think it useful in closing to recall, if only briefly, my point about how representations of Stephen illustrate the broader ambitions of Joyce's narrative. He shows us Stephen in a number of situations, revealing a range of attitudes, assumptions, and inclinations. Some are commendable. Some are deplorable. Yet all represent him as a figure worthy of the same sort of sympathy and understanding that we would wish for ourselves.

The distinguishing feature of Joyce's characterizations in *Ulysses* is not merely the gritty representation of humanity. Rather, he infuses his descriptions with a humane respect, highlighting complementary features of their natures that mitigate reader responses to their dominant attitudes. In this fashion representations of Bloom, Molly, Stephen, and even a number of the minor figures in the narrative capture the quotidian concerns of modern fiction trace the defining interest of contemporary society. This result is not merely a depiction of a paragon or even the representative "l'homme moyen sensual." Rather Joyce's characters encompass the spirit of the age by revealing their all too human natures, and in doing so they underscore the diverse features of their humanity that we cannot fail to recognize in ourselves.

Notes

1 Margot Norris and I are roughly contemporaries, and over that time we both thought, spoke, and wrote about James Joyce. During that period I have gained enormously from her invaluable insights into how a scholar engages the intellectual community, fosters her own ideas and those of others, and celebrates the joy and intensity that literature brings to us. From the superlative analyses of *The Decentered Universe of Finnegans Wake*, through her analysis of the deconstruction of Modernism in *Joyce's Web* and her marvelously oscillating sense of the possibilities of understanding the short fiction in *Suspicious Readings of Dubliners* to a stunning recollection of her scholarly engagement over the years in *Simply Joyce*, and of course with her scrupulous editing of the Norton Critical Edition of *Dubliners*, time and again she has personified the best elements of critical writing: insight, wit, and generosity. Margot's effect on Joyce studies has been like that of Bob Boyle or Walt Litz. They all have written brilliantly, but they have done so in ways that do not simply impose insights. Rather, they have made clear to the rest of us how many unique points of view Joyce's canon supports and how much great pleasure we can derive from engaging it. I am deeply grateful for all she has done for me, for my students, and for so many other Joyceans in making accessible to us with such marvelous clarity a sense of the depth, breadth, and delightfulness in all of Joyce's works. I am honored to participate in this tribute to her scholarly life.

2 For a detailed list, see Michael Patrick Gillespie, *James Joyce's Trieste Library: A Catalogue.* (Austin: Humanities Research Center, University of Texas, 1986), 38–42.

3 *A Portrait of the Artist as a Young Man*, ed. John Paul Riquelme. Norton Critical Edition. (New York: W.W. Norton, 2007), 5. All subsequent quotations are taken from this edition and appear in parenthesis in the body of the text.

4 James Joyce, *Ulysses.* Edited by Hans Walter Gabler with Wolfhard Steppe and Claus Melchior. (New York: Vintage Books, 1986), 1.01 &.08. I follow Gabler's citation suggestion: chapter number appears as an Arabic numeral, period, and the line numbers in Arabic follow. All subsequent quotations are taken from this edition and appear in parenthesis in the body of the text.

5 I must confess that the first time I read that passage, the verisimilitude of Stephen's description led me to the assumption that he actually was visiting the Goulding family, though I realize that may reveal as much about my abilities as a reader as it does about Stephen's talents as a mimic.

Chapter 13

CHANGING PERSPECTIVE: WHY STYLE AND STRUCTURE MATTER IN *ULYSSES*

Vicki Mahaffey

I would like to start by clarifying something about the nature of freedom, as Joyce was fighting for it. Joyce's main concern was not with freeing Ireland from British control, but with freeing the mind. As a writer, his technique for doing so was to challenge the (learned, socially conditioned) assumptions of his readers. As Stephen says in "Circe," pointing to his forehead, "In here it is I must kill the priest and the king."[1] And in his early essay "Ireland: Island of Saints and Sages," Joyce makes a related point about Catholicism, which enslaves the soul: "I do not see what good it does to fulminate against English tyranny while the tyranny of Rome still holds the dwelling place of the soul."[2] In 1967 in the U.S., Martin Luther King said something very similar: "As long as the mind is enslaved, the body can never be free."[3] In *Portrait*, the prequel to *Ulysses*, Stephen wonders in his youthfully superior idiom about freeing the minds and touching the conscience of "the patricians of Ireland" sitting in Maple's Hotel, along with their daughters: "How could he hit their conscience or how cast his shadow over the imaginations of their daughters, before their squires begat upon them, that they might breed a race less ignoble than their own?"[4] Stephen again expresses his determination to create a conscience for his compatriots at the end of the novel, when he vows to "encounter the reality of experience and to forge in the smithy of [his] soul the uncreated conscience of [his] race" (*P* 213).

In *Portrait*, Stephen is angry, seeing his contemporaries as ignoble and without a conscience. In *Ulysses*, though, haunted by the pathos of his mother's death and humbled by the pricks of his own conscience as he recalls his treatment of her, Stephen is trembling on the brink of greater self-awareness and concern for the other: "Pain, that was not *yet* the pain of love, fretted his heart" (*U* 1.102). He does not yet know how to do what Leopold

Bloom can do so admirably, or what Joyce positions the reader to do over and over in *Ulysses*: to look again, not only at the other but also at himself.

Ulysses teases its readers for hundreds of pages, prodding them with persistent playfulness to look again: to respect otherness as well as the self (literally look at it again); to revise assumptions (look again); to change perspective. To review what they've seen, or think they saw, from a different angle. To correct for the distortions of parallax. To adopt an unfamiliar point of view: not just once, but over and over again, throughout a day, a season, a year, a lifetime. Doing this can be exhausting, especially at first, but as it gets easier it becomes both revitalizing and funny. *Ulysses* is, after all, a comic novel, but it can only be experienced as such once the reader can feel that this is not a test, but an opportunity. Sometimes the process of learning to translate an ostensible test into an invitation (to increase mental and emotional agility) can take the whole novel, or a second reading (look again). And what stimulates it is Joyce's relentless array of narrative techniques all designed to restore flexibility to points of view that have become automatic, the results of social conditioning repeatedly reinforced over time. *Ulysses* takes aim at the well-worn grooves along which movements of the mind and heart have been taught to run.

Learning to practice respect is the most pressing challenge of our present moment. Lack of respect—or appreciation—for the autonomy and difference of the other is the heartbeat of racism, sexism, homophobia, and other social ills that have currently risen to critical levels.[5] One prerequisite for the desire to respect others (to want to take a second look, to challenge one's first impressions or question toxic generalizations) is curiosity. And curiosity, above all, is what makes Bloom heroic—not physical strength, youth, or a naïve disregard of danger (the usual attributes of a male hero).[6] It is often said that Bloom isn't the only character on an odyssey in *Ulysses*; the reader is also participating in one. Can he or she get home, to the "Ithaca" chapter and beyond? Will the reader make it to the end, or go the way of Odysseus' crew: overboard?

Let me do what I am advocating and change perspective by saying this another way, by approaching it from a different angle. Joyce is the most rhetorical of writers. By that, I mean he is always acutely, sometimes eerily, aware of the impact of his writing on the reader's expectations and probable reactions. How can he know what the reader will think or feel? Obviously, he cannot predict individual reactions, but he *can* predict conditioned ones, ones that are prompted by previous experience, habit, and expectation. Joyce's alchemy can work to transform the reader's consciousness and feeling[7] only if the reader is willing to participate in an imaginatively daring, active way. The reader is the *tertium quid*, the unidentified third thing amid two known ones (writer and text). How, then, does Joyce unsettle the reader's habitual and even mechanical way of understanding a text? To answer this, let me borrow an analogy from the game of pool: Joyce banks his shots. The shooter (here the writer) seems to be aiming at telling a given story, but the book is a means, not an end in itself. The story (or bank) is where Joyce directs the reader's gaze in order to put the ball—a transformed understanding or awareness—in the pocket, which is in a corner on the opposite side of the table. That pocket is the reader's mind and imagination; the method one of calculated indirection. The calculated indirection of the writer is designed to stimulate the reader to change perspectives, the way the ball on the pool table changes direction. My goal is to try to demonstrate exactly how this works and why it matters. Before I begin, I will say that Joyce has the same aim in all his books, but *Ulysses* is the one that has the greatest chance of succeeding. *Dubliners* and *A Portrait of the Artist* seem too familiar—why attempt to probe beneath the surface when the surface is clear enough?—and *Finnegans Wake* seems too strange (there isn't enough in it that is familiar for most readers to play along).

One of the ways Joyce banks his shots at the reader's minds is by bouncing each hour of the day off something from Homer's *Odyssey*. As Stephanie Nelson has argued, one of the unexpected parallels between Joyce and Homer has to do with the way that Homer highlights the difference in perspective between the gods and human beings. As she argues, in *Ulysses* the changing styles act as a hinge between two such perspectives: the diegetic and what might be described as a meta-perspective, the overarching plane of awareness on which the minds of author and reader may meet.[8]

The process of learning respect begins, perhaps unexpectedly, with respecting the self—learning to see oneself from a different angle. Joyce highlights his fiction's capacity to offer new opportunities for self-recognition by referring to them as mirrors (he calls *Dubliners* a nicely polished looking glass, whereas in *Ulysses* that looking glass is significantly cracked). As Bloom thinks in "Nausicaa," with a nod to Robert Burns, there is a value in "See[ing] ourselves as others see us" (*U* 13.1058). Joyce himself didn't yet have this ability to see himself objectively when he was writing the autobiographical, or more accurately hagiographical, *Stephen Hero*. He was doing as a writer what most readers do when they identify with the protagonist of a novel: he made himself the hero of his own story. That is the initial impulse of most people until they learn to look again. Stephen continues to lack accurate self-awareness throughout the books in which he appears, although he has periodic realizations (only in retrospect) that he has inflated his own importance.

In *Ulysses*, Stephen is just beginning to look at himself again, as is apparent when he thinks of his remorse of conscience through the Middle English phrase,

"Agenbite of inwit." He who wanted to forge a conscience for all his race is discovering that he himself has escaped the pangs of conscience. Seeing again here takes the form *biting* again, because when Stephen takes a second look (backward) at his behavior toward his mother, that new perspective is painful (and "agenbite," which sounds like "again bite," underscores the etymological meaning of "remorse," which means to bite again). Everyone wants to be a hero, and secretly fears being a schmuck, a failure, a loser, or simply ordinary. Literature panders to this desire-cum-denial, with this drive to categorize oneself once and for all in a reassuring and even flattering, non-contradictory way. Joyce seems to have learned this from Oscar Wilde, who wrote that "It is the spectator, not life, that art really mirrors." (Wilde also called the dislike of realism "The rage of Caliban at seeing his face in a mirror"—thoughtless readers are here portrayed as Calibans who only want to see an image of themselves that flatters).[9] The irony of readers not seeing themselves reflected by what they read reaches back to Jonathan Swift, who wrote that "Satire is a sort of glass, wherein beholders do generally discover everybody's face but their own."[10]

Joyce learned to "look again" at his narcissistic self-portraits by revising. He was not only a writer but also his own first reader, able (in retrospect) to see in the mirror of his fiction the youthful frailties partly concealed beneath the mask of egotism: self-absorption, lack of compassion, ruthlessness of purpose. He used that recognition to anticipate what readers would do—to look for heroes that they could use as masks for themselves, to conceal disavowed psychic and social blemishes—and then to frustrate that desire by giving them dynamic, inconsistent characters who were admirable in some ways and flawed in others.

Here we get to the trickiest part of the argument, which is my claim that the stereotyping, categorizing, and hierarchical valuing of *groups* of people that we know as racism, sexism, etc., begins with an oversimplified, wishful elevation of the self, as if the self were only one thing and were capable of being stamped and graded, like eggs or meat. This is a view that angered the young Joyce and amused the older one, and it is a view that much literature panders to by allowing readers to identify with a narrator who has neatly ordered the past in a "retrospective arrangement."[11] I propose that the impulse to oversimplify or categorize other people and to classify and rank them is rooted in a wishful oversimplification of oneself, the desire to view the self as a hero. Joyce tries to disrupt this understandable preference for an idealized self-image by cracking the mirror of his art: the image of the spectator that it reflects is imperfect. And the person who "owns" this looking glass—the writer—is not himself a master but a servant. He is a servant not only to the British state and the Holy Roman Catholic and Apostolic Church, but to the reader, who often, at least initially, declines his service, misreading it as Joyce's assertion of "superiority."[12]

The first challenge, then, is for readers to change their perspective when looking at their own image as it is reflected in the cracked mirror of Joyce's art: to see themselves as flawed, but not without value, and as capable of learning. This is how we are asked to see the characters in *Ulysses*: not as heroes, not as villains, but as human works in progress. They have surprising and sometimes wonderful capabilities, and they also have blind spots, along with other characteristics that readers may find repellant. In my teaching of *Ulysses* this past year, I encountered several students who were vocally disgusted by Bloom's masturbation in "Nausicaa." They insisted it was "public" because it occurred in the open, on a beach. Never mind that it was dark enough to see fireworks and that Bloom's hand was discreetly in his pocket and the beach was almost empty and that Gerty half-consciously participated by swinging her leg. The point is not whether someone is disgusted by Bloom's release or glad that he was able to find some relief on an emotionally trying day: the point is that one or more of Bloom's activities is bound to disgust *someone*. That is intentional, because readers will see the protagonist as a reflection of themselves.

Many readers object to the detailed description of Bloom's trip to the outhouse in "Calypso." What they are actually objecting to is the solicitation to accept, with full sensual and cognitive awareness, the fact that they too defecate, which is only seldom integrated into the typically airbrushed self-image.[13] Others call Bloom a "wimp" for not going home and forbidding Molly to see Boylan, or for not interrupting their tryst; instead, he sits in the Ormond Hotel listening to songs that inspire self-pity. Some readers dislike Bloom's masochistic tendencies. Others object to his voyeuristic interest in other women. Or his status as a cuckold. There are readers who might not be delighted by Bloom's perceived "foreignness" (although he was born in Ireland, his family is Hungarian) or his perceived "Jewishness" (his father was Jewish). What matters is that Bloom—like most people—is a heterogenous collection of attributes and tendencies. Joyce described him to his friend Frank Budgen as "an all-round man" and a "good man." One must look at Bloom from all sides to really see him, and this is also, by extension, a model of how one should regard oneself: as three-dimensional but always changing, shot through with great potential in some areas and capable of stupidity and error in others. What makes Bloom ultimately a good man is his ability to do exactly that: to change perspective. His habit of considering matters "on the one hand" and "on the other hand" that the unnamed narrator of the "Cyclops" episode lampoons is what makes him both admirable and capable of learning. I am always particularly struck by what Bloom thinks when he passes a sex worker: it must be hard for someone new to the trade to experience so many rejections before she gets hardened. Instead of looking down on a woman because she is selling herself, he imagines what it must be like to be a rookie in her position.

We could read Stephen and Molly the same way, by identifying their unique talents as well as their limitations without excising the aspects of them that some readers will find repellant: Molly's adultery, Stephen's lice; Stephen's egghead thoughts while picking his nose and taking a leak in "Proteus"; Molly's desire to take the cock of a statue of Narcissus in her mouth or have sex with a priest. It takes an effort to integrate these qualities—not usually narrated in literature, let alone a book that was considered the most important book of the twentieth century—with the same characters' unique and extraordinary talents: Stephen's facility with language or his brilliant reading of Shakespeare (that his listeners are determined to resist and do not make an intellectually generous attempt to understand). Molly's wit, facilitated by the deficiencies of her education, such as when she calls Ben Dollard a "base barreltone" instead of a "bass baritone" (*U* 18.1285). Or Molly's ability to sustain her appreciation for Bloom's sensitivity and openness only hours after her sexual liaison with another man. For most readers, this operation of keeping all these contractions alive in their minds and hearts is extremely difficult. But when one learns to do it, one enters the world of the comic, which "delights in the self-contradictory."[14]

The sheer difficulty of shifting perspectives is counterbalanced, then, by the playfulness and humor of splitting people into their dynamic component parts. Joyce displays this by the way he verbally disarticulates the body in the "Sirens" episode. Characters are identified less frequently by pronouns that reinforce the impression of their unity ("he" or "she") and more by the piece of themselves that is involved in a given action.[15] In place of "Miss Douce said" we get "miss Douce's wet lips said" (*U* 11.72). She is next identified with her hair color, which also suggests the metal of a musical instrument: "A haughty bronze replied" (*U* 11.97). The boots, employed by the hotel, becomes the boots he is responsible for cleaning: "loud boots unmannerly asked," and even "bootsnout" (*U* 11.94, 100). Instead of Miss Kennedy, we are presented with her throat, from which laughter springs like a living animal: "Shrill shriek of laughter sprang from miss Kennedy's throat" (*U* 11.143). Miss Kennedy is split into her voice and gaze: "Miss voice of Kennedy" and "Miss gaze of Kennedy" (*U* 11.237, 240). Miss Douce is dismembered in Lenehan's eyes; he sees "bronze's teabathed lips," "listening lips and eyes" (*U* 11.266). Later, "Shebronze [...] syrupped with her voice" (*U* 11.365–6]. After she snaps her garter for him, Boylan becomes all "spellbound eyes" and "fat lips" (*U* 11.420, 419). There are dozens of examples of body parts acting with unexpected autonomy, splintering the coherence of the imagined self. In "Circe," even objects join the fun, such as when Lynch's cap speaks and the soap Bloom bought sings to him from the sky to which it has risen in place of the sun.

The self is recast as a multiplicity of moving parts, like the body, from which the illusion of personal unity arguably originated. If we exaggerate and extrapolate this idea of individual multiplicity, it becomes more apparent how Bloom can come to represent the entire city of Dublin. Another way Joyce splits the self-conception (or cracks the mirror into which the reader peers) is through the use of a triple protagonist, with the narrative emphasis moving from one to each of the others in succession. The fact that there are three protagonists is essential to the perspective-changing technique of *Ulysses*. (Woolf does something similar a few years later when she gives *Mrs. Dalloway* a double protagonist in Clarissa and Septimus.) Most readers turn with relief from Stephen's picturing of what happens to the penis of a drowned man as "A quiver of minnows, fat of a spongy titbit, flash through the slits of his buttoned trouserfly" (*U* 3.475–6) to Bloom's preparation of breakfast in the "gelid light" of his kitchen. Significantly, though, the first thing Bloom does is change the perspective on himself by envisioning himself from the perspective of his cat. "Wonder what I look like to her. Height of a tower? No, she can jump me." (*U* 4.28–9). Readers may have more difficulty moving from the lyrical description of Bloom's loss of consciousness in bed, "the childman weary, the manchild in the womb" (*U* 17.2317–18) to the beginning of Molly's mental soliloquy, if only because of the lack of punctuation in her run-on multi-page sentences and the ambiguity of her pronouns. The radically different style of "Penelope" once again forces a change in perspective. This shift brings with it a solicitation to transfer our narrative allegiance to someone whose actions we may have heretofore seen primarily as unfaithful and hurtful.

The shock of changing perspective, of being prodded to alter our imaginative allegiance, is something readers experience more and more frequently as *Ulysses* progresses and June 16, 1904 wears on: the styles become increasingly intrusive and disruptive, forcing the reader not only to change points of view *between* episodes but also *within* them. There are the "wandering sentences" in "Wandering Rocks" and the two narrators of "Cyclops": the deflating oral narrator who is periodically interrupted by inflating, stylistically varied, written interpolations. "Nausicaa" switches from a narrative that imitates Gerty's self-elevating mode of thinking to the post-orgasmic, uncompromising realism of Bloom's thoughts. Worst of all for most readers is "Oxen of the Sun," with its parodies of many different narrative styles representing the evolution of English prose. There is "Ithaca's" question and answer format, with its dispassionate precision, strikingly at odds with a heartbreaking homecoming to a bed so recently utilized by another man. Increasingly, more attention is being drawn to the mode of narration than to the diegetic features of the story readers thought they were following, because the real focus of *Ulysses* is to make us conscious of the lenses through which we see everything. Every lens is a distortion, which is why we need many of them to construct a more comprehensive view.

The reader's perspective is further fractured and/or multiplied not only by the episodic structure, but by each episode's connection to the *Odyssey*. What do the Odyssean parallels do to the experience of reading the book? It is certainly possible to read without them, and I have several colleagues who insist, with Ezra Pound, that the parallels to the *Odyssey* simply served Joyce as a scaffolding on which to build the book, to be kicked away when it was finished. Adopting this perspective impoverishes the experience of reading the book by depriving the reader of another way to change perspective.

To appreciate the technical brilliance of Joyce's use of the Homeric parallels, it is helpful if we refer back to features of his earlier books. Joyce knew, from the very beginning of his writing career, how fiendishly difficult it is for readers to wean themselves away from the perspective of the narrator or protagonist, and to do so while retaining the ability to sympathize with him or her. How can you stimulate a reader to want to see more than the character being depicted does? The stories in *Dubliners* aren't difficult to follow, but they can be difficult to appreciate, difficult to interpret, for the simple reason that readers aren't typically in the habit of trying to see more than the characters do, or more than the narrator tells them. Joyce helped them by framing the collection with a boy (in "An Encounter" and "Araby") and Gabriel (in "The Dead") who are briefly able to change the angle at which they see themselves. This ability is rare, and its effects can be fleeting. Most of the characters in *Dubliners* never accomplish it, and most readers don't know how to get beyond what those characters can see. This makes the collection feel depressing, but to say that it is depressing to read *Dubliners* is like saying it is depressing to be a doctor because you see so much disease. The point of *Dubliners* is not the disease itself, the imaginative impoverishment of the characters and their lack of self-awareness, but the implied invitation to readers to look more deeply at their own plight and to look more broadly for what they might be missing.

A Portrait of the Artist as a Young Man presents readers with a similar but arguably even more formidable challenge. Once again, it is easy to see what is happening, but difficult to see its significance, to chart its implications. That is because Joyce doesn't package and deliver the meaning along with the story but invites the reader to (re)construct it. And to do that, the reader must learn to read on two different levels, one that imaginatively and empathetically identifies with the protagonist (here Stephen) and one that ranges beyond Stephen's limitations, learning to access a perspective he cannot yet attain. How can a writer stimulate that response in a reader?

By inspiring a change of perspective. In *Dubliners*, Joyce used music to do this, alluding to songs to provide an emotional soundtrack to what could otherwise easily seem like a dispassionate critique. Joyce continued to use musical allusions, but when he scrapped *Stephen Hero* to write *Portrait* he found something that would work intellectually as well as emotionally: allusion to a "metanarrative." In *Portrait*, the main metanarrative is provided by Stephen's surname in combination with the epigraph: the story of Daedalus from Ovid. When the reader measures the story of Daedalus and Icarus against Stephen's perspective of himself as a great artist and inventor (Daedalus), it gives the reader access to another interpretive possibility than the one Stephen has claimed for himself: he *could* be Daedalus, and he could also be Icarus. He could have done something extraordinary, or he might be flying too high, the prelude to a fall. This is an example of a banked shot: by directing the reader's attention to another story, Stephen's version of his own story is called into question: not dismantled, exactly, but no longer certain, as it is in Stephen's own mind.

In *Ulysses*, Joyce went on to use a similar technique, but he deployed it in much more intricate ways. The episodes of the *Odyssey* work roughly the way the Daedalus story did in *Portrait*, except that the characters are unconscious of any parallels. All the Homeric chapter titles were removed before publication, and there is no epigraph. Instead, there is only the title—*Ulysses*—to point to a metanarrative. It seems to refer to the *Odyssey*, and for the most part it does, but even the allusion to Homer is routed through Dante, because "Ulysses" is the form of the name used in the *Inferno*. In the *Inferno*, Ulysses has been relegated to hell, with Diomedes. One man's hero can be another man's villain. As is the case with Bloom, the polytropic Odysseus has an admixture of qualities that can make him heroic from one perspective and culpable (or damned, mostly for the death of his crew) from another.

A few examples help to show how the Homeric parallels draw the reader's attention to richer modes of interpretation that those that could be drawn from the story itself. One of my favorites is "Calypso," because without the Homeric parallel it is almost impossible to realize that Bloom, like Odysseus at the outset of his odyssey, is being held captive by a goddess, who can be identified if we read the details of the episode against the story of Odysseus's captivity. Bloom's Calypso is an idealized image of Molly, drawn from memory but airbrushed into a slimmer, divine, and naked version of her as a Greek nymph cut out of the magazine *Photo Bits*. If Bloom is to make it "home" to the present moment, with all of its potential and humiliation, he has to escape from this idealized image, which is framed and hung above his bed, titled "The Bath of the Nymph." This is the nymph who will try to kill Bloom in "Circe," motivated by anger when he is no longer cowed by her claims of purity. Bloom tells her, after his trouser button bips, "You have broken the spell [...] If there were only ethereal where would you all be, postulants and novices?" (*U* 15.3449 500). The nymph then strikes at Bloom's loins with a poniard but he seizes her hand, calling for fair play, which causes her plaster cast to crack, allowing her hidden stench to escape: "Rut. Onions. Stale. Sulphur. Grease" (*U* 15. 3477–8). The nymph is unveiled as a whited sepulcher, subsequently replaced by Bella Cohen (the opposite, whorish version of Molly) saying, "You'll know me the next time."

Another particularly revealing parallel is the one drawn to Scylla and Charybdis in the library episode. The Scylla of the episode is Aristotle (championed at first by Stephen), whereas the Charybdis is Plato (represented by George Russell, oracling out of his shadow). Gradually, however, the attentive reader is prodded to realize that the most important point about Scylla and Charybdis in the *Odyssey* is not only that they are structural opposites (one an upward-tending rock, the other a downward-tending whirlpool), both deadly. It is that Odysseus ends up encountering *both* of them, at different times. He has experienced or encompassed opposite extremes over the course of his odyssey, a feat that Joyce attributes to relatively few people (or characters) in his schema for the episode: Socrates, Odysseus, Shakespeare, Jesus. Half of these people were executed (and one sent to hell). By implication, it is a mark of genius to refuse to take sides unilaterally, instead experiencing mutually exclusive perspectives, but it is also intensely dangerous, even lethal.

When Joyce pops the reader up from Stephen's exposition of his Shakespeare theory to what he called the "splendid parable" of Scylla and Charybdis in the *Odyssey*, he gives the reader another perspective for appreciating Stephen, who is able to move from adopting an Aristotelian perspective ("Hold to the now, the here, from which all future plunges to the past," *U* 9.89) to a more transcendent or Platonic one in response to Mulligan's overly literal jokes about masturbation as "a honeymoon in the hand." Stephen may be Telemachus in many respects, but intellectually he is capable of Odyssean adaptability. He is his (ghostly) father's son.

If we turn to the "Oxen of the Sun" episode of *Ulysses*, we can see how a knowledge of the Homeric parallel again makes new interpretive possibilities available. Bloom has gone to the Rotunda, a maternity hospital, to inquire about the labor of Mina Purefoy, a woman who is enduring the third day of unanesthetized labor before the birth of her ninth child. Bloom is sympathetic, solicitous. We are told, in Anglo-Saxon alliterative prose, that a man stood at the door of "the high sunbright wellbuilt fair home of mothers" at night's oncoming. We realize it is Bloom: "Of Israel's folk was that man that on earth wandering far had fared. Stark ruth of man his errand that him lone led until that house." (*U* 14. 68–9, 72–3). Bloom is concerned: "he felt with wonder women's woe in the travail they have of motherhood" (*U* 14. 119–20). In the background we may recall the loss of his own son 11 days after his birth, 11 years earlier. Through the unfamiliar but often beautiful locutions of early English prose we learn that Mrs. Purefoy is suffering, but a group of male med students are loudly carousing in a nearby room, fantasizing about impregnating as many women as possible. Stephen is among them; Bloom joins them. As the styles of English prose evolve through time, the spotlight of narrative attention shifts, moving from the magic of glasses blown out of molten sand though gothic terrors and opium dreams and the hidden fears of both Bloom and Stephen as they contemplate their respective failures to reproduce (a son and a work of literature, respectively). Eventually, Mrs. Purefoy gives birth, and it is to a son. The males make their way to a pub to celebrate, and the episode ends in an orgy of broken, drunken sounds—an almost incomprehensible jumble of patois.

What is the episode about, though? In the schema, Joyce identifies the crime against the Oxen of the Sun as being the breaking of a vow. What vow? Who are the oxen of the sun? Who are the murderous crewmembers? It is important to remember that, as always, the Homeric parallel is not the key to an allegory; there is never a simple one-to-one correspondence between the different players in the *Odyssey* and *Ulysses*. But the minute we re-spect or re-view the story from the perspective of its Homeric metanarrative, the interpretive possibilities multiply. The oxen of the sun could be women—the sacred cows that men repeatedly sacrifice against all warnings. They can also be babies, if we read "sun" as "son." Killing the sacred oxen can refer to the "sin" of contraception, violating the dictates of the sacred Catholic church. (It may or may not be relevant that during the Renaissance condoms were made of animal bladders or intestines, usually those of sheep, but sometimes cows.) If the killing of the oxen is comparable to the breaking of a vow, could the crime anticipate that of a "good" Catholic husband who chooses to follow the teachings of the church by saving the baby rather than his wife if both are in danger? It isn't just the Homeric parallel that changes a reader's perspective in "Oxen." One of the reasons it is considered the most challenging episode to read is that the reader keeps moving through centuries via the changes of style.

So, why is it important to change perspectives as we read? To some extent, all fiction solicits readers to do this: the imaginative world being entered offers a new perspective from the outset. To the extent that readers see through the eyes of different characters, each of their points of view constitutes a different perspective. What Joyce understood is that an omniscient narrator governs, reconciles, unifies these different perspectives, which leaves us ultimately with that narrator's point of view. There is value in entertaining a narrator's perspective, but the imaginative challenge is a relatively simple one, and the reader's experience of the narrator's perspective is often limited to the time actually spent reading that book. Joyce had a much more ambitious goal for literature: to redesign it so that the reader is repeatedly, frequently jolted into changing his or her point of view. In *Ulysses*, this must be done every hour of the day, or even more frequently as the day wears on. When we change our perspective, it calls our assumptions of what is normal and universal into question. Kind of like a pandemic on a much smaller scale. We see with a thousand eyes.

Joyce pricks his readers to experience a more imaginatively attuned concern for the Other. This is perhaps the most important imperative of our time. Practicing changes of perspective wouldn't magically eliminate poverty, racism, homophobia, or sexism, because all of these have deep-rooted structural components that are long established in our society, but it *could* reduce hate crimes. For a writer or a reader, being imaginatively attuned to the other means having the flexibility to change positions—for the writer to imagine being the reader, for the reader to imagine being the writer. This exchange of roles can only happen, though, if the reader is willing to acknowledge and attempt to revise the heroic story he or she is expecting to read and identify with. Recognition of the other as a complex, promising, flawed collection of possibilities and past actions is only possible if one can forgo the desire to encounter only self-flattering reflections of the self. It is all too easy to see the mote in the other fellow's eye and not see the beam in one's own. As Jesus put it in the sermon on the mount (King James version), a passage Joyce alludes to in "Cyclops": "Thou hypocrite, first cast out the beam out of thine own eye; and then shalt thou see clearly to cast out the mote out of thy brother's eye" (Matthew 7:5).

Ulysses, however, is not a sermon. It is a comedy, one in which the humor begins with the reader—with the reader's ability to laugh at himself. *Ulysses* is comic *because* comedy is predicated on radical equality.

The biggest and most common mistake readers make about *Ulysses* is to see it as the work of a virtuoso: a lengthy display of Joyce's stylistic and linguistic mastery, practiced at their expense. Such readers fail to appreciate the rhetorical purpose served by the multiple stylistic devices Joyce uses to prompt readers to learn to change perspective. We can see traces of Joyce's disappointment over the reception of *Ulysses* in *Finnegans Wake*, where he refers to it as the "usylessly unreadable blue book of Eccles." But it is helpful in this context to remember another of Oscar Wilde's one-liners: "What do we mean when we say something is unreadable? We mean that it is new." *Ulysses* was written in an extravagantly, comically, uproariously egalitarian spirit. It is at war with mastery *and* with slavery. Joyce, like Stephen, would not be the master of others nor their slave, and he invites his readers to join him.

The value Joyce placed on changing perspective, and on crafting fiction that spurs readers to abandon their own heroic self-narratives in order to see with both compassion and accuracy the yearnings and limitations of others, is something that Margot Norris illustrated in the 1980s with successive game-changing readings of two stories from *Dubliners*. The first, "Narration under a Blindfold: Reading Joyce's 'Clay'" (1987),[16] startlingly revealed something that critics had missed for over 50 years: that the narrator of "Clay" had adopted Maria's own wishful, self-aggrandizing perspective, designed to compensate for her social insignificance as "a poor old woman without family, wealth, or social standing."[17] Maria's narrator represents an "objective" voice telling a flattering story about her to compensate for the grim truth she understandably finds it difficult to face.

Joyce, I argue, does not promote the old maid to metaphoric status as much as he explores her need, and her strategies, for promoting herself. These strategies are narrational and rhetorical, as "Clay" becomes her defense against all the derision and contempt she has internalized from those around her.[18] Norris goes on to demonstrate how the reader becomes "a critical actor in the story"[19] whose response to the narrator's "self-defense" reinforces the fact that the origin of her shame (and attempted self-aggrandizement) is social, and that the social devaluation of unmarried women contributes to the (unrealistic) psychological compensation of the woman who is thereby devalued. In the language of the essay, "narrative speech in 'Clay' is mostly uttered in the language of Maria's desire; it is Maria's desire speaking" [trying to restore her significance]. Norris is describing what I have called a "banked shot": the narrative is "putatively directed toward us, to tell us about Maria, but its true beneficiary is Maria herself, whose prestige is being 'recognized' by objective and autonomous 'others.'" The next twist implicates the reader in Maria's plight, as "the text reflect[s] the reader's smug superiority like a mirror." The reader's defection from the rhetorical program is coaxed, then implicitly judged. In the end, the reader of 'Clay' is read by the text.[20]

The reader, Norris shows, is complicit with the social structure that turns people into caricatures who can be easily sorted: Maria must either be the independent, tidy woman she imagines herself to be or a witch, unattractive and desperate to attain the attributes that give women meaning or value in society. The text traps the reader into complicity with the system that presents these alternatives as mutually exclusive, while introducing gaps and silences that allow us to see the text differently, as a criticism of the way social values insinuate themselves into the psyches of its members, including our own. Does Maria touch "clay," as the title suggests, or shit? Is clay the narrator's euphemism for what Maria actually chooses, not just the earth that suggests her death, but excrement, a representation of her own worthlessness?

Margot Norris deftly changed the critical perspective on Joyce's point of view in these stories in a single stroke. She disclosed a partially occluded subtext in Joyce's writing, one that operates both as social critique and psychological interrogation. The reader, conditioned to trust the narrative voice as objective, gets tricked into making assumptions that preclude deeper investigation, unconsciously filling in the gaps in the narrative in order to fulfill prior expectations.

Two years later, Norris turned to "The Dead," revealing how the Morkans' party is designed to operate by the same rules of normative social behavior and discourse that have stifled the lives of the three sisters, along with most of their objections, although to a lesser degree than it constrains the lives of those who are oppressed by class or race as well as sex (such as Lily or the black tenor at the Gaiety theatre).[21] She argues that "Joyce dramatizes in 'The Dead' the politics of art's determination to conceal its own politically oppressive functions,"[22] objections to the status quo that in the story are all female. The "ubiquitous oppression of women is both blatant and discounted, unmistakable and invisible at the same time,"[23] and the conventions of art make it complicit with such politics. Norris highlights the crucial distinction between what a text says and what the author means,[24] arguing that Joyce's meaning is subversive in ways that most critics had overlooked. Focusing on Gabriel's question to himself about what a woman symbolizes, Norris offers Joyce's tacit answer, which differs significantly from Gabriel's: "when woman is transformed into a symbol by man, woman becomes a symbol of her social detextualization, her silencing, the occlusion of her suffering, the suppression of her feeling."[25] Woman is a central locus for the political unconscious of a society. Her thoughts and feelings provide the subtext which is also the implicit meaning of the story. Norris is particularly insightful about the (easily discounted) beauty of Aunt Julia's singing: "Joyce embeds in 'The Dead' itself a kind of shadow text, a counternarrative that provides a 'back answer' or articulation of Julia's grievances, a complaint necessary for the critique of the social function of art to be heard."[26] She importantly insists that "art reproduces political ideology and social relations,"[27] that it "is the product of social forces that operate on the same principles of privilege and exclusion that categories such as gender, race, class, and age produce in other areas of social and cultural life."[28] Implicitly, this is why Joyce's art is different: on the surface, it beckons the reader to do what art usually does, to seduce the reader into feeling superior to the characters, especially women (as Gabriel does). But it does this with a fiendishly subtle irony. Readers willing to dig beneath the surface will find there a set of radically egalitarian values, a change of perspective comparable to that advocated by the historical Jesus. Jesus, who flouted contemporary

Jewish law by touching menstruating or adulterous women and Samaritans, advocated love for all others, reserving intolerance for those who abused their privilege. Like Dante, he understood Christianity as a divine comedy, fiercely egalitarian and just as fiercely at war with the world as it stands. Such a change of perspective helps to illuminate why Joyce gave his Odyssey a Jewish (or half-Jewish) hero who is not heroic in any of the conventional ways, and why he celebrated his masculinity as leavened with womanliness. Like Ibsen, as Joyce described him, Bloom is not simply a man, but has a "curious admixture of the woman about him."[29] The cracked looking glass would fracture (and mar) not only the viewer's self-image, but also the artificially exclusive categories of identity.

Notes

1 James Joyce, *Ulysses*, ed. Hans Walter Gabler with Wolfhard Steppe and Claus Melchior (New York: Random-Vintage, 1986), episode 15, lines 4436-7. Hereafter cited in the text as *U* followed by the episode and line numbers.

2 In James Joyce, *Occasional, Critical, and Political Writing*, ed. Kevin Barry (Oxford: Oxford University Press, 2000), 125.

3 Martin Luther King, Jr., "Where Do We Go from Here?," address delivered at the Eleventh Annual SCLC Convention, April 16, 1967, The Martin Luther King, Jr. Research and Education Institute, Stanford University, available at kinginstitute.stanford.edu/king-papers/documents/where-do-we-go-from-here-address-delivered-eleventh-annual-sclc-convention.

4 James Joyce, *A Portrait of the Artist as a Young Man*, ed. Jeri Johnson (Oxford: Oxford University Press, 2000), p. 200. Hereafter parenthetically cited in the text as *P* followed by the page number.

5 Ibram X. Kendi argues that what precludes such respect is not primarily hate, but self-interest. *How to Be an Anti-Racist* (New York: One World, 2019), 42.

6 For an account of how Joyce positions his protagonists against conventional models of heroism, see my "*Ulysses* and the End of Gender," in *A Companion to James Joyce's* Ulysses (Case Studies in Contemporary Criticism), ed. Margot Norris (New York: Bedford Books, 1998): 151–68. Republished in *European Joyce Studies*, 10: *Masculinities in Joyce*, ed. Christine Van Boheemen and Collen Lamos (Amsterdam: Rodopi, 2001): 137–62.

7 Joyce himself refers to his writing as attempted alchemy in *Finnegans Wake*, when he describes the semi-autobiographical artist figure, Shem the Penman, as the "first till last alchemist" (*FW* 185.25). See Barbara DiBernard, "Alchemy in *Finnegans Wake*," *JJQ* 14 (Spring 1977), pp. 274–89, for a fuller account of his use of the metaphor. She also published a book on the subject: *Alchemy and* Finnegans Wake (SUNY Press, 1980).

8 See Stephanie Nelson, *Time and Identity in* Ulysses *and the* Odyssey (Gainesville, University of Florida Press, 2022), especially the last chapter.

9 Oscar Wilde, "Preface," *The Picture of Dorian Gray*.

10 Jonathan Swift, *The Battle of the Books* (1704), preface.

11 This phrase is one of Tom Kernan's elaborate locutions that Bloom first recalls in the "Hades" episode (*U* 6.150). The phrase occurs seven times in *Ulysses*.

12 See *U* 1.636–44. I am suggesting that Stephen's insistence to Haines that he is a double or triple servant, not a master, also characterizes Joyce's experience as a writer.

13 Joyce's technique here recalls Jonathan Swift's poem "The Lady's Dressing Room," in which a lover steals into his beloved Celia's dressing room and discovers everything she conceals to produce her image as a goddess. The lover is disgusted, repeating in amorous fits "Oh! Celia, Celia, Celia shits!" and he subsequently recoils from the hidden foulness of all women. The narrator takes a different attitude. He pities the disillusioned lover, contrasting Strephon's revulsion with his own appreciation for the whole reality of women. He "bless[es] his ravished sight to see/ Such order from confusion sprung, / Such gaudy tulips raised from dung."

14 Stephanie Nelson, *Aristophanes and His Tragic Muse: Comedy, Tragedy and the Polis in 5th Century Athens* (Leiden: Brill, 2016), 14.

15 The best critical treatment of this phenomenon is Derek Attridge's section on "Lipspeech" in *Peculiar Language: Literature as Difference from the Renaissance to James Joyce* (Ithaca: Cornell University Press, 1988), 160–72.

16 *PMLA* 102 (March 1987), 206–15.

17 Ibid., 206.

18 Ibid., 206–7.

19 Ibid., 207.

20 Ibid.

21 Margot Norris, "'Stifled Back Answers': The Gender Politics of Art in 'The Dead,'" *Modern Fiction Studies*, vol. 35 (Autumn 1989), 479–503.

22 Ibid., 480.

23 Ibid., 482.

24 Ibid., 481.

25 Ibid., 483.

26 Ibid., 492.

27 Ibid., 501.

28 Ibid., 502.

29 In "Ibsen's New Drama," Joyce says of Ibsen that "there is a curious admixture of the woman in his nature" (*CW* 64).

Part VI

Possible Worlds

Chapter 14

HOBGOBLINS IN DUBLIN: JOYCE'S "CIRCE" AND THE WORLD OF THE WORK

Gregory Castle

The idea that literature transports readers to another place, a world apart from the one in which they live and breathe, has long been supported by anecdotal evidence. Narrative theorists have, since the 1990s, been trying to understand and codify this feeling of occupying, for however long a time, a world that seems to emerge out of the text itself. Drawing on semantic theory, analytic philosophy and the philosophy of logic, theorists such as Lubomir Doležel and Marie-Laure Ryan have developed sophisticated tools for describing literary worlds. Their approach, possible worlds theory, requires the reader to negotiate among different kinds of worlds. Doležel draws a distinction between a *possible world*, one "that is thinkable," and an *impossible world*, one "that contains or implies a logical contradiction."[1] The emphasis on the "thinkable" refers to the foundations of possible-worlds theory in semantics, philosophy, natural science, historiography, and fiction. Doležel writes that "[f]or various cognitive aims various kinds of possible worlds can be stipulated."[2] "Thinkable" fictional worlds differ from the other kinds, primarily on the basis of "truth conditions." Semantic, logical, scientific, and historical discourses are *world-imagining*, while fictional discourse is *world-constructing*; the former, "as representations of the actual world[,] are subject to truth-valuation"; the latter, is "outside truth-valuation," because fictional sentences "are neither true nor false."[3] Fictional worlds cannot be inhabited by the reader, according to Doležel; however "[a]ctual persons, authors and readers" who wish to cross "the world boundary between the realms of the actual and possible"[4] can find access through the very material of textual art. One starts with "semiotics and text theory," for "fictional worlds are accessed through semiotic channels and by means of information processing."[5]

Ryan's study of possible worlds depends, like Doležel's, on semantic theory and philosophy of logic. The difference is largely a matter of emphasis; while Doležel considers fictionality and fictional worlds ("narrative macrostructures"[6]), Ryan is more interested in narrativity as such and the broader range of possible worlds that arise out of narrative forms. Her work is interdisciplinary, "a perspective which may be called semiotic, since [her] approach is largely formalist, and [her] concern is signification in all kinds of texts, not just in literary ones."[7] From this perspective, "possibility is synonymous with accessibility: a world is possible in a system of reality if it is accessible from the world at the center of the system."[8] The text, fictional or otherwise, projects an "image of a system of reality" that constitutes the "textual universe." The actual world at the center of the system forms a "textual reference world [...] [t]he world for which the text claims facts."[9] The "textual actual world" is the image in the text of this reference world, "a textual representation of the world external to itself."[10] Ryan helpfully offers a way of understanding this constellation or collision of worlds based on the types of access to them, specifically the "accessibility relations" formed between readers in the "actual world" and multiple possible worlds in the work.[11] She develops these relations "into a system of semantic classification" that help us understand what "makes a world possible."[12] For her, as for Doležel, possible-worlds theory is as much about how the "actual" world comports with fiction as about how fiction creates its own autonomous worlds. More than this, as Ryan especially underscores, the possibility of other worlds raises new questions about the ethics of reading, particularly the reader's responsibility to grasp the nature of these worlds even when they are only partially visible, only partially open to the reader's aesthetic experience. For as Doležel and Ryan both point out, literary worlds are always *incomplete* worlds.

In two articles from 2007, Margot Norris explores the potential of possible worlds theory for understanding the function of narrative in Joyce's work, specifically the extent to which it "semantically represents a mental or virtual world in its entirety."[13] In her study of *Finnegans Wake*, she seeks to account for its "plausible realism" as part of a world-constructing fiction.[14] Multiple possible worlds occupy the *Wake*'s textual universe, and they maintain contact with each other through relations of access that open up various "virtual domains."[15] One form of access is through "knowledge-worlds," private nonfactual worlds associated with fictional characters. Two other kinds of possible worlds form around obligations felt by characters and desires they might have that conflict with their obligations.[16] Norris examines the first chapter of the *Wake* using "Ryan's accessibility relations and her private-world or possible-world modalities to produce a clearer sense of how, precisely, the *Wake* functions as a work of fiction."[17]

Norris concludes that the worlds of the *Wake*—and the "ontological realms that conflict and collide in these worlds"[18]—are not evenly balanced between real and unreal realities. For one thing, "[t]he narrator's hybrid status of a voice fluctuating between anonymous and impersonal third person, yet endowed with a logic resembling stream of consciousness, creates an indeterminate knowledge-world." Moreover, "wish-worlds," which are usually part of the inner life of a character, are "imputed to figures rather than expressed directly and are, therefore, also indeterminable with respect to their status as a private possible world. These contradictions can further be ascribed to the text's failure to represent a textual actual world."[19]

Norris's article on the "Wandering Rocks" episode of *Ulysses* focuses on a more successful, if problematic, representation of a "textual actual world." The passage featuring Father John Conmee is a good example of the phenomenon of an actual historical figure appearing in fictional form and among fictional characters. "[W]hat is the consequence," Norris asks, "of inventing imaginary, or possible, worlds for fictional figures drawn from real life"?[20] One consequence is that the reader is put in the position of trying to understand the mystery surrounding one Lady Maxwell, whom Conmee has seen just before we meet him in the narrative (perhaps for confession, perhaps for something more intimate), and the uncertainty of the outcome of Conmee's visit to the Dignam family, which takes place outside the narrative frame. These indeterminacies, which are native to the fictional worlds that Doležel and Ryan describe, make it difficult for readers to responsibly gauge Conmee's character, a difficulty exacerbated by his status as an actual historical figure. We glean from his thoughts that his obligations to Patrick Dignam's widow and child are bound up with other obligations, like "fundraising for the African missions."[21] We glimpse in his walk "one of Conmee's private worlds, his *obligation world*, as Ryan calls the 'system of commitments and prohibitions defined by social rules and moral principles'."[22] However, because we cannot know the extent of his visit with the Dignams or the amount of leverage he exerts elsewhere to fund his missions, we cannot rely on this textual glimpse to form a judgment of him *as a priest*. We see a sense of self-satisfaction as he moves in his private world, but the indeterminacy and incompleteness of the text—what came before and what happened after Conmee's walk—"may complicate the reader's judgment of [his] charity."[23] At issue here is the precarious balance between "the incomplete world of fiction" and the "complete and factual" historical world.[24] The fictional Conmee's "trans-world similarity" to his actual world counterpart is at the heart of a secular modern myth "in the sense that it displays a natural world peopled by visible figures and an invisible domain that implies relationships and connections among them that the figures themselves can neither divine nor control."[25] The gaps and indeterminacies of the narrative belong to this second invisible domain.

For Norris, possible worlds theory enables a rigorous description and interpretation of virtual worlds wholly constituted by formal, semantic, or logical propositions and relations. It also "offers readers and critics strategies for clarifying with greater rigor and precision interpretative assumptions that are generally made intuitively" and creates the conditions of "an enabled ethical position to make responsible determinations about actual and possible events in the fictional world."[26] My reading of Norris, and of the possible-worlds theory she engages, has led me to another question about readers and the fictional worlds they engage: Is it possible that readers respond to the invitation issued by the work not only so that they might better understand its textual universe and the worlds it contains—and to recognize more fully their responsibility to other worlds—but also so that they might enter into and enjoy its atmosphere, to feel an affinity with the work as well as its creator, as part of an aesthetic experience? The creation of a world in art, an impossible world with a definite existence, requires this affinity, which is nothing other than a mutual depth of feeling. This point of view about art, put forward by Mikel Dufrenne in *The Phenomenology of Aesthetic Experience* (1953), offers an alternative to the semantic and logical approaches of possible-worlds theory, but one that is at bottom complementary, in the sense that for many aspects of the latter there are corollaries in Dufrenne's phenomenological method. As I will show later in this chapter, the "Circe" episode of *Ulysses*, like *Finnegans Wake*, invites the reader to assent to, even to participate in, an impossible world, for such a world exists in almost total isolation from a "textual actual world" that might recenter or stabilize it.[27] Dufrenne's approach to artistic worlds allows for, perhaps even requires, logically impossible worlds. Though unreal in the sense that they are not actual, the worlds he describes are substantial in that they exist.

In Dufrenne's exploration of the ontology of textual worlds, the reader's aesthetic experience plays a decisive role, for without it the work does not open up to reveal its being *as a world*. The reader, as the subject of an aesthetic experience, approaches a work of art as a specific kind of object, "an eminently real object," but one that "does not pretend to produce the real within itself or even to copy the real. The aesthetic object *says* the real and thus discovers it."[28] Unlike an "ordinary object," which "appears against the background of the world," the aesthetic object, "in signifying, [...] does not exist to serve the world. It is, rather, the source of a world which is its own" (*PAE* 166–67). This world is really two worlds dialectically entwined: a *represented world*, which corresponds closely to the actual world outside the work, and an *expressed world*, which is native to the work and is concerned not with representation but with the expression of the work's "being-in-depth" (*PAE* 398). The expressed world is not so much a separate world as "the expansion of the represented objects to the dimensions of a world" (*PAE* 186). In Ryan's possible-worlds framework, the represented world is the result of an "analytical compatibility" between the "textual actual world" and the actual world itself, that is, in both worlds "objects designated by the same words have the same essential properties."[29] From the point of view of phenomenology, the key point is that the "expressed," which has no analogue in possible-worlds theory, "is like the effect of the represented"; at the same time, "the expressed precedes and heralds the represented." Thus, "the expressed is, as it were, the possibility of the represented, and the represented is the reality of the expressed. Together with the style which gives them body, they compose the world of the aesthetic object" (*PAE* 185).

For Dufrenne, the world of the work—not just a novel but any work of art—is the construction of a creator whose subjectivity or inner life informs it. Expression is the work's "characteristic quality," which "also appears to designate its creator"; it serves as the "mark of what is genuinely human in the work," a "living bond" and a living dialogue. "Our comprehension of the work consists in a dialogue which we take up with its creator. In this respect, expression is the foundation of inter-subjectivity" (*PAE* 326).[30] Feeling is a vital element in this intersubjective aesthetic experience because it is the facet of the work that attracts the attention of the reader by an expression of a certain depth. The "depth of the object," which Dufrenne also calls "being-in-depth," is "the plenitude of a meaning":

> [T]he aesthetic object's inexhaustibility is, in the end, a function of its depth. This object does not exist in the manner of a thing which cannot be fully viewed in the course of a single glance but, rather, in the sense of a consciousness whose depths are unfathomable. (*PAE* 398)[31]

Depth designates temporal unity within the work but it also designates the "unfathomable" depths of the reader's "inner life," which is manifested above all in its power of "laying open the self" to the aesthetic object (*PAE* 405). In this capacity for openness, which correlates to the work's incompleteness, the reader gains access to the world of the work.[32] Such access is relatively frictionless in works dominated by the represented world, for representation serves the world of the work in part by furnishing it with familiar objects and personages.[33] "The represented world," Dufrenne notes, "possesses, in its own fashion, the spatiotemporal structure of the perceived world. Space and time here fill a dual function. They serve both to open up a world and to ordain it objectively by creating a world common to the characters and the readers" (*PAE* 171).

In the aesthetic experience, the reader discovers "an entire world"; and while this world may resemble an actual social environment (as in, say, a realist novel by Dickens or Balzac), it is no less a world for that. In the realist novel, the represented world dominates, and readers' responsibility to it goes no farther than to affirm the representation and enjoy its fidelity to the real world around them. And while the expressed world of an experimental novel, such as Joyce's *Finnegans Wake* or Virginia Woolf's *The Waves*, may strike us as more otherworldly, this is mostly an effect of style. In the case of many experimental fictions, the focus on inner life, as Dufrenne understands it, makes a direct appeal to the reader to enter into the world of the work and in this way affirm not a representation but an "alternative possible world."[34] The reader exists in a pact with the creator, both of whom generate the world of the work by virtue of their shared aesthetic experience, their shared capacity for recognition and expression. Moreover, the protagonists of literary works, particularly when they are conveyed in free-indirect style, become, as it were, signatories to this pact. The responsibility of readers to a fictional world, their complicity with protagonists and creators alike, is based on the capacity for inner life, the world generating power of aesthetic perception and attentiveness to remain open to another way of being, to an atmosphere and temporality that together form the substance of a world.

When I speak of "the reader," I mean also to speak of the spectator of the work. Dufrenne mostly talks about the spectator of temporal arts like music and dance in which performance ushers the spectator into "the presence of the work," thereby making it "manifest and present" (*PAE* 4). The performer embodies the aesthetic object—"the qualities of the dance are those of the dancer" (*PAE* 75)—and through performance the spectator is invited into the world performed onstage. With respect to literary texts, performance can take place as recitation, but more often, especially in modern times, it is a matter of "inner speech" that approximates, though abstractly, the kind of live performance seen in the dramatic arts.[35] In a sense, then, literature exemplifies what is true of any encounter with an aesthetic object, that "every spectator is a performer in his own fashion" (*PAE* 341). The spectator is "a performer, indeed, the only performer, when he is a reader; for the reader is one who perceives, but who, in uttering sounds, presents himself to himself to be perceived" (*PAE* 45). In this self-presentation, one's whole being becomes swept up into a moment of profound attention to a work of art. "If the reader turns performer," Dufrenne writes, "it is, in every case, in order to confront the work, to be its witness [...] without leaving his post in physical space" (*PAE* 55, 57).

Reader, spectator, performer, witness: "Circe," unlike any other episode of *Ulysses* requires us to think of all of these roles, and does so largely by invoking dramatic forms in the midst of a novelistic experience. The reader is invited to become a character in a drama in which other characters from other episodes are themselves spectators, sometimes witnesses, of what transpires in Nighttown. Because "Circe" takes the form of a closet drama, the aesthetic experience it offers is very close to that of a novel or poem; but the slight difference between them—in the closet drama, the reader is meant to imagine that the world of the work could exist *yet again* on some impossible, unreal stage—is magnified in Joyce's text by the abrupt shift from prose to drama and by the use of stage directions. The world presented in "Circe" is almost entirely the expressed world of the text, with little support coming from the represented world (in Ryan's terms, the "textual actual world"). The reader is thus confronted with the spectacle of an impossible world enabled by dramatic form, which heightens and deepens the textual atmosphere, suggesting vitality by stylistic exorbitance and presentness by the illusion of performance. Dramatic form also amplifies the reader's role in the aesthetic experience and draws out the intersubjective relations made possible by the act of creation and by the reader's acceptance of the invitation made by the work.

In "Circe," an atmosphere of permutation (often following the logic of free association) and a recursive temporality accommodate the re-emergence of characters, images, and phrases from the textual past of *Ulysses.* The episode is a "temporal no-man's land," with little connection to the "textual actual world," despite the familiar Dublin street geography.[36] Permutation takes place without duration, even as the episode unfolds dramatically, through time and space. On the imaginary stage of "Circe," gestures and speech acts take place in such a way that time is suspended; gesture and dialogue, subject to permutation, break free of ordinary organizations of action and statement. This temporal and cognitive elasticity creates tension in an atmosphere in which everything comes and goes, an endless transmutation of beings. Stage directions, crucial to creating this atmosphere, generate meaning—"eloquent signification" as Dufrenne puts it (*PAE* 152)—and give substance and contour to an unreal impossible world in which nothing, human or otherwise, is deprived of its vital existence.

For generations, "Circe" has puzzled scholars who cannot with confidence locate the narrative or textual consciousness that motivates it. Clive Hart's theory of a non-human "Arranger" is one way to talk about the structure of "Circe"[37]; others speak of a collective dream or the unconsciousness of the text itself.[38] Others still attribute narrative form and agency to textual repetitions, the phantasmagoria of language, or the "odyssey of style."[39] In most of these cases, the argument for narrative authority tends to favor a solution involving a nonhuman agent, like Hart's "Arranger," but this argument—which is, broadly speaking, poststructuralist—leaves the reader and the author with little to do. What possible-worlds theory and Dufrenne's phenomenological aesthetics provide is a way of including both author and reader as crucial components of an explanation for the progressive increase in stylistic performance over denotative representation. I am suggesting, following Dufrenne, that we might profitably view this progression as evidence of the mounting tension of the text's expressiveness, which is to say, the increasing visibility of the world indigenous to the work.

What transpires in the fifteenth episode is the depiction of a world in which the unreal cohabits with the real or, as a possible-worlds theorist might say, an impossible world coexists among other possible worlds of a textual universe in which characters—and, arguably, readers—acquire a "transworld identity."[40] Given the relation of "Circe" to the rest of Joyce's text, this identity is very often achieved in conjunction with prior versions of a character's self. Thus, Bloom transforms into his son, who has just castigated him for coming home drunk: "*(In youth's smart blue Oxford suit with white vestslips, narrowshouldered, in brown Alpine hat, wearing gent's sterling silver waterbury keyless watch and double curb Albert with seal attached, one side of him coated with stiffening mud).* Harriers, father. Only that once."[41] What is deep in ourselves, Dufrenne writes, "is not so much the past per se as it is our present experience of unifying ourselves with this past and identifying ourselves with what we have been, aided by a peculiar perception testifying to the past" (*PAE* 400). In order to get the most out of their aesthetic experience, readers should try to achieve this "peculiar perception," which arises out of the "plenitude and authenticity of [their] being" (*PAE* 401). Bloom's transformation into Rudy is an identification of himself with his own past that could only take place in the impossible world of "Circe."

This kind of unity, in which time resembles a corkscrew driving the mutated return of what has come before, is given eloquent expression when Virag Lipoti, Bloom's "granpapachi," appears to harass him about his past, referring derisively to his "stockingette gusseted knickers" and "complicated combinations" (*U* 515). Bloom is used to this kind of treatment. When he is brought up on trial for having overstepped the bounds of propriety and decency he appeals to the "Gentleman of the jury" (one of many surrogates for the reader in "Circe") for understanding: "let me explain," he says. "A pure mare's nest. I am a man misunderstood. I am being made a scapegoat of. I am a respectable married man, without a stain on my character. I live in Eccles street" (*U* 457). He then goes on to describe the glorious military career of his father-in-law, "a gallant upstanding gentleman," and to invent a similar career for himself. The desire to explain his past leads, under the pressure of a rapidly permutating and illogical legal procedure, to the invention of a self from which he might draw the plenitude and authenticity he needs for an acquittal. It does not help.

But when standing before the undead Virag, he is finally able to come up against himself and to weave his past self into the rhythms of his present speech act: "I wanted then to have now concluded. Nightdress was never. Hence this. But tomorrow is a new day will be. Past was is today. What now is will then tomorrow as now was be past yester" (*U* 515). This is just the sort of "peculiar perception" about himself that Bloom has been avoiding all day—an understanding of his past as united to his present ("*Past was is today*"). If he were to grasp this, as he can in the world of "Circe," the belief that his past could be retrieved from its temporal backwater, verified, and offered up as evidence against him would be shattered.

The temporal unity Bloom achieves takes place in a performance space in which another kind of unity is asserted, for "Circe" uses dramatic form to make one of the main points of the text: "Everything speaks in its own way. Sllt" (*U* 121). In this spectacle of appearance, "mere" inanimate objects achieve dialogical and ontological parity with human subjects. Mingling human and nonhuman speaking beings implicitly articulates a theme of reconciliation and equanimity, a strange, dream-like equality that is expressed—and actually achieved—in the world of the work: "Jewgreek is greekjew," says the Cap. "Extremes meet. Death is the highest form of life. Bah!" (*U* 504). Though the Cap speaks "*[w]ith saturnine spleen*," the reconciliation it exemplifies remains germane to an episode whose time signature is permutation without duration. This signature is expressed primarily in stage directions that describe mutations of character, scene, and dialogue that, more often than not, undermine conventional notions of duration, on stage and off. Unlike G. B. Shaw's *Man and Superman*, in which stage directions serve as editorial elaborations that have little to do with staging, Joyce's exorbitant directions in "Circe" serve a quite different purpose: they reinstate formally the physical movement and material supports (including stage design, setting, costumes) of a live performance; they become the locus of the work's overt expression of another world, one in which Bloom can become his own son and address himself from a past that has never existed.

In the uncanny world of "Circe," everything seems to happen at once, to mutate without a moment's notice and without a reliable sense of the temporal distance between speech acts. The very idea of the past, understood as a time before the present, is superseded by a sense of it as part of a present unity of feeling, whose depth and significance are called forth and amplified in stage directions. Bloom models this unity, though not always successfully and, as I have suggested, serves as a surrogate for the reader who also confronts Nighttown with some knowledge of what has already transpired in early episodes. That Joyce meant for this temporality to be recognized—and shared—by the reader is evident in several key scenes in which Bloom and Stephen appear to offer the reader access to the world of the work by performing their own experience of Nighttown. In Stephen's case, reflection on the nature of aesthetic experience and the aesthetic object (or "esthetic image" as he calls it in *A Portrait of the Artist as a Young Man*) leads him to a theory of gesture that welcomes the reader; in Bloom's case, a confrontation with mirrors—that is to say, with himself—suggests another way for the reader to access the world and to grasp its permutating environment and temporal logic.

Beneath the streetlamps of Nighttown, Stephen "*flourishes his ashplant shivering the lamp image, shattering light over the world*" (*U* 432). In this instant, the world of the work is illuminated, and the "shattering light" reveals the cohesion of an expressed world, one in which the actual world has no stable image in the text and in which the "textual reference world for which the text claims facts"[42] (the actual world of Dublin) shivers like the "lamp image" into fragments. Stephen's gesture, like a swordsman's, clears a space for advance; but it is also a performance meant to invest the world of the work with depth and meaning, particularly when later he calls out "*Nothung!*" (*U* 583) and actually shatters a lamp. His initial attempt is witnessed by his friend Lynch, who has been patiently listening to a recitation of the antiphon "used with asperges (the ceremony of sprinkling the alter) during paschal time."[43] When Stephen finishes with "*(Triumphaliter.) Salvi facti i sunt*" [And they are made whole (saved)] and Lynch prompts him with "So that?" (*U* 432), the reader may as well be in the world of *A Portrait*, where these two characters engage in similar verbal hijinks. Once prompted, Stephen continues in the same vein as that earlier text: "So that gesture, not music, not odours, would be a universal language, the gift of tongues rendering visible not the lay sense but the first entelechy, the structural rhythm" (*U* 432). He essentially calls for rendering visible that which is usually invisible, the cause or soul of things whose existence can only be alluded to in the "structural rhythm" of gesture. The "shivering of the lamp *image*" is a gesture without contact with an actual lamp, for the shattered light it emits illuminates a world in which time is governed by gesture, not the other way around.

According to Dufrenne, rhythm in a work of art determines the duration of harmony. Speaking of painting, he notes that in the work there exists a kind of harmony that creates a "theater of movement" (*PAE* 291). In the ordering of harmony, rhythm "manifests a duration which is born of the animation of space." Yet rhythm does not "inscribe a real becoming in objective time. [It] does not preside over a temporal progression but over the unification of a spatial manifold" (*PAE* 291–92). In fiction, as in painting, this manifold is not the representation of duration in the actual world, but the expression of a duration that unfolds in the reader's experience of a virtual world. Stephen's aesthetic pronouncements, which are meant to explain reality as such—"Metaphysics in Mecklenburg street!" Lynch cries (*U* 432)—suggest a way of understanding the logic and temporality of permutation that animate the "spatial manifold" of the episode. He philosophizes about art and life, and even makes a grand gesture when he strikes out at the world of Nighttown with his ashplant, rechristened *Nothung*, the sword of legendary Germanic warriors. But he remains, as perhaps the reader ought to remain, strikingly like himself, adapting to permutation so quickly that it seems like the natural expression of his personality, which is "fluid and lambent," on the cusp of "refin[ing] itself out of existence."[44] This is true even when he puppets his own prior speech acts and "*[g]abbles, with marionette jerks*" (*U* 569):

> *(He points about him with grotesque gestures which Lynch and the whores reply to.)* Caoutchouc statue woman reversible or lifesize tompeeptoms virgins nudities very lesbic the kiss five ten times. Enter gentlemen to see in mirrors every positions trapezes all that machine there besides also if desire act awfully bestial butcher's boy pollutes in warm veal liver or omellete on the belly *pièce de Shakespeare*. (*U* 570)

The "peculiar perception" of his own past that Stephen offers here reveals a depth of feeling absent in his early theorizing in *A Portrait* and in his performance of Shakespearean criticism in "Scylla and Charybdis." His appeal goes out to those who are listening—Lynch, Zoe, Flurry, Bella, the reader—who may recognize in themselves the same depth of feeling, the same "plenitude and authenticity" of being (*PAE* 401).

Bloom's entry, unlike Stephen's, is announced in a florid description of Mabbot street, in which "*[t]he swancomb of [a] gondola, highreared, forges on through the murk*" (*U* 429). Bloom too moves through the "murk," where a "*navvy lurches against the lamp*" and frightens Tommy and Jacky Caffrey, who "*scuttle off in the dark.*" Then, swaying and staggering, the navvy moves through a shadowy, fetid atmosphere where, amid the "*stagnant fumes,*" "*[a] glow leaps in the south beyond the seaward reaches of the river.*" Into this weird scene of scrambling, scuffling, clasping, lurching, climbing, and scuttling life, "*Bloom appears flushed, panting, cramming bread and chocolate into a side pocket*" (*U* 433). He is immediately confronted with a portrait of Admiral Nelson in a hairdresser's window and next to it a "concave mirror," which serves as a portal for his—and the reader's—otherworldly adventure in Nighttown. By virtue of his greater attentiveness and susceptibility to his environment, Bloom more credibly than Stephen ties the "universal language" of gesture to the universalizing temporality of permutation that governs the world of "Circe." In the window of a hairdresser's shop, he sees "*gallant Nelson's image*" (*U* 433). Then everything alters dramatically, and he enters into a fluctuating gallery of historical figures who join Admiral Nelson in a funhouse of misrecognition.

He sees himself in a "*concave mirror at the side*," which presents to him "*lovelorn longlost lugubru Booloohoom*" (*U* 433–34). As he passes, "*grave Gladstone sees him level*" and he suffers "*the stare of the truculent Wellington.*" He is then confronted by a "*convex mirror*" in which a "*grin unstuck the bonham eyes and fatchuck cheekchops of Jolly-poldy the rixdix doldy.*" He appears on the scene then disappears, then "*[i]n a moment he reappears and hurries on*," only to disappear again "*into Olhousen's, the pork butcher's under the downcoming rollshutter*" from which he emerges after a few moments "*from under the shutter, puffing Poldy, blowing Bloohoom*" (*U* 434). In the temporality of permutation, time is less about progression than appearance and reappearance, changes that illuminate the space of a world, in which duration resolves into a continuous tableau, as when "*the night hours link, each with arching arms, in a mosaic of movements*" (*U* 577).

Under the pressure of the expressed world, the world of representation, which in the previous episodes constitutes a fairly stable "textual actual world," undergoes distortions and permutations that transform this world into "the murk," a zone of indistinction that blurs boundaries between objects and people, but also between the various private worlds or knowledge-worlds that constitute the textual universe of the episode. In the absence of a stabilizing "textual actual world," narrative authority in "Circe" is less like an Arranger than like the Hobgoblin who "*whirls round and round with dervish howls*," forming worlds in order to gamble them away: "*Tiny roulette planets fly from his hands*" and "*rush together, uttering crepitant cracks* [...]. *The planets, buoyant balloons, sail swollen up and away*" (*U* 506). In the scene featuring Nelson, the mirrors reflect a changeling Bloom, who suddenly occupies a world in which everything else is changing too, "*uttering crepitant cracks.*" Reflection does not fail; it simply takes this other world as its object. In a concave mirror, an object is reflected in the form of an *actual* image. Image, object, and focal point take their place along the same line of sight *in front of* the mirror, as when Bloom sees *Booloohoom* while Gladstone and Wellington look on or when he and Stephen "*gaze in the mirror*" and "*[t]he face of William Shakespeare, beardless, appears there, rigid in facial paralysis, crowned by the reflection of the reindeer antlered hatrack in the hall*" (*U* 567). In a convex mirror, the image and focal point are *behind* the mirror. The image created is a *virtual* one. Thus Bloom is transformed into an unreal self, "*Jolly-poldy the rixdix doldy*," a permutation that is neither distortion nor reflection but an original, if virtual, source of light. In a sense, he joins the statues of goddesses he admires in "Lestrygonians," a denizen of another world "drinking electricity: gods' food" and lounging among the "[l]ovely forms of woman sculped Junonian. Immortal lovely" (*U* 176).

The double-mirror of "Circe" permits both virtual and actual realities. This may be why, in Nighttown, Bloom recognizes Stephen, and Stephen and Lynch fall into their usual schtick amid an otherwise chaotic and unreal *mis en scène*, in which animated objects take their place among people. Both sides of the mirror exist on the native ground of the work. The reader in this funhouse world, like Bloom himself, sees the distortions of a represented world famously furnished by real names of people and places, and in which real products and publications circulate. But she also sees "*Jolly-poldy the rixdix doldy.*" In a sense, the reader takes a position in front of and behind the mirrors at once and thus becomes a witness to a world in which permutating characters and animated objects coexist, ontologically equal, each given a speaking role, that is to say, a *voice.*

Nowhere is this voice more pronounced than in the scenes depicting Bloom's rapid transformation into "alderman Sir Leo Bloom" (*U* 479), who invites everyone, including the reader, to join the denizens of an impossible world: "My beloved subjects, a new era is about to dawn. I, Bloom, tell you verily it is even now at hand. Yea, on the word of a Bloom, ye shall ere long enter into the golden city which is to be, the new Bloomusalem in the Nova Hibernia of the future" (*U* 484). Earlier, he had been indicted for gross indecency and faced humiliating punishments. Now he is able to call forth a whole new world grounded on little more than his lewd suggestion, after Zoe asked him for a "swaggerroot," that "[t]he mouth can be better engaged than with a cylinder of rank weed." His ludicrous swagger, quite unlike his usual self-doubting and circumspect approach to women, sparks a riposte—"Go on," Zoe says. "Make a stump speech out of it" (*U* 477–78)—that leads to the New Bloomusalem. When it is all over—"Talk away till you're black in the face"—just before he is pilloried once again, he blends into yet another world, "*[i]n caubeen with clay pipe stuck in the band, dusty brogues, an emigrant's red handkerchief bundle in his hand*" (*U* 499).

Having been invited into a seemingly chaotic world by one of the protagonists— who is himself an emigrant, or at least for the moment—the reader is surrounded by characters whose appearance is initially jarring but ultimately comforting, if only because their *re*appearance weaves threads of consistency throughout the episode. But what is the reader's responsibility to these characters and their world? Possible worlds theory, and Margot Norris's use of it in her reading of Joyce, suggests that this responsibility has its roots in the "actual world," which is reflected in the relations of accessibility that make responsible reading possible. But when, as in "Circe," these relations, and the obligation- and wish-worlds they sustain, are confounded in a process of permutation that has neither duration nor extension, responsibility becomes, for both reader and characters, a purely textual matter. In a telling scene, Bello, while engaged in his sadomasochistic *contretemps* with Bloom, insists on being told a story: "Tell me something to amuse me, smut or a bloody goodghoststory or a line of poetry, quick, quick, quick! Where? How?

What time? With how many? I give you just three seconds" (*U* 538). Perhaps our responsibility, as readers, is to our own amusement, our own enjoyment of the world in which we find ourselves while reading, a world in which we, like Bello, are transformed utterly.

Notes

1 Lubomír Doležel, *Heterocosmica: Fiction and Possible Worlds* (Baltimore: Johns Hopkins University Press, 1998), 180–81.
2 Ibid., 44. On impossible worlds, 163.
3 Ibid., 24. See Doležel's *Possible Worlds of Fiction and History: The Postmodern Stage* (Baltimore: Johns Hopkins University Press, 2010), in which he elaborates on the status of "historical possible worlds," which "have to be truth-functional because [historical texts] stipulate possible worlds that serve as models of the actual past" (43).
4 Doležel, *Heterocosmica*, 20.
5 Ibid.
6 Ibid., 33.
7 Marie-Laure Ryan, *Possible Worlds, Artificial Intelligence, and Narrative . Theory* (Bloomington: Indiana University Press, 1991), 3.
8 Ibid., 31. Ryan summarizes the work of analytic philosopher Saul Kripke.
9 Ibid., vii.
10 Ibid., 24–25. Such a world is a "version of a world" according to Nelson Goodman, in *Ways of Worldmaking* (Indianapolis: Hackett, 1978).
11 On these "accessibility relations, see ibid., 31–33.
12 Ibid., 31.
13 Margot Norris, "Possible Worlds Theory and the Fantasy Universe of *Finnegans Wake*," *James Joyce Quarterly* 44.3 (Spring 2007), 457.
14 Ibid., 456.
15 Ibid., 457.
16 Ryan calls these "obligation-worlds" and "wish-worlds" (*Possible Worlds*, 111).
17 Norris, "Universe of *Finnegans Wake*," 458.
18 Ibid.
19 Ibid., 467–68.
20 Norris, "Possible-Worlds Theory and Joyce's 'Wandering Rocks': The Case of Father Conmee," *Joyce Studies Annual* 7 (2007), 22.
21 Norris, "The Case of Father Conmee," 28.
22 Ibid., emphasis in original. Norris quotes from Ryan, *Possible Worlds*, 116.
23 Norris, "The Case of Father Conmee," 28.
24 Ibid., 33
25 Ibid., 28, 38. On this "modern myth," see Doležel, *Heterocosmica*, chapter VIII.
26 Ibid., 39.
27 On recentering as a means to stabilize fictional worlds, see Ryan, *Possible Worlds*, 21–23.
28 Mikel Dufrenne, *The Phenomenology of Aesthetic Experience*, trans. E. S. Casey (Evanston: Northwestern University Press, 1966), 516; emphasis in the original. Subsequent references will be cited in the text parenthetically as *PAE*.
29 Ryan, *Possible Worlds*, 33.
30 J. Hillis Miller, in *Charles Dickens: The World of His Novels* (Cambridge: Harvard University Press, 1958), echoes Dufrenne when he writes that a "poem or novel

is indeed the world refashioned into conformity with the inner structure of the writer's spirit, but at the same time it is that spirit given, through words, a form and substance taken from the shared solidity of the exterior world." Literature thus becomes a "self-sufficient reality beyond which the critic need not go" (x).

31 This inexhaustibility corresponds to the incompleteness and indeterminacy described by possible-worlds theorists.

32 Possible-world theory regards the opening offered by the work in terms of a narrator's presentation: "For the duration of our immersion in a work of fiction," writes Ryan, "the realm of possibilities is [...] recentered around the sphere which the narrator presents as the actual world," that is, "the actual world of the textual universe projected by the fictional text" (*Possible Worlds,* 22–23).

33 On furnishing and the idea of a "furnished world," see Umberto Eco, "Small Worlds," in *The Limits of Interpretation* (Bloomington and Indiana: Indiana University Press, 1994), 65–67.

34 Ryan, *Possible Worlds*, vii.

35 This is possible because the means of execution are not vital to the experience of the performance. "Execution—i.e. production, technical making, or rendering—is a necessary but not a sufficient condition of the aesthetic object" (Dufrenne, *PAE* 17, translator's note 9).

36 Norris, "Fantasy Universe of *Finnegans Wake*," 461. In Doležel's terms, "Circe" has almost "zero texture" with respect to the share of the "actual world" in the narrative (*Heterocosmica*, 169–70).

37 Clive Hart, "Wandering Rocks," in *James Joyce's* Ulysses: *Critical Essays*, eds. Clive Hart and David Hayman (Berkeley: University of California Press, 1974), 181–216.

38 See, for example, Brandon Lamson, "Orpheus Descending: Images of Psychic Descent in 'Hades' and 'Circe,'" *Joyce Studies Annual* (2010): 254–61 and Michael Bruce McDonald, "'Circe' and the Uncanny; or Joyce from Freud to Marx," *James Joyce Quarterly* 33.1 (Fall 1995): 49–68.

39 See, respectively, Ronan Crowley, "Fusing the Elements of 'Circe': From Compositional to Textual Repetition," *James Joyce Quarterly* 47.3 (Fall 2010): 341–61; Daniel Ferrer, "Circe, regret and regression" (trans. Gilly Lehmann), in *Post-Structuralist Joyce: Essays from the French*, eds. Derek Attridge and Daniel Ferrer (Cambridge, England: Cambridge University Press, 1984): 127–44; and Karen Lawrence, *The Odyssey of Style in* Ulysses (Princeton: Princeton University Press, 1981). Gerald L. Bruns, in "What's in a Mirror: James Joyce's Phenomenology of Perception," *James Joyce Quarterly* 49.3–4 (Spring–Summer 2012), writes that freed from the Law of the Father, "we enter the 'Circe' episode [...] in which everything is as meets the eye and is not to be understood otherwise. [...] In 'Circe,' whatever can be placed into language is the case" (582).

40 Doležel, *Heterocosmica*, 16–17. Norris, "The Case of Father Conmee," 22ff.

41 James Joyce, *Ulysses* (New York: Vintage, 1990), 438. Subsequent citations will be given in the text. Unless otherwise noted, the emphasis in quotations from "Circe" is Joyce's.

42 Ryan, *Possible Worlds*, vii.

43 Don Gifford, with Robert J. Seidman, *"Ulysses" Annotated: Notes for James Joyce's "Ulysses,"* 2nd rev. and enlarged ed. (Berkeley: University of California Press, 1988), 453.

44 James Joyce, *A Portrait of the Artist as a Young Man*, ed. John Paul Riquelme (New York: Norton, 2007), 189.

Chapter 15

FINNEGANS WAKE AS FICTIONAL WORLD REFUSAL

Paul Saint-Amour

Few literary scholars have thought as restlessly or as generously as Margot Norris has about novels and the world. We might look at how her *Joyce's Web* (1992) torques its author's early deconstructivist reflexes toward feminist, historicist, and political accounts of Joyce.[1] Or we could consider how *Writing War in the Twentieth Century* (2000) brings the ethical demand of action and intervention to bear on the scene of reading war novels, lighting up literature's capacity to shape "the ideological constructions that legitimate attitudes that inform public policy."[2] In both these books, and in many others, we find Norris wrestling fiction, alongside other modes and media, into different angles of engagement with the world. Her work's restlessness inheres in how often we find a given project rounding on, probing, and complicating the central impulses of those that precede it. Its generosity lies in the rich intellectual sustenance it sets before its readers and in the openings created by its internal twists and rotations—the pockets of air where new impulses and projects can get their start.

In the mid-2000s, Norris's work began to address *world* as a theoretical term by engaging with possible worlds theory, an interdisciplinary precipitate of philosophy-of-language and narratology that formed in the early 1990s. As possible worlds theorist Lubomír Doležel put it, this approach shifted attention from "narrative as story to narrative as fiction"—that is, from narrated events and their emplotted sequence to the ontologies of fictional worlds. Possible worlds theory places special emphasis on how a work of fiction may host many "non-actual" worlds (in the shape of characters' plans, wishes, fantasies, etc.) while typically designating one world as "actual" within the fiction.[3] Joyce's *Ulysses* offers a vividly illustrative example: even as it offers us multiple "non-actual" worlds (from characters' daydreams and hallucinations to episode-long stylistic distortions), the novel implies the baseline existence of an "actual" June 16, 1904, which in turn differs ontologically from the historical June 16, 1904. Norris's possible worlds scholarship to date has been drawn primarily to this rich literary example, culminating in *Virgin and Veteran Readings of "Ulysses"* (2011), whose methodology is rooted in possible worlds theory.[4] But in one essay, Norris has also brought possible worlds theory to bear on *Finnegans Wake*, whose liquidation of novelistic realism makes it an unlikely object for a theory grounded in the realist novel. The present essay follows Norris in carrying the lamp of possible worlds theory into the labyrinth of the *Wake*. I follow a different path from Norris, taking up the question of diegetic coincidences, whose impossibility in Joyce's book points, I argue, to its broader refusal of an internally consistent fictional worldedness. But I go on to suggest that in sweeping narrative coincidence off the table, *Finnegans Wake* also clears space for other kinds of coincidence, particularly between individual readers and the highly localized place names with which the book teems. The essay ends by rejoining Norris, connecting the *Wake*'s trans-world coincidence to her recent ecocritical reading of the book's "Anna Livia Plurabelle" chapter, which I read by *her* light as a pioneering instance of weak environmentalism.

In some respects, *Finnegans Wake* appears to be densely worlding and worlded. It's produced dozens of encyclopedias, concordances, annotations, censuses, indices, maps—all genres of ancillary work that attest to the strong world-making of the primary work to which they pertain. The *Wake* has prompted Carol Shloss to affirm its "integrity" and to engage in geovisualization projects, mapping the text onto a terrestrial globe in "book-world-space."[5] Other *Wake* scholars have read the book as an experiment in literary many-worldedness—as a quantum world or multiverse or, in the book's own words, "this world or the other world or any either world."[6] And the recurrence within the text of identifiable narrative elements, scenarios, and vignettes—the crime in Phoenix Park, the gossiping washerwomen, the Mookse and the Gripse, the Ondt and the Gracehoper, and dozens more—creates the impression of a cumulative and self-conversant whole. Treating the *Wake* as a world likely accords with many readers' instincts, given both the widespread use of "world" to trope complex but integrated systems and the *Wake*'s reputation as a singular literary "chaosmos," to use one of the book's more famous portmanteau words (*FW* 118.21). Even considering the *Wake* a "dreamworld" underscores, rather than weakens, its status as a world.

All of the foregoing uses of "world" gesture broadly toward the *Wake*'s distinctiveness, fullness, self-communion, and extensivity. However, if we consider literary worldedness as a matter not of plenitude or holism but of fictional ontology, we discover that Joyce's last work of fiction is not a fictional world. Here, I invoke the concept "fictional world" in the specific sense it enjoys in possible worlds theory. In philosophy of language, possible-worlds thinking presupposes that things could have been otherwise than they are in actuality. It goes on to ascribe modes of utterance—possible, necessary, nonexistent, counterfactual—to worlds in which they can be said to inhere. To say that something is possible, for example, is in effect to say that there exists a possible world in which it is true. As Ruth Ronen puts it in *Possible Worlds in Literary Theory*, "non-actual possibilities make perfectly coherent systems which can be described and qualified, imagined and intended and to which one can refer. [...] [T]he non-obtaining or non-actuality of a state of affairs does not preclude or stipulate one's ability to make propositions about this state of affairs."[7] For philosophers of language, possible worlds branch causally or "ramify" from the one world that actually obtains; they are distinguishable from the actual world but not ontologically autonomous with respect to it. Fictional worlds, in contrast, are ontologically independent of the actual world and have their own self-sufficient arrays of modal structures. These include the fictional (or textual) actual world—that which did occur within the fictional world—as well as a populous set of things that could have occurred in the fictional world. In one of the daydream-worlds of *Ulysses*' "Proteus" episode, Stephen Dedalus drops in at the home of his maternal uncle, Richie Goulding; in the fictional actual world, he does not. Ronen again: "A fictional world, like any possible world, is analogous to the actual world in that it has its own set of facts and its own subworlds and counter-worlds. As a *world* it contains an 'actual world' and a set of possibilities, alternatives, predictions, and forecasts non-actualized in the fictional world."[8] Fictional worlds are constructed *as worlds*—that is, as ramifying modal systems independent of the actual world yet resembling it in their basic architecture of possibility and consequence.

In her essay "Possible Worlds Theory and the Fantasy Universe of *Finnegans Wake*," Norris characterizes Joyce's book as "Wonderland minus the Victorian [frame narrative]"—in other words, as a fantasy- or dream-world without moorings in a textual actual world accessible to the reader.[9] The question of readerly access is a crucial one, as it marks the difference between textual worlds whose existence I might infer or imagine and those about which I can make testable, refutable claims to another reader. Possible-worlds theorist Marie-Laure Ryan has gone as far as to develop a set of "accessibility relations"—criteria that determine the nature and degree of a reader's access to a fictional world. According to Ryan, the accessibility relations common to the greatest number of fictional genres are three kinds of compatibility between the reader's world and the domain of the text: linguistic compatibility, logical compatibility, and analytical compatibility. In her discussion of the three, Norris posits that "in spite of its many portmanteaus and neologisms, the *Wake* exhibits general linguistic compatibility with

English" thanks to its grounding in English syntax.[10] It's the *Wake*'s analytical and logical properties that Norris finds more incompatible with those of the reader's actual world. If, in Ryan's formulation, analytical compatibility exists when "objects designated by the same words have the same essential properties," Norris observes that we look in vain for many such objects, or for standard words whose semantic consistency across both real and textual worlds can be verified.[11] And because logical principles such as noncontradiction and the excluded middle are either defunct or made fun of in the *Wake*, the text cannot be said to be very logically compatible with the real world. From these incompatibilities follow others—violations by the text of real-world physical laws, taxonomic systems, and chronological constraints. All of these incompatibilities contribute, says Norris, "to the negation of a textual actual world in the *Wake*." The book's peculiarity, she observes, "may be ascribed to its status as an entirely virtual construction that makes no attempt to present itself as actual but rather flaunts its virtuality."[12]

Rather than disqualifying the *Wake* from a possible worlds approach, the absence of a waking actual world in Joyce's book could be said to call attention to the variety of churning, often clashing non-actual worlds—wish-worlds, knowledge-worlds, obligation-worlds—that constitute the dream. For Norris, the work of Ronen, Ryan, et al. offers *Wake* readers "a semantic rather than a psychological analysis" of the-world-of-the-dream, which we encounter as "an alternate world where logic and norms fail to hold sway, where physical laws may be broken and knowledge breaks down, where taxonomies may become confused and identities and properties may shift and merge."[13] But if the semantic dream-world can provide a model for the *Wake*'s fictionality, as Norris suggests, I submit that the book's liquidation of the modal systems of world-making—its relinquishing of consequence and possibility-structures, its being ungrounded in a textual actual world—are exactly the sites at which the *Wake* declines to be a fictional world full stop, for all that it may partake in other traits of fictionality and other varieties of worldedness.[14] Further, although this world refusal manifests in the *Wake*'s analytical and logical incompatibility with its readers' actual world, I suggest it's rooted in the book's linguistic incompatibility with our world, which I understand to be more severe than Norris does.

To illustrate what I mean by the *Wake*'s wholesale refusal to be a fictional world, I'd like to introduce a new term into the conversation: coincidence. If you've read Joyce's *Ulysses*, you know that it is full of coincidences both lexical and diegetic. Derek Attridge notes that the word "coincidence" and its cognates occur 14 times in the novel, every one of which is associated with Leopold Bloom's consciousness and is triggered by some surprising convergence of persons, things, or circumstances in the world represented by the text.[15] In the "Lestrygonians" episode, for example, Bloom walks through the center of Dublin musing on the late parliamentarian Charles Stewart Parnell only to catch sight of Parnell's brother, John Howard Parnell, walking along the opposite side of the street. Bloom thinks: "There he is: the brother. Image of him. Haunting face. Now that's a coincidence. Course hundreds of times you think of a person and don't meet him."[16] It's a minor moment that doesn't presage anything more important at the level of symbol or event. Far from being the Dickensian portal to an inheritance or genealogy plot, coincidence here is a reality effect in a city small enough that you're liable, from time to time, to run into the brother of the man you're thinking about, particularly if the latter man is, as Charles Stewart Parnell would have been to a Dubliner in 1904, often on your mind.

But try, now, to imagine what coincidence at the level of event would look like in any part of *Finnegans Wake*. The mind jams at the thought. To be legible as an event in the diegesis, coincidence requires that both human and nonhuman actors remain discrete and identifiable, that the words describing the coincidence exhibit a fairly high degree of lexical stability and integrity, and that the consequence and possibility structures of the fictional world be intelligible and essentially consistent. The *Wake*, by contrast, offers us passages like the following:

> Now let the centuple celves of my egourge as Micholas de Cusack calls them,—of all of whose I in my hereinafter of course by recourse demission me—by the coincidance of their contraries reamalgamerge in that indentity of undiscernibles where the Baxters and the Fleshmans may they cease to bidivil uns [...]. (*FW* 49.33–50.02)

One sort of coincidence is obviously at work here: the kind represented by "Micholas de Cusack," which fuses Michael Cusack, the founder of the Gaelic Athletic Association and one of the models for the Citizen in the "Cyclops" episode of *Ulysses*, with Nicholas de Cusa, the fifteenth-century philosopher and theologian who posited the coincidence of opposites. The neologism "Micholas" allows two words—here "Michael" and "Nicholas"—to occur together thanks to the happenstance of their partial homophony. Such portmanteau words, the nucleotide bases of which *Finnegans Wake* is built, are thus double coincidences: accidents of orthography and/or sound that permit multiple words to coincide in a single one. The word "coincidence" (coming from *coincidere*, the Latin for "fall together") is a good description, too, for what the words "merge," "emerge," "reëmerge," and "amalgamate" are doing in the portmanteau "reamalgamerge"; and what "indent," "indenture," "indemnity," "identity," and something like its opposite, "in-identity," do in the word "indentity."[17]

A "coincidance" indeed, in which—ashes, ashes—we all fall down. And yet from these phonic, orthographic, and semantic "coincidances" no discrete dancers can be extracted at the level of fictional event, nor a sense of what separates possible and actual, contingency and necessity in the narrative. I'm calling here on Attridge's definition of *coincidence* as "an instance of contingency bearing the marks of necessity," which nicely captures the frisson that coincidences give us in seeming planned or providential.[18] By the strictures of that definition, we can discern nothing in the *Wake*'s diegesis as straightforward as the coincidences of *Ulysses*—nothing as clear-cut as a man happening to see the brother of the man he's thinking of.

What we can do is to posit an inverse relationship between semantic coincidence and the intelligibility of diegetic coincidence—an inverse relationship, that is, between the falling together of units of meaning into portmanteau words such as "chaosmos," "Micholas," "reamalgamerge," and "indentity" and the capacity of fictional events to fall contingently but eerily together in ways a reader can parse. We could say that the more saturated a work is with semantically super-dense words, the harder it is to extract from them the particular alloy of contingency and necessity that is the diegetic coincidence. Of course, there are fictional worlds in which coincidences don't happen, or don't happen to happen. But a fiction whose individual words are as indeterminately and densely polysemous as the *Wake*'s is a fiction in which coincidences, at least at the level of events, *can't* happen. Its characters, actions, and circumstances are too unstable for their concurrences to register, much less for those concurrences to register as remarkable, still less for them to tempt a reader to misattribute them to causality or necessity. This point gestures toward a still more interesting corollary: a novel in which diegetic coincidences cannot happen is not a fictional world in the possible-worlds sense. A modal system in which everything bearing the marks of necessity is in fact necessary, and in which contingency can only sail under the flag of contingency, cannot sustain the misrecognition of contingency as necessity—or of necessity as contingency—that makes for coincidence. Nor can such a modal system ramify through necessity's interaction with contingency. The capacity for coincidence, I suggest, is a key node in worldedness, a ganglion where the indispensable strands of fictional worldedness meet.

A second relation of inverse proportionality can help us think further about coincidence as an index of world. In an essay on cheap plot tricks, Marie-Laure Ryan posits that "the degree of probability of a coincidence is inversely proportional to the size of the pool of events that are possible in a certain situation; hence the 'small world' effect when the coincidence occurs: it is as if a large world had shrunk, leaving fewer possibilities."[19]

Think of those Dickens novels in which the sheer density of happenstance makes it seem as if there are only three people in all of London—crowded street scenes notwithstanding. A fictional world in which improbable coincidences too frequently occur comes to seem poor in characters, independent causal chains, and/or possibilities. Too many improbable coincidences threaten to reduce all contingency to necessity, collapsing the world into a monad whose sole causality is heavy-handed authorial plotting. Moving in the other direction, a fictional world in which a few not-so-improbable coincidences occur, or in which none occurs, will appear large—replete with characters, independent causal chains, and/or possibilities. But a fiction in which coincidences *cannot* occur is too large and unbounded to be a world. Its bar on coincidence disarticulates necessity and contingency, the forces whose interaction constitutes the modal system that possible worlds theory calls a world. Such a fiction can no more constitute a world than two skew lines can limn a plane.[20]

What I have been saying about the *Wake*'s fictional world refusal also illustrates something counterintuitive about the laboriousness of fictional worldmaking. As difficult as it is to write a complex, fully-realized work of fiction, the creation of rudimentary fictional worlds is quite easy. Get pen and paper or open up a new document. Write, *If the young moisture-farmer had looked up from his work just a moment later, he would not have seen the imperial cruiser gleaming in the light of the twin suns.* In a single sentence you've set in motion a ramifying modal system independent of the actual world, a system in which a possible world has branched, at the word "if," away from a fictional actual world in which the protagonist *did* look up in time to see the cruiser's gleam. Now sit down and try to write a rudimentary work that is recognizable as fiction but declines a ramifying modal system independent of the actual world. Such a work requires much more effort, both to write and to read. It turns out that we spawn fictional worlds as profusely and carelessly as a swimmer climbing out of the pool sheds rills of water. Fiction defaults to ontological independence from the actual world. To go against this gradient—to create self-unworlding fictions that are ontologically dependent on the actual world—is the uphill work.

By arguing that *Finnegans Wake* is a work of fiction but not a fictional world, I may sound as if I were trying to deny it some crucial literary entry visa. To the contrary, I would insist that the *Wake* becomes all the more curious and important as a work of fiction when we recognize its refusal of fictional world-creation. By declining to secede ontologically from the actual world—by forgoing a fictional actual world of its own—the *Wake* lets our actual world be *its* actual world. This semantically otherworldly text may, paradoxically, be more *ontologically* of-this-world than any other work of fiction.

One consequence of this ontological dependence is that *Wake* readers do not experience anything like the mimetic, often intensely visual immersion that can attend the reading of a book endowed with a discrete fictional world—the kind of reading in which we feel we are no longer decoding signs on a page but rather observing the unfolding of events in another universe. Here's Ryan, a last time, on what she calls the immersive versus the interactive reading experience:

> The textual incompatibility of the two types of experience can be traced back to several factors. While immersion in a textual world depends on the forward movement of a linear plot, interactivity involves (and creates) a spatial organization. While immersion presupposes pretended belief in a solid extratextual reference world, interactivity thrives in a fluid environment of changing relations. While immersion looks through the signs toward the reference world, interactivity exploits the materiality of the medium. Textual representation behaves in one respect like holographic pictures: you cannot see the worlds and the signs at the same time. Readers and spectators must focus beyond the signs to witness the emergence of a three-dimensional life-like reality.[21]

Rita Felski could be speaking for readers of *Finnegans Wake* when she observes, in objecting to the above passage, that readers may also be enchanted by "a cadence of tone, by particular inflections and verbal rhythms, by an irresistible combination of word choice and syntax."[22] For that matter, most *Wake* seminars and reading groups experience moments of a kind of immersive interactivity, when the group simultaneously produces and falls under a spell of collective interpretation. But these are not the same thing as immersion in a fictional world. We may be transported, held captive, or swept away by the *Wake*, but not because we have misrecognized it, even for a second, as a world.

Yet it is just this check on fictional world-immersion and misrecognition that intrigues me most about the *Wake* at this moment in literary study, at least in the U.S. academy. We're in a position, first of all, to see the *Wake*'s refusal of fictional world-creation as one reason that ideology-critique has never found much purchase with it. During the last several decades, while one or another version of ideology critique has cycled through U.S. literary studies, we have had the sense that the more world-immersive a text is, the more resolutely we must turn to a hermeneutic of suspicion in order to undo the ruses of ideology and/or the unconscious that cluster most thickly at the sites of misrecognition I have been describing, where signs are to be taken for worlds.

By the same token, the less immersive the world—the less, that is, that we are in the thrall of the fictional world's modal structures—the less purchase ideology enjoys. Again, this is why the ideology critique surrounding *Finnegans Wake*, to the extent it exists at all, has tended to focus on the actual-world history of the book's reception and institutional consecration rather than on its ideological gambits at the level of mimesis and diegesis. Since about 2007, though, a growing number of literary scholars in the U.S. have been faulting ideology critique (along with other varieties of "symptomatic reading") for reproducing its own findings in stale, flat, and unprofitable ways. Many of these scholars have also proposed alternatives to the hermeneutic of suspicion, such as Eve Sedgwick's "reparative reading," Sharon Marcus's "just reading," Marcus and Stephen Best's "surface reading," Heather Love's "close but not deep" reading, and Timothy Bewes's "reading with the grain."[23] Why go trawling the hidden depths of the text for the truth about power, these critics ask, when the world affords us so many naked, unencrypted, even spectacular examples of power's abuses?[24]

Finnegans Wake can participate, I think, in this conversation in at least two ways. First of all, it can act as a limit case for surface reading insofar as its surface is not legible in the same way as that of other texts. Because it asks its readers in effect to produce its surface in the course of reading it—because a significant amount of decryption or at least unpacking is entailed even in a with-the-grain traversal of the text—the *Wake* interferes with the dichotomy of surface-versus-depth. It may even be the case that the surface and the depths are continuous or fused in Joyce's book; that the *Wake*'s integrity lies in sparing its reader from having to translate it into a theoretical metalanguage because that act of translation is immanent to the operation of the text, not a conversion of inside to outside, latent to patent. By these lights, much *Wake* criticism—maybe even the majority of it—since the book's publication has exemplified the kind of thick-descriptive "surface reading" that has only more recently come to seem necessary or timely to critics who work on other texts. Yet at the same time, the apparent fusion of surface and depth in the *Wake* may have had something like the opposite result. In rushing into the arms of unpacking, elaboration, and decryption, we may have failed to do justice to that sensuous integument that surrounds the work's constitutive signifiers without being quite identical to them. We have yet to produce, in reference to the *Wake*, anything like the "erotics of art" for which Susan Sontag called in "Against Interpretation"; we know virtually nothing about the affective dimensions of the *Wake*.[25] We may be in a unique position, then, to begin exploring the integrity of a work of fiction that plays upon our senses and elicits a range of powerful affective responses from us without asking us to misrecognize that work for a world.

I don't mean to claim that *Finnegans Wake* is alone in being a fiction without a fictional world, much less that its ontological dependence on the actual world makes it necessarily more "real," less "escapist," more "committed," more "political" than works endowed with a fictional world. When the *Wake*'s scheduled May 1939 publication seemed likely to be delayed, Joyce himself complained, "They had better hurry. War is going to break out, and nobody will be reading my book any more."[26] It was as if the book's ontological dependence on the actual world made it part of the closed economy of that world's self-scrutiny—as if, lacking a fictional world, it could not be escaped into but only shelved in favor of more pressing actual-world events. It's possible that in order to receive news of the world from a novel, we need it to be discrete from our world, to bring news by way of analogy rather than through contiguity. We may need a novel's forms of ease in possible-world-creation, its unstrenuous and casual modeling, to stand in contrast to the difficulty of creation in the actual world. We may need novels to offer relief, as well, from the world's illegible consequence and possibility structures, its distribution of contingency and necessity. To the extent that a novel is a model of the world, there are advantages to that model's having edges, however engagingly what goes on inside those boundaries might replicate, distend, or overclarify the modal structures of what we call the actual world. The fantastic condensations and encryptions of the *Wake*, the laborious piercings that constitute its world refusal, may be perforations we cannot quite tear.

This very question of fiction's continuity with the actual world is centrally at stake in book I chapter 8 of *Finnegans Wake*, "Anna Livia Plurabelle," where we'll shortly rejoin Norris. As the chapter opens, two washerwomen—identified later in the book as "queer Mrs. Quickenough and odd Miss Doddpebble" (*FW* 620.19–20)—are gossiping as they do laundry on opposite banks of the Liffey somewhere in Dublin, through which the river runs from its source in Wicklow to join the Irish Sea. The subjects of their gossip are predictably human, featuring Chapelizod denizen Anna Livia Plurabelle, her early sexual exploits, her midlife tolerance for her husband's philandering, her many children. Yet as the dusk deepens, the two laundresses begin to have trouble hearing one another above the sound of the river and the flittering of bats. Their human gossip tapers off and soon they find their feet grown heavy, rooted in the muddy banks. As night falls, Mrs. Quickenough is transformed into an elm tree, Miss Doddpebble into a stone, and they lapse into silence. I.8 is thus an appealing tale for us at a moment when environmental humanists are attending to the vibrancy of stone, to mushroom–human affiliations, and to the manner in which forests think; a moment that invites us to see ourselves as coplanar with nonhuman beings and with the inorganic, such that the old metamorphoses in Ovid—petrification, arborification, ornification, and the like—begin to seem more than fanciful.[27] In Joyce's tale a woman may incarnate a river, but she may also become, like Baucis and Philemon, a tree, or like Echo a stone. Such transformations hint not only at what Jeffrey Cohen has called "the anthropomorphic in the stone" and "the petric in the human" but also at intimate and active partnerships between things and beings.[28] For it is in collaborating not only with one another but also with water and rocks that Joyce's washerwomen undergo their transformation into "petrock" and "laurals" (*FW* 203.30–31)—into the lovers Petrarch and Laura, yes, but also into a stone enfolded in social relations (a pet rock) and the laurel tree Daphne became.

Norris's essay "Fluid Figures in 'Anna Livia Plurabelle'" takes up Finn Fordham's call for an ecocritical reading of the *Wake*, as other scholars have since done.[29] But her approach remains unique among these in being informed by possible worlds theory. The washerwomen, she observes, "should anchor the chapter in a more or less conventional fictional world"—one with a stable, unitary setting in a fictional actual world patterned on Dublin and focused on the acts and utterances of human characters (even as they undergo a transformation into nonhumans).[30] But I.8 can only be paraphrased as I did above if we ignore its most conspicuous attributes as a piece of writing. These include the lexical and semantic traits the chapter shares with the rest of the *Wake* as well as a layer of reference particular to the chapter: the incorporation of some 1000 river names, many of them stashed in puns or portmanteau words or otherwise blended into the text. In Norris's reading, the river names have a purpose beyond euphony for its own sake or as a means to subliminal environmentalism, as other scholars have opined.[31] The river names, she says, turn the reader's attention less to the signifiers themselves than back "to their referents, not merely as concepts but as moving, rushing, winding, coursing, ubiquitous, global phenomena in the real world that speak themselves in the form of sound," obliging us "to place them on our mental map of the world, and to remember their function and role in human lives all over the planet."[32] This turn from signifier to referent is abetted by the chapter's not, after all, being anchored in a more or less fictional world.

Norris goes on to describe a host of human–nonhuman entanglements in "Anna Livia Plurabelle." I want to tarry, though, with the chapter's river names as offering an alternative to the strong environmentalism performed by the washerwomen's metamorphosis. That transformation has attracted ecocritics for the reasons I've just adduced—because it forgoes the anthropocentric masterplot of human agency acting in and upon nature, producing, instead, a fungibility between character and environs. Yet this same Ovidian layer in I.8 also says that magic or divinity alone may re-entangle human and nonhuman. By reviving the mythological trope of radical transformation, it makes environmentalism a function of credulity, leaving none for the reader who refuses the premise that a person can turn into a stone or an elm. In this, Joyce's tale approaches the strong quasi-theological gatekeeping question that frames the largest-scale environmental issue of our own day, the question of whether one "believes in" global climate change. A strong theory of environmentalism is addressed exclusively to those who answer that question in the affirmative. Only a weak theory of environmentalism can even imagine a question like the following: what is the environmentalism of the climate-change denier?

It's just such a weak environmentalism—"weak" not as in fragile but as in local, provisional, contingent, low-bar—that I.8 exhibits in bubbling with river names. Taken together, these can seem like a stunt or eccentricity to be either embraced or dismissed as a totality. But if we approach this feature as part of a phenomenology of reading the chapter, we're reminded that each river name is primed with a charge that can be released only by a certain subset of readers. When one of the laundresses exhorts the other, saying "I amstel waiting. Garonne, garonne!" (*FW* 205.14–15), you release its charge in a specific way if you happen to be in the Netherlands, reading by the banks of the Amstel river, or in southwest France where the Garonne flows to the sea north of Bordeaux. If you've spent time in Zürich and know the names of the Sihl and Limmat rivers whose confluence is just downstream from the city center, reading the exclamation "Yssel that the limmat?" (*FW* 198.13) causes a little burst of recognition. And if you know the border country between England and Wales, or you're a reader of Wordsworth, the phrase "wyerye rima" (*FW* 200.23) summons the River Wye apostrophized in "Tintern Abbey." One scholar of the *Wake* has written in a revealingly personal manner about being hailed by a familiar river name in I.8:

> Rereading the "Anna Livia Plurabelle" chapter recently I came upon the phrase "bakereen's dusind" (*FW* 212.20), and there before me was the name of the South African river near whose banks I grew up (the Umsindusi, or in its familiar abbreviated form, the Dusi), and, like the small boy Joyce imagined in just such a situation, I felt a momentary pleasure in this unlooked-for bond between the work and me—a pleasure in no way diminished by my awareness that, if asked whether I was responding to an intended allusion or to a coincidence thrown up by the chapter's dense web of names, I would probably have to answer, like Bloom in his response to Stephen's story set in the Queen's Hotel, "coincidence."[33]

For Derek Attridge, the author of this passage, encountering the Dusi in "dusind" exemplifies his frequent experience, as a reader of Joyce, of "being surprised at the sudden public manifestation of what one took to be a private memory or quirk."[34] The frequency of that experience is a function less of the sheer scope of *Ulysses* and *Finnegans Wake* than of how they fuse systematicity and chance, necessity and contingency. They are, in other words, coincidence-generators. But the *Wake*'s coincidences, as I argued earlier, are lexical and semantic rather than diegetic. As Attridge's anecdote reveals, the experience of recognition and attachment produced by these coincidences occurs not between characters in the story world but between individual readers and a text supersaturated with unique words and with the names, albeit frequently distorted ones, of unique places. To the extent his encounter with the Dusi works as coincidence—again, as "an instance of contingency bearing the marks of necessity"—it is because it produces the feeling that here, in this arbitrary field of names, is the one addressed to me, the name with my name on it.

If collecting and deploying the names of rivers as Joyce does in the *Wake* can be considered environmentalism, it's not an environmentalism of suasion or argument. For that very reason the chapter's weak environmentalist gambit is immune to denial or refutation. Far from asking readers to believe a narrative of radical transformation, it uses the humbler magic of the name to construct a text dense with potential recognition-triggers that, when tripped, bind particular readers to particular waters. It's not an environmentalism that fears anthropocentrism, either. What aspect of a river could be more anthropocentric than the name given to it by humans? Yet in distorting its river names by fusing them with other words, often in multiple languages, "Anna Livia Plurabelle" and its tributaries in other chapters project these fluvionyms not just in space but also in time, enacting something like the process of linguistic drift, the morphing of words through shifts in usage and practice, cross-linguistic influence, etc. When the narrator of "The Mookse and the Gripes" says of Nuvoletta in I.6, "her muddied name was Missisliffi" (*FW* 159.12–13), that voice not only conflates the rivers of Huck Finn (Mississippi) and Fionn mac Cumhaill (Mrs. Liffey) but also invokes the drift from the Algonquin *Misi-ziibi* to the French *Messipi* to the English *Mississippi*. Linguistic drift like this is the deep time of language. Joyce's speculative use of it in the river chapter and elsewhere unpetrifies the very proper nouns that trigger recognition, unbinding us from our presentism even as it binds us to the banks and flows we know. What's more, this convergence of diffusive spatial recognition and linguistic deep time might be said to epitomize the *Wake*'s project overall. Joyce's last work, by these lights, is a speculative fiction angled toward a future in which what reads today as nonsense, neologism, paleologism, or hapax legomenon might become common parlance—and vice versa.

And it's in this crossing of diffusiveness, recognition, and applied anti-presentism that "Anna Livia Plurabelle" can stimulate our thinking about environmentalisms that lie to the side of the strong models that predominate today. These strong environmentalisms tend toward the normative, the global, the epochal, the apocalyptic. Motivated by a sense of urgency, they can be so strong in their conceptual gatekeeping as to impede just the kinds of broad and loosely tied coalitions that urgency requires. We need to keep attending, then, to weaker, lower-intensity environmentalisms, both for their own sakes and with an eye toward moving weak and strong into relation. The kind of weak environmentalism I've touched on here—and, in a twilit dialogue with Norris's pathbreaking work on Joyce, heard burbling through I.8—neither presumes nor impugns world-scaled commitments. Instead, it starts with local attachments that catch one off-guard and set one quietly wobbling off the axis of presentism and present-bias. It's an environmentalism that says, "Of all the rivers in the world, *this* one claims me *now* in the long drift of language and matter."

Notes

1 See Margot Norris, *Joyce's Web: The Social Unraveling of Modernism* (Austin: University of Texas Press, 1992).

2 Margot Norris, *Writing War in the Twentieth Century* (Charlottesville: University of Virginia Press, 2000), 4.

3 Lubomír Doležel, *Heterocosmica: Fiction and Possible Worlds* (Baltimore: Johns Hopkins University Press, 1998), ix.

4 See, for example, Margot Norris, "Possible-Worlds Theory and Joyce's 'Wandering Rocks': The Case of Father Conmee," *Joyce Studies Annual* 18 (2007): 21–43; "The (Im) possible Worlds of Joyce's 'Oxen of the Sun' Episode in *Ulysses*," *Genre* 41.1–2 (2008): 95–123; and *Virgin and Veteran Readings of 'Ulysses'* (New York: Palgrave Macmillan, 2011).

5 I have in mind Shloss's unpublished presentation, "The Ecology of *Finnegans Wake*," which she delivered at a roundtable on "The Integrity of *Finnegans Wake*" at the International James Joyce Symposium in Prague in 2010.

6 On the *Wake* as multiverse see, for example, Strother B. Purdy, "Is There a Multiverse in *Finnegans Wake*, and Does That Make It a Religious Book?" *JJQ* 36.3 (1999): 587–602. The quotation from the *Wake* is James Joyce, *Finnegans Wake* (New York: Viking, 1939), 91, line 25. Further references will be cited parenthetically in the text as *FW* followed page number and line number.

7 Ruth Ronen, *Possible Worlds in Literary Theory* (Cambridge: Cambridge University Press, 1994), 25.

8 Ibid., 29. The *Wake*'s recurrent narrative elements and scenarios (the washerwomen, the crime in the park, etc.) may appear to constitute a kind of minimal worldedness through their recurrence, as if to say, "Here is a world in which these things are

held to have happened." However, the text's semantically and logically destabilizing operations, beginning at the scale of the individual word, make it impossible to locate these scenarios within a modal system—as belonging, in Ronen's terms, to a set of facts versus a subworld versus a counter-world. Recognizable narrative elements, even recurrent ones, are not the same thing as a modal system, and without it do not constitute a fictional world.

9 Margot Norris, "Possible Worlds Theory and the Fantasy Universe of *Finnegans Wake*," *JJQ* 44.3 (2007): 462.

10 Ibid., 459.

11 Marie-Laure Ryan, *Possible Worlds, Artificial Intelligence, and Narrative Theory* (Bloomington: Indiana University Press, 1991), 33; qtd in Norris, "Possible Worlds Theory," 459.

12 Norris, "Possible Worlds Theory," 461, 462.

13 Ibid., 468.

14 For a neighboring discussion of Norris's work on the *Wake* and possible worlds theory, see Tony Thwaites, "'Through the Windr of a Wondr in a Wildr is a Weltr as a Wirbl or a Warbl is a World': *Wake*ing Worlding," *Autralasian Journal of Irish Studies* 14 (2014): 11–28. Thwaites argues not that the *Wake* declines worldedness altogether but that it is concerned with "that impossible, liminal state at which there is *not yet* any separation between something we could call a 'textual actual world' and some other things we could call 'embedded private virtual worlds.'" The *Wake*, in other words, is occupied with world-emergence, with "*world* as verb rather than noun: worlding" (17–18; emphasis in original).

15 See Derek Attridge, "The Postmodernity of Joyce: Chance, Coincidence, and the Reader," *Joyce Studies Annual* 6 (1995): 15.

16 James Joyce, *Ulysses: The Corrected Text*, ed. Hans Walter Gabler with Wolfhard Steppe and Claus Melchior (New York: Vintage Books, 1986), 8.502–4.

17 See Scarlett Baron, *'Strandentwining Cable': Joyce, Flaubert, and Intertextuality*, 249. The phrase "indentity of undiscernibles" alludes to Leibniz's Law of the Identity of Indiscernibles, which posits that no two objects have exactly the same properties, even if they are qualitatively identical. Possible worlds theory grows out of Leibniz's view that God chose the best world for us from an infinite number of possible worlds.

18 Attridge, "The Postmodernity of Joyce," 17.

19 Marie-Laure Ryan, "Cheap Plot Tricks, Plot Holes, and Narrative Design," *NARRATIVE* 17.1 (2009): 58.

20 Ryan has herself written about fiction's capacity to refuse worldedness. As she puts it, "an important form of experimental literature creates worlds that cannot satisfy even the most liberal interpretation of possibility because they transgress the basic laws of logic: non-contradiction (you cannot have p and ~p) and the excluded middle (you must have either p or ~p)." See Marie-Laure Ryan, "Impossible Worlds and Aesthetic Illusion," in *Immersion and Distance: Aesthetic Illusion in Literature and Other Media*, eds. Werner Wolf, Walter Bernhart, and Andreas Mahler (Amsterdam: Rodopi, 2013), 129. Although it might be more accurate to refer to these as fictional nonworlds on the grounds that "an entity cannot be logically impossible and still remain a world," Ryan elects to call them "impossible worlds" to reflect the fact that "readers of literary fiction have a broader sense of what is a world than logicians" (130). But it's with her logician's hat on that she singles out Jonathan Safran Foer's "Here We Aren't, So Quickly" (2010) as exemplifying world-refusing logical contradictions both

between and within individual sentences. One wonders what she might have said about the co-presence of p and ~p in a single *Wake* word such as the aforementioned "chaosmos."

21 Marie-Laure Ryan, *Narrative as Virtual Reality: Immersion and Interactivity in Literature and Electronic Media* (Baltimore: Johns Hopkins University Press, 2001), 98.

22 Rita Felski, *Uses of Literature* (Oxford: Blackwell, 2008), 63.

23 See, respectively, Eve Kosofsky Sedgwick, "Paranoid Reading and Reparative Reading, or, You're So Paranoid, You Probably Think This Essay Is About You," in *Touching Feeling: Affect, Pedagogy, Performativity* (Durham: Duke University Press, 2003), 123–51; Sharon Marcus, *Between Women: Friendship, Desire, and Marriage in Victorian England* (Princeton, NJ: Princeton University Press, 2007); Sharon Marcus and Stephen Best, "Surface Reading: An Introduction," *Representations* 108.1 (2009): 1–21; Heather Love, "Close but not Deep: Literary Ethics and the Descriptive Turn," *New Literary History* 41.2 (2010): 371–91; and Timothy Bewes, "Reading with the Grain: A New World in Literary Criticism," *Differences: A Journal of Feminist Cultural Studies* 21.3 (2010): 1–33.

24 Here I'm paraphrasing the opening paragraphs of Sedgwick's "Paranoid Reading," 123–24. For a fuller discussion of the so-called post-critical turn in relation to modernist studies, see my "Weak Theory, Weak Modernism," *Modernism/modernity* 25.3 (2018): 437–59, as well as the other essays in the special issue my essay introduces and the subsequent responses to the special issue published in 2019 on the journal's online Print+ platform.

25 See Susan Sontag, "Against Interpretation," in *Against Interpretation and Other Essays* (New York: Farrar, Straus and Giroux, 1966), 10.

26 Richard Ellmann, *James Joyce* (New York: Oxford University Press, 1982), 721.

27 I refer here, respectively, to Jeffery Jerome Cohen, *Stone: An Ecology of the Inhuman* (Minneapolis: University of Minnesota Press, 2015); Anna Lowenhaupt Tsing, *The Mushroom at the End of the World: On the Possibility of Life in Capitalist Ruins* (Princeton: Princeton University Press, 2015); and Eduardo Kohn, *How Forests Think: Toward an Anthropology Beyond the Human* (Berkeley: University of California Press, 2013).

28 See Cohen, *Stone*, 10.

29 Finn Fordham, *Lots of Fun at Finnegans Wake: Unraveling Universals* (Oxford: Oxford University Press, 2007), 20. For ecocritical studies of I.8, see Bonnie Kime Scott, "Joyce, Ecofeminism, and the River as Woman," in Robert Brazeau and Derek Gladwin, eds., *Eco-Joyce: The Environmental Imagination of James Joyce* (Cork: Cork University Press, 2014): 59–69; Alison Lacivita, *The Ecology of "Finnegans Wake"* (Gainesville: University Press of Florida, 2015); and Rachel Nisbet, "James Joyce's Urban EcoAnarchism," *EcoZon@* 7.2 (2016): 10–28.

30 Margot Norris, "Fluid Figures in 'Anna Livia Plurabelle': An Ecocritical Reading of I.8," in Kimberly J. Devlin and Christine Smedley, eds., *Joyce's Allmaziful Plurabilities: Polyvocal Explorations of "Finnegans Wake"* (Gainesville: University Press of Florida, 2015), 135.

31 See, respectively, John Bishop, *Joyce's Book of the Dark: Finnegans Wake* (Madison: University of Wisconsin Press, 1986), 336; and James S. Atherton, *The Books at the Wake* (Carbondale: Southern Illinois University Press, 1959), 45; qtd. in Norris, "Fluid Figures," 136.

32 Norris, "Fluid Figures," 136.

33 Attridge, "Postmodernity," 121.

34 Ibid., 121.

Part VII

Epilogue

Chapter 16

THE REEL MARGOT

Moshe Gold

Why do some critical works on film not receive their proper acknowledgement until years after their publication?[1] Many essays have appeared on Joyce and film, and quite a few books on the subject.[2] But what does "Joyce and film" mean here? It could mean James Joyce and film adaptations, the use of Joycean techniques in the history of film, the ways films influence our reading of Joyce, Joyce's own attempts to launch a movie house, Joyce's associations with early cinematic giants,[3] the filmic qualities of Joyce's writing, allusions to films and film stars in Joyce,[4] or the medium of film and the (moving) art of Joyce. It could also mean applying a specific film (or critical) theory to the works of Joyce, or perhaps a digital archive devoted to updating references pertaining to film and Joyce. It could even be a title of a course: *Joyce and film*. None of these meanings captures the uniqueness of Margot Norris' book *Ulysses*, a work that surpasses each of the individual meanings listed. Yet, other than scattered references to her short book in later books on the topic(s), there needs to be what I will call an inheritance of Norris on *Ulysses*/film.

The opening dedication to Norris' gem of a book suggests the kind of autobiographical and self-reflective (philosophical) musings and recollections of Stanley Cavell: "For my son, Josef Norris, whose love of films and filmmaking when he was young inspired me" (v). This non-saccharine dedication addresses an other's love, a clear distinction between films and filmmaking, the memory of youth, and personal inspiration. In her "Acknowledgements" (a Cavellian term in other discourses), Norris once again invokes her memory of her own youth and inspiration: "I first saw the 1967 Joseph Strick film of James Joyce's *Ulysses* while I was an undergraduate at the University of Florida, and before I had yet read the novel. The film inspired me to read the book, and set me on my way to becoming a life-long scholar of the works of Joyce" (ix): Strick's *Ulysses* prior to Joyce's *Ulysses*, prior to Norris' *Ulysses*.

The personal intensifies when Norris tells us that she was "in touch with Joseph Strick [. . .] [which] allowed me to ask hundreds of questions by e-mail, to which I received full, interesting, often funny replies" (ix). Moreover, her autobiographical narrative continues, when Strick visited LA, "he kindly agreed to meet my class at the University of California, at Irvine, and satisfy my students' endless curiosity about his choices in making the film" (ix). Note the oxymoron in satisfying something that is endless! Yet, because she situates others' desires in a pedagogical situation, Norris provides us with a replicating form of postponed desire—after all, she first experiences Strick's film in an undergraduate class, an experience that became expressed as a desire to become a Joycean scholar. To students, there is something gratifying, yet endless, when encountering Joyce (no matter the medium). I am not choosing to focus on satisfaction from any perspective other than the one Norris herself reveals to her readers. She expands the educational occasions (with Norris as teacher—almost parallel to Stephen changing from student in *Portrait* to teacher in *Ulysses*). Strick's meeting with her class "was followed by an extensive interview with follow-up calls and e-mails, which *satisfied my own endless curiosity* about how the film was made" (ix, my emphasis). At this point, the vertiginous zigzagging of satisfaction and endless curiosity among teacher and student displays not just interacting with, but actually exchanging positions with the other. Norris performatively navigates oscillating pedagogical perspectives.

The "generosity [. . .] openness and candor" of Strick, made writing her *Ulysses*, in fact, "one of the most pleasurable scholarly experiences of my career as a Joycean" (ix). Such an experience of pleasure and satisfaction derives, in part, from writing a book inspired by her son "Josef" and film, and by her relationship with "Joseph" Strick and film—in addition to her clearly inspired relationship with her students (and the student she herself still is)! Norris, having seen Strick's *Ulysses* before reading Joyce's *Ulysses*, presents her readers with another, this time biographical, parallel to Strick:

> Joseph Strick told interviewer Stephen Watts that his parents enjoyed keeping the book [Joyce's *Ulysses*] on view at home in the hope of stirring up debate with visitors. They challenged friends and argued with them if they judged the novel "dirty." Strick's father showed himself to be a wise reader of *Ulysses*. "It's about life and people—you and me and all the rest," he used to say. To young Joseph himself the book initially just "like an artifact, an interesting object that lay around the house," but when he was sixteen, he picked it up and finally read *Ulysses* himself. Watts reports: "He didn't understand it but was fascinated. He had found something completely new, and he says he has been finding new things in it ever since" (16).[5]

Joseph Strick's father (amazingly like Leopold Bloom's father) is a Jewish immigrant, and Joseph grows up in a house in which his parents keep Joyce's *Ulysses* on view to stir up debate (akin to several Joycean debates?). Joseph the filmmaker reads Joyce's *Ulysses* when he's 16 years old, is fascinated by the "artifact, an interesting object," and, ostensibly for the rest of his life, continues to find new things in Joyce's *Ulysses.* Of course, along the way, he makes his own (film) *Ulysses.*

As Norris points out in her third chapter, "Strick pointedly titled his film *Ulysses by James Joyce* in the opening credits," but rather than uncritically accept this detail, Norris poignantly ends her sentence by stating that "the question of what his film does and does not accomplish as an adaptation of the novel is none the less legitimate" (31). Unsatisfied with this comment, though, Norris—lucidly, and with pedagogical insight for all readers of Joyce—unsettles the question: the "chief difficulty with this question is that it presupposes James Joyce's *Ulysses* to be a stable and identifiable entity, rather than a text whose realization as a piece of writing that is *read* makes it finally a product of interpretation" (31, Norris' emphasis). Rather than applying a popular theory or name-drop a famous theorist, Norris, being an unending mix of student and teacher, makes, what I claim, is a self-reflective comment: "We might say that each reader *constructs* his or her own *Ulysses*, and that there are as many *Ulysses* (plural) as there are scholars and readers of the text" (31, Norris' emphasis). Norris has, in fact, constructed her own *Ulysses.* Perhaps this claim partially addresses the first question in this essay. Each reader's "own" *Ulysses* might be difficult for others to place neatly into a pre-given category. Does Norris' *Ulysses* fit only one category? More importantly, might Norris' insight not provide students with an effective way to read/view Joyce's/Joseph's *Ulysses* (plural)?

Norris returns to Strick's title at the very start of her fourth chapter. Not satisfied with her prior comments, Norris now writes, the "opening title of Joseph Strick's film of *Ulysses* makes it clear that this film is inextricably linked to Joyce's novel: 'Ulysses by James Joyce', it reads, printed in a style of type that imitates the covers of the early editions of the work" (47). While seemingly a fact-filled sentence written in a clear style, the truth-claims embedded here are submerged like most of a Hemingway iceberg. Why should Norris incessantly—throughout her book—refer to Strick as "Joseph Strick"? Why should she repeat the observation about Strick's title? If Strick's film were entitled *Ulysses*—without the phrase "by James Joyce"—would it not be "inextricably linked to Joyce's novel"? We can infer an answer from a phrase in the same paragraph: "Joseph Strick's direction of *Ulysses* complicates his fidelity to the text with interpretive and inventive enhancements that produce a singular vision of the novel" (47). I submit that Norris here circuitously, again, crafts a self-reflective truth-claim: the title of Norris' book is not "Strick's *Ulysses*," nor is it "Joseph Strick's *Ulysses*," nor is it "James Joyce's *Ulysses*," nor is it "Joyce and film." Instead, if one looks at the cover and the title page, the title contains a single word: *Ulysses*. This short book is Norris' constructed *Ulysses* that itself "complicates [Norris'] fidelity to the text [both Joseph Strick's and James Joyce's] with interpretive and inventive enhancements that produce a singular vision of the novel" (47). The inclusion of many still photographs from the moving film (in such a short book), the rich background in drama and cinema, the focus on the "Modern Avant-Garde" and "a Cinematic Medium," the lucid exploration of Ireland and Dublin in relation to both film and novel, and the very fact that this book is published in a series called "Ireland Into Film," all lead scrupulous readers to construct their own world of Norris' world-making *Ulysses*. Pedagogically, Norris performs for her readers the claims in her "Acknowledgments." A student/teacher/scholar can craft prose and visual styles addressed to *Ulysses* that actually construct their own *Ulysses*.

In the middle of her fourth chapter, Norris explains how Strick first confronts viewers with Bloom "as a Jew" (53). Bloom's "introduction into the film as a Jew is accomplished by two cleverly ironic transitions" (53). The first happens when Strick cuts to Bloom in the kitchen immediately after Haines states "I don't want my country to fall into the hands of the Jews." The second "ironic transition" occurs cuts to Bloom "by a store window emblazoned with a Star of David, his identity intensified with Semitic music" (53). Viewers encounter this scene after Mr. Deasy presents his joke to Stephen about the Irish never persecuting the Jews since the Irish never let them in. Rather than focusing on the explicit content of her description of these two juxtapositions, I argue that, again, Norris here, vigilantly self-reflective, invites her readers to observe how this *Ulysses* first introduces Joseph Strick "as a Jew" in her constructed world.

Of the abundance of "illustrations" (so called at the start of the book)/ pictures in Norris' book, all except one come from Joseph Strick's film *Ulysses*. In fact, the very first picture displayed to readers is none other than "Plate 1. Joseph Strick" (15). Readers are confronted by the director's smiling face looking directly at them; Strick's eyes in the shot are clearly looking directly at the camera. This is not Strick directing a film; this is not Strick reading *Ulysses*[6]; this is not Strick teaching Norris' students; this is not Strick in Dublin or Ireland, etc. It is a photograph of a personal nature. One can barely see anything other than a friendly looking face resting a cheek on his arm, suggesting a relaxed and personal pose, almost akin to a photograph of a family member displayed somewhere in one's home. Where precisely does this illustration appear? In what Norris later calls "a cleverly ironic transition" (53). Most of page 14 (the very last page of Chapter 1) is white space.

The few lines on the top of this page end with the following comment: "many of the formal features of *Ulysses* might be thought to have predicted the cinema, which was in its infancy at the time of the novel's setting but which was undergoing rapid maturation at the time of the novel's writing" (14). We might expect the next page to then discuss such "formal features," how they somehow "predicted the cinema," the "infancy" of cinema, or the "novel's writing." No. The next page/chapter introduces into Norris' *Ulysses* Joseph Strick as a Jew. Norris accomplishes this introduction by crafting her own "cleverly ironic transition." Rather than shifting into the non-stable text of James Joyce's *Ulysses*, or the non-stable text of Joseph Strick's *Ulysses*, Norris cuts to the personal history of Joseph Strick "as a Jew" parallel to Bloom's personal history "as a Jew."

Recall that in her third chapter, Norris challenges the "presuppos[ition that] James Joyce's *Ulysses* [is] a stable and identifiable entity" (31). The instability of Joyce's *Ulysses* mixes into the instability of Strick's *Ulysses*, which here mixes into the instability of Norris' *Ulysses* (and endlessly continues with each reader's own constructed voyage and world-making). The clever transition to Strick "as a Jew" does not simply follow immediately from the last sentence of her first chapter. Rather, Norris constructs her world in such a way as to challenge any stable relationship among all the *Ulysses* (plural) here. The friendly photograph of Joseph Strick appears beneath prose introducing Joseph Strick "as a Jew" by way of his father:

> Joseph Strick was born in Braddock, Pennsylvania, near Pittsburgh, in 1923 and grew up in Pennsylvania. His father was a Jewish immigrant from Poland who worked for the steel industry and had a talent for engineering and inventing. The family had great respect for the arts, and Strick's father smuggled a copy of *Ulysses* into the United States from France while it was still banned. (15)

The paragraph continues with the biographical anecdote discussed above concerning a 16-year-old "Joseph himself" reading Joyce's *Ulysses*. Just as Norris' *Ulysses* displays the histories of "Drama and Cinema," "the Modern Avant-Garde," the "Literary Challenges of *Ulysses*," a "Cinematic Medium," and "Ireland and Dublin" (all the last phrases from each of her five chapters), so too does Norris' *Ulysses* display the "inextricabl[e] link" (47) to personal histories of Joseph/Josef and memories of the educational (and family) histories of Margot Norris. In other words, Norris crafts clever transitions in her *Ulysses* to ensure that, pedagogically, her readers/students challenge the notion that her *Ulysses* remains fixed as a "stable and identifiable entity" (31). This claim also, I suggest, helps answer the first question of this essay.

In "Ulysses in a Cinematic Medium" (Chapter 4), Norris claims that "[arguably, the film's greatest challenge was the invention of devices for representing the vast amount of interior experience offered by the book" (57). For Norris, Strick's "film invented an array of tactics for filling the screen with visual images suggested by the verbalized thoughts" (58). Norris herself constructs her *Ulysses* in similar fashion. She has invented an array of tactics for filling her text/screen with visual images and verbalized thoughts. The picture of Joseph Strick, the personal memories of her own educational experiences, the dedication to her son Josef, the desire to address the unending curiosity of her students and herself, the relationship between Strick and Norris, etc., all exhibit an array of tactics for constructing and interpreting her *Ulysses.*

Norris ensures that her readers pause (something one is not quite able to do if one attempts to watch Strick's film in an uninterrupted single viewing—but perhaps Norris would challenge even this ability, as one is unable to read Joyce's *Ulysses* in an uninterrupted single reading) over the exhibition of revealed bodies. The second illustration/picture in Norris' book is simply entitled "Plate 2. Mulligan" (41). This "Plate" does not reveal Mulligan at the tower, or Mulligan talking to Stephen or to Haines. Instead, we look directly at the nude body of Mulligan with arms lifted, naked derriere facing readers, about to plunge into the waters below. The prose on that page explains that the "film was able to portray *Buck Mulligan's stately* backside poised to dive into the Forty Foot swimming hole (Plate 2), but the focused frontal genital nudity required to present Bloom's 'limp father of thousands' would have been impossible in a 1967 film, as would reproduction of the delicate lassitude of the prose" (41, emphasis added). Note how Norris deftly weaves, unravels, and reconstructs Joyce's introduction to Buck Mulligan in the opening four words of Joyce's *Ulysses* (after the title, of course): "Stately, plump Buck Mulligan." Norris visually introduces her readers to Mulligan with a "stately backside" nude picture, but not of Mulligan's genitals. Unclothed, ostensibly on full display to her readers, the body of Mulligan also, simultaneously, remains hidden. One might argue, in terms of the history of cinema, about frontal nudity in film, but that is not my point here. My claim is that, again, Norris performs an education tactic/transition for readers of her *Ulysses*: remember the lacunae, remember the missing parts, construct your own interpretation of what is not there, yet there.

Norris uses this clever tactic again in her chapter on "Ulysses in a Cinematic Medium" when she confronts readers with "Plate 14. Bloom in the operating theatre." The picture/still presents the naked body of Bloom on an operating table. Except for shoes and socks on his feet, Bloom's body is fully exposed/revealed. Only, the body is not fully displayed. Strick has Milo O'Shea (the actor playing Bloom) cover his genitals with (what appears to be) a hat.

We are duped again into thinking we can finally see Leopold Bloom's real and complete physical body. But we cannot, Norris teaches us, ever see the complete or real bodies of Mulligan, Bloom, or Molly. As Norris argues about the presentation of Molly in *Ulysses* (plural), a successful *Ulysses* contains what people get wrong—in terms of none other than photographic shots of one's body. For Norris, the

> film succeeds in making Molly Bloom not a sex object, but a sex subject in our contemporary sense of the word—that is, a thinking agent who has her own vision of the world with her own views on men, women, sex and gender roles. Sometimes she gets things wrong. When she wonders why Bloom showed Stephen her photograph ('what is he driving at now showing him my photo'), she imagines them leering and guffawing in the kitchen, when the film had earlier shown us Bloom's pride and Stephen's nonplussed and uncomfortable response." (69)

A photograph, a personal still, "my photo," drives one's imagination to construct a world (or a world viewed) that appears to reveal, but actually also covers. Nevertheless, however "wrong" such a constructed view might be, it is too late. It has become part of the interpreter's *Ulysses.* The "leering" at a photograph mixes into ("driving at now") the constructed *Ulysses.*

Something very personal always remains present in its absence. And yet, while the desire to satisfy endless curiosity, or the "love of films and filmmaking" (from the dedication) will drive us on continually, that desire or love also inspires us. Indeed, I would claim that both the endless drive and the love that inspires are cut/interspersed shots of personal history that make this book so pleasurable for Norris to write and for us to read.

Let us return to my first question. In her *Ulysses,* Norris wonders why "Academic criticism of the film has been surprisingly scant and [...] surprisingly negative" (70), and she ends her fourth chapter quoting extremely positive reviews of the film. The very last sentence of that chapter reads, "They [the positive reviewers] may not have been vindicated in their predictions ['one of the great classics of cinematic art'/'a remarkable achievement'],[7] but perhaps their judgments deserve renewed consideration in the twenty-first century" (71). I have argued that readers apply this last type of comment to Norris' *Ulysses* (plural), which itself deserves renewed consideration. The attention to Norris has been too scant.

Perhaps readers will realize the stylistic self-awareness of Norris' *Ulysses.* Indeed, if one were to glance at the works of Norris, one would see that she began at the end. Her *Decentered Universe of Finnegans Wake* (1977), the first book by Norris—which is on Joyce's last work—has become a classic of Wakean scholarship. Toward the end of Norris' *Ulysses* (2004), she reveals one of Joseph Strick's memories about the film, a memory that parallels Norris' own career trajectory—"Strick recalls that he filmed Molly's monologue first: 'Once we had it, I knew we had a movie'" (79). Strick begins at the end, as Norris begins at the end. But such endings are endless.

Norris ends her book with a focus on memory, what we do not see, physical bodies, youth, and love:

> The Blooms as young lovers on a holiday running along the ridge of the hill appear free of all earthly cares [...] and free to give themselves over to pure beauty and pure pleasure.
>
> We may not see the rhododendrons Molly remembers so vividly in memory, but we do see the grasses stirring in the wind in the film. And their mild agitation serves as a subtle analogue for the agitation of their bodies ("and his heart was going like mad") as the lovers both make love and love. (87)

This beautifully crafted (endless) ending challenges us to remember (and reexperience) the multiple beginnings of Norris' *Ulysses* (plural). But more importantly, intimately, and personally is youth, inspiration, and love: "For my son, Josef Norris, whose love of films and filmmaking when he was young inspired me." If this essay reads like a celebratory panegyric, that's because (at least in terms of etymologically) it is an all-assembly-flattering-laudatory discourse that, I hope, motivates others to attend, with more vigilance, an inheritance of the reel Margot Norris.[8]

Notes

1 Stanley Cavell's *The World Viewed* might be among the more prominent instances of such initial misreadings and problematic (if not faulty) receptions. In fact, Cavell wrote a new forward when he published the enlarged edition, at the end of which he adds a biographical note. Moreover, he added a long last chapter entitled "More of *The World Viewed*," in which he acknowledges the frustration early readers experienced, and his ongoing desire to address difficulties readers encounter.

2 The plethora of effective essays on "Joyce and film" need their own checklist. In terms of volumes, Philip Sicker's *Ulysses, Film and Visual Culture* is an excellent book; however, due to the intended focus, there is no mention of Norris' *Ulysses* in this wonderful work. Burkdall's *Joycean Frames* was published before Norris' book, so obviously there are no references to Norris in that work. The superb collection of essays entitled *Roll Away the Reel World: James Joyce and Cinema* (edited by John McCourt) remains a standard for any book or volume devoted to "James Joyce and Cinema." However, within that collection, though Keith Williams crafts an outstanding piece on "Odysseys of Sound and Image: 'Cinematicity' and the *Ulysses* Adaptations," in which he lucidly and persuasively compares film versions of *Ulysses*, Williams never mentions Norris' *Ulysses*. I would submit that John McCourt astutely recognized this Bloomian anxiety

of influence since he explicitly writes in his "Introduction" to that collection, "Keith Williams turns our attention to film versions of Joyce's *Ulysses* in an essay that benefits from being read in parallel with Margot Norris' study of Joseph Strick's *Ulysses* [...]" (McCourt 10). This half of a sentence displays the acumen, erudition, careful critical reading, and editorial sharpness of McCourt, but in the entire *Roll* volume, there is no additional reference to Norris' *Ulysses*. Cleo Hanaway-Oakley's monograph *James Joyce and the Phenomenology of Film* provides a significant contribution to "Joyce and film," particularly in terms of her fabulous elucidation of Merleau-Ponty's phenomenology (as well as her focus on Charlie Chaplin and Joyce), but, again, due to the author's intended focus, Norris' *Ulysses* has been elided. Indeed, Hanaway-Oakley references Keith Williams' fascinatingly insightful essay (from *Roll*) on the adaptations of *Ulysses*, but there is no mention of Norris' *Ulysses*.

3 Joyce and Eisenstein come to mind. Norris includes an extremely reader-friendly summary of the encounter between these two inventors.

4 *Finnegans Wake*, of course, has received much attention in terms of cinematic allusions.

5 See Stephen Watts, "Movies: 'If you Censor "Ulysses" There Will be a Scandal,'" *New York Times* (Sunday, 2 October 1966), p. D11. Norris provides this source in her second chapter's first footnote.

6 Recall the famous photograph of one of the world's most famous actresses, Marilyn Monroe, reading *Ulysses*!

7 On page 71, Norris refers to the comments by Louis Cook of the *Detroit Free Press*, Charles Champlin of the *Los Angeles Times*, and Robert Sullivan of the *Capital Times*. Also see Norris' endnote # 33 on page 97.

8 Perhaps this is the moment, in this public collection, to acknowledge my own endless debt, as a student, as a teacher, and as a Joycean to all the work crafted by Margot Norris.

INDEX

Abraham, Nicolas 34
Adorno, Theodor 144, 152–53
Albert, Prince 126
Alexandra, Queen 135
Althusser, Louis (Althusserian) 159
Anderson, Margaret 58
Angenot, Marc 152
Aristotle 198
Attridge, Derek 9, 31, 35, 42, 87, 159, 226, 228, 235
Ausonius (poet) 95

Bachelard, Gaston 84
Balzac, Honoré de (Balzacian) 10, 175, 178, 180, 212
Barnacle Joyce, Nora (*see also* Joyce, Nora) 114
Barry, Sebastian 38
Barthes, Roland 41
Batchelor, Frederick 133
Baym, Nina 65
Beckett, Samuel 94, 121–22
Beecher Stowe, Harriet 61
Beegan, Gerry 58
Beja, Morris 85
Bellew MacManus, Terence 128, 130
Bender, Abby 166
Bénéjam, Valerie 10, 143
Bergson, Henri 150
Bewes, Timothy 231
Best, Stephen 28–29, 231
Bien, Peter 76
Birnbaum, Nathan 150
Bishop, John 68
Bishop, Ted 83
Bök, Christian 94, 99
Boyle, Robert 176
Brabant, Joanna Duchess of 124
Brooke, Arthur 112
Brower, Reuben 88
Browning, Robert 4, 51
Budgen, Frank 57, 76, 193
Burns, Robert 191
Butler, Samuel 67
Byron, Lord George Gordon 125

Castle, Gregory 11, 207
Castlereagh, Lord 125
Catton, Eleanor 9, 87, 95, 97–99
Cavell, Stanley 241
Cheng, Vincent 15
Clarke, Suzanne 68
Cohen, Jeffrey 233
Coleridge, Samuel Taylor 88
Connelly, James 135
Cummins, Maria 58–61, 63, 65–68, 70

Dante, Alighieri 112–13, 119, 197, 203
de Cusa, Nicholas 227
de Medici, Lorenzo 109
Deppman, Jed 57
Derrida, Jacques 155
Devlin, Kimberly 15, 60–61
Dickens, Charles (Dickensian) 35, 62, 212, 227, 229
Dionysos (Dionysian) 110–12
Doležel, Lubomír 207–209, 223
Donoghue, Denis 60
Drew, Sir Thomas 131
Dufoix, Stéphane 151
Dufrenne, Mikel 210–14, 216
Dürer, Albrecht 125

Eagleton, Terry 20
Edward VII (king) 124, 133–35
Eliot, T.S. 88

Ellmann, Maud 164
Emmet, Robert 131, 133–34
Empson, William 88
Enright, Ann 38
Epstein, Edmund 176
Erlls, Astrid 169

Felski, Rita 230
Ficino, Marsilio 109
FitzGerald, Edward (lord) 131
FitzGerald, Gerald 126
Flanagan, Fionnula 19–20
Fogarty, Anne 8–9, 31, 35, 57
Fordham, Finn 233
Freud, Sigmund (Freudian) 17, 20, 105

George IV, (king) 124–25
Gilbert, Sandra 5
Gilbert, Stuart 76
Gilbert and Gubar. *see* Gilbert, Sandra, Gubar, Susan
Gillespie, Michael 10
Goethe (Johann Wolfgang von) 183
Gogarty, Oliver St. John 170
Gold, Moshe 241
Gonne, Maud 131
Graham, Sir James 127
Grattan, Henry 132
Greenaway, Peter 94
Griffith, Arthur 134, 165
Groden, Michael 9, 75
Gubar, Susan 5

Hart, Clive 213
Heap, Jane 58
Hemingway, Ernest 243
Henke, Suzette 60
Herzl, Theodor 150, 168
Homer (Greek poet) 11, 81, 83–84, 91–93, 95, 98–100, 191, 196–99
Huston, Angelica 121
Huston, John 121

Ibsen, Henrik 5, 105, 120, 203

Jewett, John P. 61
Johnson, B.S. 94
Johnson, Jeri 53
Jones, Ellen Carol 9, 10, 124
Joyce, James (Joycean) 3–12, 15–22, 28–30, 32, 34–37, 41–52, 57, 59–62, 65–70, 75–76, 81–85, 87–94, 98–100, 105–107, 114, 116, 118–23, 128, 130–38, 143–55, 159–60, 162–63, 165, 167–71, 175–77, 179, 181, 184, 186, 189–203, 208, 212–15, 219, 223–26, 231–36, 241–48
Joyce, Nora. *see* Barnacle Joyce, Nora

Kavanagh, Patrick 84
Kendrick, Walter 58
Kenner, Hugh 3, 9, 30, 42–44, 46–47, 49, 53, 60, 91–92
King, Martin Luther, Jr. 189
Klemperer, Victor 144, 149

Lacan, Jacques (Lacanian) 28, 105, 159
Larbaud, Valéry 91
Lawrence, Karen 8, 15, 18, 60, 160, 176
Leavis, F.R. 88
Le Lionnais, François 94
Lecercle, Jean-Jacques 153
Ledbetter, Kathryn 58
Leo XIII (pope) 134
Linati, Carlo 91
Love, Heather 231

Mahaffey, Vicki 3, 10–11, 189
Malraux, Andrew 17
Marcus, Sharon 28–29, 231
Martyn, Edward 133
Marx, Karl (Marxist) 7, 27
Maximilian I (emperor) 125
Mayo, Michael 44–45
McCabe, Colin 3
Méliès, Georges 134–35
Meyer Spacks, Patricia 76
Michelangelo (di Lodovico Buonarroti Simoni) 109
Mierlo, Wim Van 82
Milesi, Laurent 153–54
Mitchel, John 126, 129, 132
Moore, George 80, 131
Morrison, Sir Richard 125
Mullin, Katherine 30
Munkacsy, Mihály 146

Nadel, Ira 146
Nelson, Stephanie 191
Nicholson, Robert 84
Nietzsche, Friedrich (Nietzschean) 20

Norris, Josef 241, 245–46
Norris, Margot 3–12, 15–17, 19, 21–22, 28–31, 33, 35–38, 41–47, 50–53, 66–67, 75–77, 85, 87, 90, 100, 105, 119–21, 123, 137–38, 143, 155, 159–68, 170–71, 176–77, 201–202, 208–10, 219, 223–26, 232–33, 236, 241–48
Nussbaum, Martha 78

O'Brien, Edna 38
O'Connell, Daniel 125–28
O'Donovan Rossa, Jeremiah 128
O'Neill, Jaime 38
O'Shea, Milo 246
Orpheus 110
Ovid 197, 233

Parnell, Charles Stewart 77, 126, 128, 131, 137, 227
Parnell, John Howard 227
Pecora, Vincent P. 46, 50
Peel, Sir Robert 127
Pentheus 110
Perec, Georges 94
Pius X, (pope) 134
Plato 109, 183, 198
Pound, Ezra 196

Queneau, Raymond 94

Rabaté, Jean-Michel 42
Renan, Ernest 127
Reizbaum, Marilyn 10, 159
Richards, I.A. 88
Richardson, Dorothy 90
Ricoeur, Paul 20
Ridgeway, Keith 38
Riquelme, John Paul 49, 53
Ronen, Ruth 225–26
Roth, Samuel 16
Rothberg, Michael 166
Rubens, Peter Paul 124
Russell, George 80, 198
Ryan, Marie-Laure 207–209, 211, 213, 225–26, 228, 230

Saint-Amour, Paul 11, 223
Sappho 106, 108–10, 112–13, 116
Schlegel, A.W. 88
Schlossman, Beryl 9, 105
Sedgwick, Eve Kosofsky 8, 27–28, 38, 231
Senn, Fritz 60, 81
Shakespeare, William 9, 80, 82, 91, 105–19, 121–22, 143, 181, 183, 194, 198, 217–18
Shaw, G. B. 215
Shloss, Carol 224
Sidney, Sir Philip 108, 112, 113
Skeffington, Francis Sheehy 144
Sontag, Susan 231
Spoo, Robert 80
Stratton, Eugene 130
Strick, Joseph 20, 241–46, 248
Sumner, John S. 58
Swift, Jonathan 192

Tone, Wolfe 130–31, 134
Torok, Maria 34

Urban, Charles 135

Vaglio, Carla Marengo 130, 135
Valente, Joseph 3, 8, 27, 44, 176
Victoria, Queen 124, 126, 129, 131–32, 135
Virgil 95

Walsh, Oonagh 136
Warner, Susan 61
Watts, Stephen 242
Weininger, Otto 82
Wellington, Duke of 127
Wenceslas of Luxembourg 124
Wexler, Laura 65
Whiting, Kezia 3, 8, 41
Wicht, Wolfgang 137
Wilde, Oscar 181, 192, 200
Williams, Susan S. 61
Wimsatt, W.K. 88
Wind, Edgar 109
Woolf, Virginia 195, 212
Wordsworth, William 234
Wright, Ernest Vincent 94

Yeats, W.B. (Yeatsian) 60, 132

www.ingramcontent.com/pod-product-compliance
Lightning Source LLC
LaVergne TN
LVHW040739130826
845500LV00025B/107
* 9 7 8 1 8 0 1 3 6 0 5 2 4 *